Building the City Beautiful

The exhibition and catalogue are supported by grants from the National Endowment for the Arts and The Pew Charitable Trusts.

Funds to conserve the architectural drawings in the Museum's collection were provided by a grant from the National Endowment for the Humanities.

Building the City Beautiful

The Benjamin Franklin Parkway and the Philadelphia Museum of Art

David B. Brownlee

Philadelphia Museum of Art

Distributed by the University of Pennsylvania Press

Published on the occasion of an exhibition shown at the Philadelphia Museum of Art, September 9–November 26, 1989

Frontispiece: Borie, Trumbauer, and Zantzinger, *Philadelphia Museum of Art*, close perspective of arcuated variant from east, 1914 (fig. 41, detail)

Designed by Phillip Unetic
Edited by Sherry Babbitt
Map by Thomas Jackson
Composition by Southern New England Typographic Service, Hamden, Connecticut
Printed by Meriden-Stinehour Press, Lunenburg, Vermont

Distributed by the University of Pennsylvania Press
Blockley Hall, 418 Service Drive
Philadelphia, Pennsylvania 19104-6097

Library of Congress Cataloging-in-Publication Data

Brownlee, David Bruce.
   Building the city beautiful: The Benjamin Franklin Parkway and the Philadelphia Museum of Art.

   "Published on the occasion of an exhibition shown at the Philadelphia Museum of Art, September 9 — November 26, 1989" — T.p. verso.
   Includes bibliographical references.
   1. Urban beautification — Pennsylvania— Philadelphia — History — 20th century. 2. Benjamin Franklin Parkway (Philadelphia, Pa.). 3. Philadelphia Museum of Art. 4. Art museum architecture — Pennsylvania — Philadelphia. 5. Philadelphia (Pa.) — Buildings, structures, etc. I. Philadelphia Museum of Art. II. Title.
NA9052.B76 1989 711′.57′097481107474811 89-22806
ISBN 0-8122-8221-3 (University of Pa. Press : hard)
ISBN 0-87633-081-2 (pbk.)

Contents

Lenders to the Exhibition

American Philosophical Society, Philadelphia

The Athenaeum of Philadelphia

Mrs. Joseph Carson, Philadelphia

CIGNA Archives, Philadelphia

City Archives of Philadelphia

The Commissioners of Fairmount Park, Philadelphia

The Franklin Institute Science Museum, Philadelphia

Free Library of Philadelphia

The Historical Society of Pennsylvania, Philadelphia

The partners of H2L2 Architects/Planners, Philadelphia

Pennsylvania Academy of the Fine Arts, Archives, Philadelphia

Philadelphia Museum of Art

The School District of Philadelphia

University of Pennsylvania, Architectural Archives, Philadelphia

University of Pennsylvania, Fine Arts Library, Philadelphia

Wesleyan University Archives, Middletown, Connecticut

Foreword

Anne d'Harnoncourt
The George D. Widener Director

Innis Howe Shoemaker
*Senior Curator of Prints,
Drawings, and Photographs*

Among the cities with great concentrations of significant architecture in the United States, Philadelphia rejoices not only in the preservation of a remarkable number of distinguished buildings but in the unexpectedly graceful coexistence and continued viability of a succession of city plans. Given the lush countryside that still encompasses and refreshes the spreading metropolis, it is not surprising that William Penn's seventeenth-century design for a "green countrie town" and the early twentieth-century plan to extend the "city beautiful" into Fairmount Park both emphasize the vital importance of the city's links with its natural surroundings. William Penn's chaste, symmetrical plan for his new city between the Delaware and Schuylkill rivers has been the focus of much scholarly attention; the complex mix of architectural, economic, and political history that produced the Benjamin Franklin Parkway and placed the vast temple of the Philadelphia Museum of Art on the hill of Fairmount is the subject of the present exhibition and catalogue.

This is one of an informal sequence of museum projects that have examined and celebrated aspects of Philadelphia architecture, from the monographic exhibition devoted to Frank Furness (1973) to the Bicentennial project *Philadelphia: Three Centuries of American Art* (1976) to the recent survey of the history of the Fairmount Waterworks (1988). It is a source of the greatest pleasure to have had David B. Brownlee, Associate Professor of the History of Art at the University of Pennsylvania, serve as guest curator for the exhibition and author of this book. Professor Brownlee's enthusiasm and energetic research have led him to the libraries, archives, and storerooms of many institutions in Philadelphia, listed as lenders at the front of this book, and we join him in expressing our profound gratitude to the colleagues who have generously shared information as well as the works of art or archival material in their care.

The initial conception of this exhibition sprang from the rediscovery of the huge and spectacular watercolor renderings of the proposed parkway by Jacques Gréber, one of which was restored and exhibited at the museum for the first time in many decades in 1976. Ann Percy, Curator of Drawings, has overseen the organization of the exhibition within the Department of Prints, Drawings, and Photographs, collaborating with Professor Brownlee and her colleagues at the museum with zeal and efficiency. Her concern for the proper cataloguing of these drawings and plans and their presentation in an elegant and meaningful context has been exemplary. This book was designed by Phillip Unetic and edited by Sherry Babbitt, who worked together and with the author with skill and style. Suzanne F. Wells, Coordinator of Special Exhibitions at the museum and herself a scholar devoted to the architecture of Paul Cret, gave the planning of this project her customary attention to detail, and the museum's registraral and installations staff ensured the careful handling and handsome appearance of the exhibition.

Many of the splendid group of plans and drawings included here have been conserved and reframed over the past two years, with the support of a grant from the National Endowment for the Humanities. We were fortunate that The Conservation Center for Art and Historic Artifacts in Philadelphia could undertake the treatment of a large number of objects, and we are particularly grateful to Elizabeth K. Schulte and Glen Ruzicka for their thoughtful work. At the museum, Denise P. Thomas and Faith Zieske, respectively Conservator and Associate Conservator of Works of Art on Paper, were responsible for coordinating this complex aspect of the project, and Ms. Zieske carried out treatments of many of the museum's objects. The matting and framing of the exhibition, at times a Herculean task, were capably taken in hand by Phoebe Toland and Kate Javens.

The exhibition and this book would not have been possible without the support of generous grants from the National Endowment for the Arts and The Pew Charitable Trusts, distinguished partners to which so many significant cultural projects in Philadelphia have had reason to be grateful.

Acknowledgments

I felt privileged when the Philadelphia Museum of Art asked me to help with the planning of an exhibition to celebrate the construction of its own building and to tell the story of the parkway and its other architecture. The project, like so much of the meritorious work that goes on within the great yellow temple on Fairmount, owes its life and vitality to Anne d'Harnoncourt, Ann Percy, Joseph J. Rishel, and Suzanne F. Wells.

In accumulating the material needed to mount the exhibition and write this catalogue, I have incurred many debts, especially to those who care for the historical record of this city and its architecture. Among those who have helped are the American Institute of Architects, Washington, D.C. (Tony Wren); American Philosophical Society, Philadelphia (Edward C. Carter II and Beth Carroll-Horrocks); The Athenaeum of Philadelphia (Roger W. Moss and Bruce Laverty); Bell Telephone Company of Pennsylvania, Philadelphia (John McBride); Mrs. Joseph Carson, Philadelphia; CIGNA Archives, Philadelphia (N. Claudette John and Leslie Simon); City Archives of Philadelphia (Ward Childs, Geraldo Maggero, and Jefferson Moak); The Commissioners of Fairmount Park (John McIlhenny); The Franklin Institute Science Museum, Philadelphia (Gladys I. Breuer); Free Library of Philadelphia (David King and J. B. Post); The Historical Society of Pennsylvania, Philadelphia (Peter J. Parker, Linda Stanley, and Carolyn Park); McNeil Gallery, Philadelphia (Sandra Lerner); the partners of H2L2 Architects/Planners, Philadelphia (William Hough, Jr.); Pennsylvania Academy of the Fine Arts, Philadelphia (Linda Bantel and Cheryl Leibold); Philadelphia Museum of Art, Archives (Louise F. Rossmassler and Alice Lefton); The School District of Philadelphia (George Edwards and Sheila O'Leary); University of Pennsylvania, Architectural Archives (Julia Moore Converse), Fine Arts Library (Alan Morrison), and Van Pelt Library, Special Collections, Philadelphia; and Wesleyan University, Special Collections and Archives (Elizabeth Swaim), Middletown, Connecticut. I thank them all.

Marc Vincent provided invaluable service to the project as my research assistant and shared his research on Paul Cret. Other assistance was rendered by Eva Aronfreed, Megan Moynihan, and Carla Yanni. Scholars who have afforded me the benefit of their advice and knowledge include Lauren Bricker, Jeffrey Cohen, Kenneth Finkel, Ruthanne Madway, Christopher Thomas, and George Thomas. Without them I should not have done as well; on their own they might have done better.

Several members of the staff of the Philadelphia Museum of Art also merit special recognition. Preparation of this manuscript for publication was helped enormously by the sage counsel of George H. Marcus, Head of Publications. Sherry Babbitt, its editor, performed her work with a verve and diligence that most authors never witness. My readers are her debtors, and they will also be grateful for the strong vision of Phillip Unetic, who designed this book. Other special assistance was provided by Irene Taurins and Anne Fuhrman of the Registrar's Office, photographers Graydon Wood and Andrew Harkins, and Steven Brett and Christina Conant of the Publications Department.

I offer this work to my parents and to all Philadelphians whose lives overlapped the construction of the Benjamin Franklin Parkway. They proved then that a civilized city, if its will is strong enough, can fulfill its dreams in spite of war, economic depression, corruption, and greed. We could learn from them.

Filius pius patri optimo matrisque memoriae

Some of my earliest and happiest memories are about Philadelphia's Benjamin Franklin Parkway and the institutions that gather around it. I remember driving into the city with my mother in the 1950s, following the exhilarating serpentine of what is now called Kelly Drive. We would pass beside the blue Schuylkill and then sweep around the bulk of Fairmount, with the art museum on top, to emerge in the sun of the Fairmount Plaza. Traffic passed much closer to the Washington Monument in those days and fountains washed its base, as the great cascades on either side of the art museum steps filled the air with a joyful cacophony. Then our car would dive into the green tunnel of the tree-lined parkway itself, and we would whisk on toward center city.

With my father I remember exploring the museums of the parkway. There were dinosaurs and locomotives and rooms full of eighteenth-century furniture, and I also recall the buildings themselves. I was especially intrigued when my father showed me how Greek "optical corrections" had been built into them and how the stony rectangular forms were actually composed of curves and inclined planes. This seemed to bring the masonry to life in a secret way, and I felt privileged to share in the mystery.

That Philadelphians still share my youthful excitement about the parkway is expressed every year when they crowd it for festivals, for bicycle races, and for parades. For them, the Benjamin Franklin Parkway is clearly the heart of a great city and the crossroads of a region. It is a work of art that has become both a cogent symbol and a durable amenity, capable of surviving the decades-old encroachment of the Vine Street Expressway and the more recent neglect of impoverished city agencies. The parkway has survived. Today the institutions that ring it are projecting the reputation of Philadelphia outward to a wider world, and that world is looking back. The library and the museums of the parkway are growing and growing more ambitious, and the parkway landscape has itself become the object of private philanthropy.

The special place that the parkway holds in the imagination of Philadelphians probably owes something to its long and turbulent birthing period. Talked about ever since the Civil War, the actual making of the new avenue occupied Philadelphia for the first third of the twentieth century. Other American cities were planning similar projects during the same years, creating what was called the "city beautiful" movement, America's first important contribution to urban design. But while progress on the parkway was slow and dogged at every step by the political skirmishing of the Reform Era, it was one of the few such projects to be completed. Philadelphia could rightly claim to have met the urban challenges of the new era, sundering the grid of William Penn's city with a grand diagonal boulevard that bespoke the energy of the twentieth century.

The story that follows is about architects, politicians, civic leaders, and those who directed the institutions that planned to relocate themselves along the parkway. They used that terrain as a battleground for ideas, ambitions, and political might. In doing so they also made the parkway into a stage for the drama of modern life. It remains that today.

Major Buildings

1. 2601 Parkway, Paul P. Cret succeeded by Aaron Colish, 1931–40

2. Fidelity Mutual Life Insurance Company (now Reliance Standard Life Insurance Company); Zantzinger, Borie, and Medary; 1925–27

3. Philadelphia Museum of Art; Borie, Trumbauer, and Zantzinger; 1911–28

4. Parkway House, Gabriel Roth and Elizabeth Fleischer, 1950–53

5. Rodin Museum, Paul P. Cret and Jacques Gréber, 1926–29

6. Youth Study Center; Carroll, Grisdale, and Van Alen; 1949–52

7. Park Towne Place, John Hans Graham and Associates, 1959

8. Philadelphia Council, Boy Scouts of America; Charles Z. Klauder; 1928–30

9. School Administration Building, Irwin T. Catharine, 1928–32

10. The Franklin Institute, John T. Windrim, 1928–34

11. Free Library, Horace Trumbauer, 1911–27

12. Municipal Court (now Family Court), John T. Windrim succeeded by W. R. Morton Keast, 1928–41

13. Academy of Natural Sciences, James H. Windrim, 1873 (new facade and south wing by Wilson Brothers, 1892)

14. Four Seasons Hotel and One Logan Square, Kohn Pedersen and Fox, 1982–83

15. Roman Catholic Cathedral of Saints Peter and Paul, Napoleon Le Brun, 1846–64 (west facade by John Notman)

16. United Fund Building, Mitchell/Giurgola, 1968–71

17. Bell Telephone Building, John T. Windrim, 1912–16

18. Insurance Company of North America (now CIGNA), Stewardson and Page, 1922–25

19. Municipal Services Building, Vincent G. Kling and Associates, 1962–65

20. City Hall; John McArthur, Jr.; 1871–1901

Sites of Proposed and Demolished Buildings

A. Fairmount Community Center (proposed), W. R. Morton Keast, 1935

B. Pennsylvania Academy of the Fine Arts (proposed). Suggested for this site beginning in 1911; design prepared by W. R. Morton Keast in 1935

C. Convention Hall (proposed), John T. Windrim, 1916
Episcopal Cathedral (proposed), Jacques Gréber, 1917
Johnson Collection Gallery (proposed), Horace Trumbauer, 1918

D. Episcopal Cathedral (proposed), Jacques Gréber, 1919

E. Municipal Court (proposed), John T. Windrim, 1920
Municipal Court and Convention Hall (proposed), John Molitor, 1926

F. Victory Hall (proposed), Paul P. Cret, 1925
Franklin Memorial (proposed), Paul P. Cret, 1927

G. The Franklin Institute (proposed), John T. Windrim, 1913–22
Concert Hall (proposed); Voorhees, Gmelin, and Walker; 1931–32

H. American Philosophical Society (proposed), Paul P. Cret, 1925–33

I. The Franklin Institute (proposed), John T. Windrim, 1908–9

J. The Franklin Institute (proposed), Cope and Stewardson, 1907 (second design by John T. Windrim, 1908)

K. Broad Street Station, Pennsylvania Railroad (demolished 1952); Wilson Brothers; 1881–82 (enlarged by Furness, Evans, and Company, 1892–94)

THE BENJAMIN FRANKLIN PARKWAY

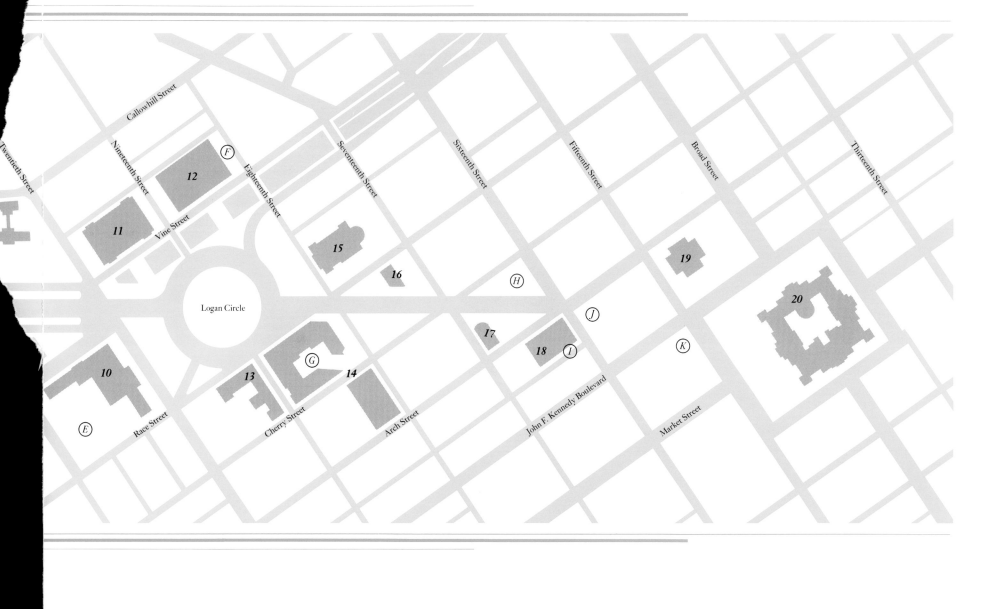

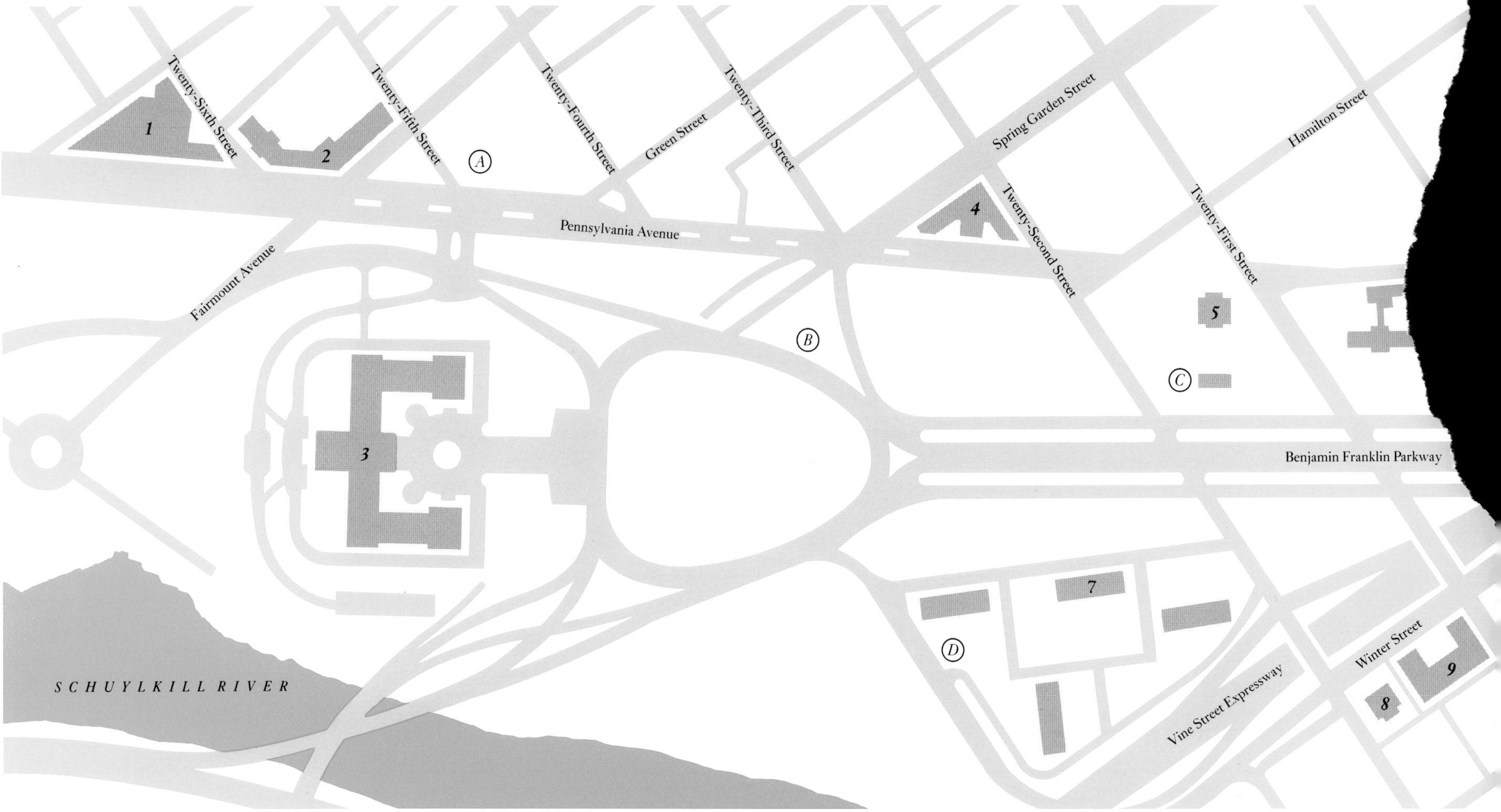

Twenty-Sixth Street

Twenty-Fifth Street

Twenty-Fourth Street

Green Street

Twenty-Third Street

Spring Garden Street

Hamilton Street

Twenty-Second Street

Twenty-First Street

Fairmount Avenue

Pennsylvania Avenue

Benjamin Franklin Parkway

Vine Street Expressway

Winter Street

SCHUYLKILL RIVER

1

2

(A)

(B)

4

5

(C)

3

7

(D)

8

9

Photograph taken from aeroplane
Sunday, August 23, 1925.

The Classical Language
of Modern Architecture

Fig. 1. The parkway from the southeast, with the end pavilions of the art museum roofed but only the foundations of the central block in place; August 22, 1925. CIGNA Archives, Philadelphia, 20/1.19

Philadelphia's Benjamin Franklin Parkway was conceived as the great symbol of a modern city—the new face of a gritty industrial metropolis as it remade itself in the complex circumstances of the twentieth century (fig. 1). Yet its modernity and complexity are not at first easily discerned, for while the parkway was designed in the very years when what is usually called "modern architecture" was invented and when America first grappled with the vexing social and technical realities of a new era, most of its buildings wear the apparently uniform garb of ancient classicism: columns, cornices, capitals, and pediments. The same is true of buildings created elsewhere as part of the "city beautiful" movement, and this great tide of American classicism is often interpreted as a bold and intentional anachronism. It is seen as a young nation's naïve appropriation of the trappings of historical legitimacy when it was first thrust into a position of world prominence.[1] It is also read as a kind of stage set, carefully obscuring the urgent and diverse forces of the modern era.

But while such classicism does present reassuring symbols from the past without displaying artistic disharmony, it was indeed modern architecture, and its creation was riven by modernist debate. In Philadelphia, the architects who made the parkway and lined it with majestic buildings called themselves "modern," and this was not a mere figure of speech or a bland synonym for "up-to-date."[2] Nor was it an offhand reference to the visual similarities between their serene and stately works and the disciplined avant-garde architecture of Europe, which, like the parkway, was just becoming visible in the 1920s (figs. 2, 3). Their modernity was not superficial. It was a matter of intent and ideology, and, like the more obvious modernists of Europe, they often disagreed with each other.

The central argument among Philadelphia's modern classicists was whether their architecture was a problem-solving science or a vocabulary of geometrical form. Almost exactly analogous to the rift that divided the more obvious modernists into functionalist and abstractionist camps, this controversy added the zest of confrontation to almost every decision about the parkway. For those observing from the perspective of the late twentieth century, it also transports the discussion of classicism into a widened territory of modern art—one that encompasses, as common children of the modern era, the Villa Savoye (fig. 3), the Bauhaus, and the Philadelphia Museum of Art.

Two Classicisms

The two factions of Philadelphia's modern classicism were both loyal to the vocabulary of ancient forms for unsentimental reasons, but each defined its loyalty by means of different modernist rationales. Like their corollaries elsewhere in America, the two camps derived their different positions from the two great forces that had forged modern American attitudes toward classical architecture: the World's Columbian Exposition, held in Chicago in 1893 (fig. 4), and the Ecole des Beaux-Arts in Paris (fig. 5). Memories of the architectural fairyland of Chicago's "White City," reinforced and extended by the subsequent work of many architects, had inspired broad public sympathy for the classical remaking of America. At the same time, the Parisian architectural school, a bastion of classicism whose foundations stretched back to the seventeenth-century system of French academies, had exerted a narrower but equally important influence. By the time the parkway was under way, the Ecole had trained hundreds of young Americans and inspired curricular reforms in most American architectural schools.

Although equally powerful, the two varieties of classicism that sprang from these sources were distinctively different. Jacques Gréber, the French city and landscape planner who worked on the parkway design in 1917–22, contrasted the "heaviness" and "coldness" of the classicism inspired by the 1893 fair with French "personality and creative instinct."[3] Not all critics used his prejudiced vocabulary, and some could identify positions that lay between the two styles, but most endorsed the fundamental truth of Gréber's bipolar interpretation.[4]

The heavier, colder classicism was apparently more indigenous, and its principal "school" was the office of McKim, Mead, and White, the preeminent American architects of the 1890s. Its Americanism prevailed despite the fact that some of its leaders had trained in Paris. These included Charles McKim himself and John Russell Pope, who designed the last great monuments of this classical style in the 1930s—the National Gallery of Art and the Jefferson Memorial in Washington, D.C.

In their approach to classicism, one could detect many themes that had long been imbedded in Anglo-American architectural practice. There was, above all, an emphasis on assembling forms as they were seen in perspective—a preference that had pushed the Gothic Revival in Britain and America toward picturesque compositions but that drove the new classicism toward strong

Fig. 2. John T. Windrim (1866–1934) succeeded by W. R. Morton Keast (1888–1973), *Municipal Court*, 1928–41. City Archives of Philadelphia, 140.3, 2336

and simple geometry. This conception of the building as seen from the outside and from afar necessarily reduced the attention paid to planning and to the rational expression of a building's structural system, again matters that had rarely been emphasized in the architecture of the English-speaking world. Finally, those who subscribed to this vocabulary were often inclined to dress their buildings in archaeological garb, evincing the sometimes naïve confidence in scholarship that was traditional among English and American architects.

Profoundly visual, this architecture had few theoretical underpinnings. But the office of McKim, Mead, and White did not need words to demonstrate its effectiveness; their geometrically strong and historically allusive architecture was sufficient. Theirs was the *romanitas* of the Agriculture Building at the 1893 fair (see fig. 4), the Florentine Renaissance of the University Club in New York (1896–1900), and the neo-Georgian of the Germantown Cricket Club in Philadelphia (1889–91). Despite its archaeology, this was new architecture for America, and its triumphant freshness overwhelmed those who first

Fig. 3. Le Corbusier (1887–1965), *Villa Savoye, Poissy-sur-Seine, France, 1928–29*

described the "American Renaissance" that grew out of the Columbian Exposition.[5] As Thomas Tallmadge recalled more than thirty years later, "When we were children and our stock of conversation had run low, we always filled the void by saying, 'Let's talk about the World's Fair.'"[6]

The other classicism was not an "American" renaissance but part of that international renaissance whose contemporary fountainhead was the Ecole des Beaux-Arts in Paris. Its adherents need not have trained in the ateliers of Paris, however, for by 1890 America's leading architecture schools—including those at MIT, Columbia, and the University of Pennsylvania—had converted to the Beaux-Arts method. Moreover, there was the Society of Beaux-Arts Architects (and after 1916 the Beaux-Arts Institute of Design), whose national network of ateliers replicated the French experience for young American men unable to afford college or go abroad. Because of the breadth of this educational system, drawing on the services of almost every talented French architect as well as many recently trained Americans, it is difficult to generalize about its character. Indeed, inclusiveness became its hallmark. The Ecole's classicism was not a "style" at all, at least in the sense that the *style Louis XIV* or the rococo were styles. Unlike the other classicism of the time, it was really not a visual phenomenon but a manner of approach or system. In the 1890s two eloquent American architects, both recently returned from Paris, explained all of this to an increasingly appreciative audience. Ernest Flagg, later the designer of the first building to stretch higher than Philadelphia's City Hall tower, the Singer Building in New York (1902–8), celebrated the openness of French training while swatting at the literalism of the other classical camp:

The school [Ecole des Beaux-Arts] not only does not encourage that dry classicism which would reduce the most noble of the fine arts to a mathematical science, but her teaching is of a directly opposite nature. She desires of her pupils that they know every-

thing, then forget all and be themselves; such teaching is inconsistent with anything but the free and liberal spirit, and such spirit pervades the Ecole.[7]

Adherents believed that this liberal spirit could produce the appropriate architecture for every age—modern architecture—by a peaceful evolutionary process. The key to this achievement was built into the Ecole's design method, and particularly into its emphasis on plan and program, matters not so vigorously considered by the other classicists. This system was repeatedly explained in the public press by the other great Beaux-Arts publicist of the 1890s, Thomas Hastings, architect, with John Carrère, of the New York Public Library (1897–1911). Hastings wrote in 1897:

Originality is a spontaneous effort to do work in the simplest and most natural way. The conditions are never twice alike; each case is new. We must begin our study with the floor-plan, and then interpret that floor-plan in the elevation, using forms, details, and sometimes motives with natural variations and improvements on what has gone before. The true artist leaves his temperament and individuality to take care of themselves.[8]

Modernity in this system was muted, however, for its practitioners believed that present-day architecture had deep cultural roots, reaching back to the fifteenth century, and so they colored their elevations with history. Hastings said forthrightly, "We are still living today in the period of the Renaissance," and he explained:

With the revival of learning, with the new conceptions of philosophy and religion, with the great discoveries and inventions, with the altered political systems, with the fall of the Eastern Empire, with the birth of modern science and literature, and with other manifold changes all over Europe, came the dawn of the modern world; and with this modern world there was evolved what we should now recognize as the modern architecture, the Renaissance . . . .[9]

Fig. 4. Daniel H. Burnham (1846–1912) and others, *World's Columbian Exposition, Chicago,* 1893. The Court of Honor, with the Agriculture Building by McKim, Mead, and White, is at left. Chicago Historical Society

One factor that kept this vocabulary from freezing into anachronism was the continuous evolutionary force exerted over it by new architectural programs, written for buildings that served a changing culture and were executed with the assistance of modern technologies. Historical detail per se was never emphasized, and in 1915 Hastings could propound that "the relation of one part of a building to another practically constitutes almost all that is beautiful in architecture."[10] His words might easily be ascribed to a much more revolutionary modernist. Equally provocative in its modernist sympathy was his passion for what he called "a universal language common to all peoples. In solving problems of modern life," he told the American Academy of Arts and Letters in 1909, "the essential is not so much to be national or American, as it is to be modern and of our own period."[11] Of course, this was partly intended by Hastings to excuse the French

Fig. 5. Félix Duban (1796–1871), *Ecole des Beaux-Arts, Paris*, 1832–40

ized design for the American Philosophical Society—represent the other side of the story. The museum of art was a prize fought over by both camps, both being represented on the team that designed it, and its story is particularly lively.

Philadelphia also produced the most eloquent twentieth-century theorists of the two positions. Cret, the French-born architect and teacher, was the most important Beaux-Arts writer and practitioner in America. The other camp at last found its spokesman in Fiske Kimball, the architect and architectural historian who became the director of the art museum in 1925.

Fiske Kimball: "The Eternal Language of Form"

Fiske Kimball (1888–1955; see fig. 6) graduated from Harvard's architecture school in 1912 and proceeded to teach architectural history and studio courses at the universities of Illinois and Michigan. At Michigan he also wrote a doctoral dissertation on Thomas Jefferson's design for the Virginia State Capitol in Richmond, and this launched his scholarly career. His ascent was rapid. Kimball was appointed chairman of the new architecture school at the University of Virginia in Charlottesville in 1919, and in 1923 was selected to head the fine arts program that New York University was establishing in cooperation with the Metropolitan Museum. This was to become the Institute of Fine Arts, and during his first year there, he was asked to accept the directorship of what was then called the Pennsylvania Museum in Philadelphia, then building its new home on Fairmount. Kimball demurred at first, but after another entreaty he took up the position in 1925.[12]

During this period Kimball established himself as the foremost scholar of the early national period of American architecture. His research included work on Jefferson, Benjamin Henry Latrobe, Samuel McIntire, and William Thornton, and in 1922 he published his *Domestic Architecture of the American Colonies and of the Early Republic*. He also published, with George Harold Edgell, a general *History of Architecture* in 1918, but in all of this time his only

training of young Americans, but such sentiment among architects was also the foundation upon which the international modernism of the next decades was erected.

These alternative classical ideals, which converged in being up-to-date and yet diverged in choosing their courses toward modernity, were both reflected in the building of the Benjamin Franklin Parkway. In Horace Trumbauer and John T. Windrim, who between them had a hand in the design of the Free Library, the Franklin Institute, the Municipal Court, and unbuilt projects for a convention hall and a gallery for the Johnson Collection on the parkway, Philadelphia possessed two powerful advocates for the more visual and archaeological classicism that had its debut at the 1893 fair. Paul P. Cret and Clarence Zantzinger, on the other hand, were both Paris trained, and their projects—the Rodin Museum, the Fidelity Mutual Life Insurance Building, and an unreal-

trip abroad was a half-year in 1911, traveling on a prize scholarship from architecture school. He even built some of his own designs, including an outdoor amphitheater (1920–21) based on antique models and a Roman-inspired gymnasium (1922–23), both at Charlottesville. They were buildings that found favor within the more historicist camp of American classicists.

The intellect that emerged from this period of incubation was powerfully directed toward certain issues. Kimball's advanced scholarship had been largely devoted to American questions, and the era that had fascinated him was that in which American architects had first accepted archaeology as the handmaid of design. Archaeology had also been visible in his own buildings. On the other hand, he had moved rapidly into the center of the emerging profession of art history in America, where Denman Ross, Kimball's friend, was proselytizing for the British formalism of Roger Fry and Clive Bell. Formalism soon modified Kimball's historicism, and he began to justify the new American taste for archaeological classicism with surprisingly formalist arguments. His synthesis of these apparently contradictory ideas was powerful.

Kimball's fresh reasoning emerged very clearly in his consideration of American modern architecture. His first approach to the subject, in his general history of 1918, was tentative and not yet original, identifying "functionalism" and the "expression of structure" as the signposts of the new era.[13] But in 1924, while still in New York, he advanced a fresh, revisionist thesis that was his own. In an essay called "What Is Modern Architecture?," he rejected his own definition of six years earlier and now explained:

It is the current view that American architecture, under the lead of designers such as McKim, Stanford White, Charles Platt, and John Russell Pope, has turned its back on modernity and reconciled itself to a barren reproduction of the classic. It is not the true or vital view. If we consider more intently the work of this contemporary classic school, we will find it is not only creative, but that

it has an underlying affinity, real though not obvious, with the progressive work in modern painting and the other arts.[14]

The Columbian Exposition finally had a philosopher.

Kimball's provocative theory began with the rejection of what he and other authors had made a commonplace: that the structural expression and functionalism of late nineteenth-century architecture was the vanguard of a new style. On the contrary, Kimball now identified those expressive and materialist forces as the last evidences of nineteenth-century romanticism and realism, movements recently eclipsed by that "purely abstract art of form and color" whose pathfinder was the painter Paul Cézanne. The architectural equivalent of Cézanne's new formalism, Kimball asserted, was classicism, wherein lay "the preeminent manifestations of pure or abstract form, as against a structural or sculptural emphasis . . . ."[15]

Fig. 6. Fiske Kimball at his desk in the museum, c. 1928. Philadelphia Museum of Art, Archives, FKP, S. 17, Ss. A, Folder 26

Louis Sullivan's efforts to express the structure of the sky-scraper were assigned to the past, while the unrevealing exterior of McKim, Mead, and White's Villard Houses (1882–85), a Renaissance *palazzo* in New York designed in their office by the young Joseph Morrill Wells, was identi-fied as the vanguard of the new. Kimball noted that by World War I even skyscraper designers had turned to for-malism, giving up Sullivan's aspirant verticality in favor of the regular patterns of Renaissance geometry.

Kimball strengthened this interpretation when he wrote "Louis Sullivan—An Old Master" one year later. The architectural equivalent of Post-Impressionism was this time defined even more explicitly, bestowing a celeb-rity on Joseph Wells (who had died in 1890) that subse-quent historians have not seconded: "Instead of the fore-runner of the new century, Sullivan, we now see, was the last great leader of the old. He was the Monet; Wells the Cézanne. Like Monet, living on into another age, he was within his life-time already an old master."[16] It was in this essay that Kimball also revealed his understanding of the deeper significance of Post-Impressionist formalism: Its abstraction had abandoned the narrowly focused specific-ities of realistic art to "speak . . . in the eternal language of form."[17] It was this universal communication through abstraction that was the common purpose of modern painting and modern classical architecture.

In 1927 in Philadelphia, Kimball drew this reason-ing together with his previous scholarship in *American Architecture* (published in 1928), a slight and rapidly writ-ten survey that nonetheless strove to make order out of the American past. On this broader canvas he could tell the story in more detail, developing the polarity that he saw arising in the late nineteenth century between the func-tionalism of the old guard and the formalism of the new. The contribution of Wells was somewhat lessened, but McKim, Mead, and White remained the architectural "standard bearers" of Cézanne's modernism.[18] The great triumph had come at Chicago in 1893, which Kimball called "a sweeping victory for the formal ideal."[19]

American Architecture continued this triumphant story up to the present. In the teens there had been the wonderful work of John Russell Pope, Charles Platt, Del-ano and Aldrich, and Guy Lowell, culminating in Henry Bacon's Lincoln Memorial (1911–22) in Washington, D.C., whose serene geometry inspired Kimball to call it "the classic ideal."[20] Frank Lloyd Wright could be shunted into a chapter called "Counter-currents,"[21] while the heroes of the twenties became skyscraper builders like Arthur Loomis Harmon and Ralph Walker, who had exploited New York's new zoning law to compose works of essential, sculptural power like the Shelton Hotel (1923–24) and the Barclay-Vesey Telephone Building (1923–26), respectively. Their sinews hidden, they retained "the basic character of our modern work—its measured simplicity and breadth, above all, its clarity."[22]

In advancing this argument, Kimball drew heavily on the writings of Roger Fry. His views on the heroic role of Cézanne in vanquishing the realism and romanticism of the nineteenth century, the Post-Impressionists' resolve to "create form," and the analogies between their incipient abstraction and the "Classic spirit" were all borrowed from an essay in Fry's *Vision and Design* (1920).[23] It was Fry's formalist vocabulary that now replaced the interpre-tation of American modernism that Kimball had offered in 1918.

Kimball recognized that the picture of classicism that he had now sketched was quite unlike that being pro-moted by those Americans who had been schooled at the Ecole des Beaux-Arts. He acknowledged that the Ecole had usefully contributed an "analytical science of plan-ning" that was not native to America, but he maintained that the indigenous style was still thriving. This could be seen in the experience of American students who had come back from abroad and were recaptured by the power of American formalism. Kimball wrote:

The scores of élèves *who have returned from the unrivaled disci-pline and emulation of the Paris school have had here to lay aside their French language of form, based on characteristic emphasis and on lavish, dynamic energy, to learn anew a language of almost mathematical simplicity and of Dorian harmony. Not one has permanently escaped the overwhelming domination of the American classic.*[24]

Paul Philippe Cret: "The Art of the Democracy"

What Fiske Kimball called the "Dorian harmony" of the "American classic" was something that Paul Philippe Cret (1876–1945) would learn to admire (fig. 7). But, trained first at the Ecole des Beaux-Arts in his native Lyons and then for six years at the great Ecole of Paris (1897–1903), Cret also knew that classicism could have other meanings. When he was plucked from the Ecole and appointed professor of design at the University of Pennsylvania in 1903, Hastings and Flagg received their most dedicated and eloquent supporter in the campaign for the Beaux-Arts system. Philadelphia, with Cret both leading the university's design program and serving as the *patron* of the local T-Square Club's independent atelier, became the center of American architectural education.[25]

Kimball arrived in the city twenty-two years later, and he and Cret became friendly adversaries, united, no doubt, by the recognition that as classicists they were necessarily allies in the wider debate over modern architecture. Nevertheless, Cret did not fail to spell out his differences, at least privately, with his younger colleague. When he read Kimball's essay on Sullivan, he rejoined immediately that the great skyscraper builder was not merely an outmoded romantic, as Kimball had argued, but "an element of trouble in the harmonious growth of American architecture . . . ." Sullivan's fault lay in his misrepresentation of steel construction, covering an equally horizontal and vertical grid of skeletal girders with a terra-cotta veneer of pure, soaring verticality. Instead of respect for the "principle of construction," which, like the program and plan, was sacred to modern Ecole men, Cret complained that Sullivan had advanced "a purely metaphysical quality" and resorted to "'literary architecture.'"[26]

Fig. 7. Adolphe Borie (1877–1934), *Paul Philippe Cret*, 1914. Oil on canvas, 29 x 22″ (73.7 x 55.9 cm). National Academy of Design, New York

Similarly, when Kimball wrote about Bertram Grosvenor Goodhue, whose bold skyscraper design had won the Nebraska State Capitol competition in 1920, Cret again faulted the direction of Kimball's criticism. Goodhue, who had begun his career as a medievalist, had been interested only in what Cret called "the picturesque element" of classicism. "The romantic in him, the old Adam, was still too strong" to allow him to see that "classicism is a discipline which requires a certain humility . . . ."[27]

And when Kimball sent him the proofs of *American Architecture*, full of admiration for the formalism of the American classic, Cret reproved him for ignoring the other camp:

There is . . . something in the French influence that you do not perhaps recognize sufficiently . . . that is, the art of planning, which has been a distinct gain in American architecture brought by the Beaux Arts men. If I had to quarrel with you, it would be on this question of the plans that you do not emphasize, perhaps, enough. They are of much more importance than is usually thought, even by those interested in facade or interior treatment, for the simple reason that they determine the volumes (solids or voids), and that is three-quarters of the appearance of a building.[28]

Kimball gracefully acknowledged that he had failed to say enough about the influence of the French system in planning, but he pointed out that such influence was slight in the work of his favorites: "My thought is that in a great many of the American buildings, such as the work of McKim, and the neo-classicists, the exterior appearance determined the plan . . . ."[29] It was plain to Cret and Kimball where the lines were drawn between them.

For Cret, the essence of the distinction between the French classic system and Kimball's classical formalism was the difference between ideas and appearances. As he made plain in 1908, in his first published explanation of the Beaux-Arts method, classicism was a "science of design" rather than a style.[30] Throughout his career he defended the disciplining power of this science with words much like those employed by Flagg or Hastings. The architect began with the client's program and knowledge of such conditions as site, finances, and technology. He then proceeded to satisfy these requirements in a plan, the preeminent part of the design process, and only when the plan was complete did he erect upon it elevations and massing studies. In the end, this method necessarily produced a building whose "character" bespoke the program as well as the times and circumstances in which it was realized.[31]

Like Hastings, Cret believed that the twentieth-century architect still lived in the Renaissance, but he was a fervent opponent of any conscious reference to archaeol-

ogy or historical style. He steered the beginning student away from the study of the classical orders—a hoary mainstay of architectural education—because it made the novice "a sort of engineer working with formulae and not with his feelings for beauty, giving to the work of all this same monotonous aspect which makes one wish for more originality and less correction." Indeed, he believed that no mention of historical precedent should be heard in the studio until the "science of design" had been mastered; until that point the history of architecture was "powerless to stimulate the mind toward the creation of new works of art." In place of the orders, the student was to devote himself to the "elements" of architecture—walls, doors, windows, porticoes, vaults—that were to be studied in plan, section, elevation, and perspective. All of this had the aim of instilling a sense of proportion, for Cret the benchmark of good design, without suggesting that it could be reduced to mathematical rules.[32]

Cret's conception of the Beaux-Arts system had been strongly shaped by his atelier master in Paris, Jean-Louis Pascal, and Pascal's friend Julien Guadet, the professor of architectural theory at the Ecole des Beaux-Arts. Guadet's lecture course, offered continuously between 1894 and his death in 1908, was published as the four-volume *Eléments et théorie de l'architecture* (1901–4), which affords the most comprehensive prospectus of the Ecole's teachings during Cret's six years in Paris. It explicates the plan-centered "science" of Beaux-Arts design and the study of "elements" that led students toward its mastery. But, as might have been expected from the architect who as a student had won the Premier Grand Prix (the "Rome Prize") in 1864 with a Romanesque design for a vast Alpine hostel, Guadet's attitude toward design was very liberal. He took pains to identify himself with the new forces in the Ecole that had overthrown "the narrow devotion to the rule" that had prevailed since the time of Louis XIV. Cret carried this new message to Philadelphia. His attack on the usefulness of assigning first-year students to work on the classical orders was an echo of Guadet's warning that the orders were not "the sole pivot of architecture nor the first stage for your studies." Similarly, Cret followed Guadet in disdaining those who "believe that architecture is an art of numbers, a table of rigid formulas and mathematics." And like Guadet, Cret subscribed to the belief that proportions were a matter of infinite possibility, wherein the artist's liberty was both "his honor itself" and his "peril."[33] On each of these points, Cret and Guadet would have found themselves at odds with French architects of the past. They would also have quarreled with some of their contemporaries, for, as always, there were several factions within the school.

Guadet had also been responsible for introducing into the Ecole some of the structural rationalism he had learned from his own atelier master, Henri Labrouste, and from the great medievalist Eugène-Emmanuel Viollet-le-Duc. In his lectures he warned that buildings must not only stand up but also *appear* to do so, thus explaining themselves to those who see them. He illustrated this point with the facade of Notre Dame in Paris.[34] In criticizing Sullivan's structural dishonesty, Cret recited this thinking to Kimball.

Most importantly, it was Guadet who set forth definitively the argument that Cret and other Beaux-Arts men would use to define the modernity of their work. Like everything else, Guadet's modernity sprang from the system that was inexorably created by the process of analyzing programs and conditions and then working out solutions. These solutions were many, for the multiplicity of modern needs created a multiplicity of responses. There was no single "truth," but rather, in Guadet's words, "a variety within truth, that is to say, character."[35] Taken together, however, a pattern would be apparent despite the varied "characters" of modern buildings; each would bear the stamp of its time. Guadet was at his most eloquent when he told his students, "The great architect of an epoch is its social state . . . . Above all the works, above all the particular programs, there is a program of programs, [and] that is the civilization itself of each century —

the faith or the unbelief, the aristocracy or the democracy, the severity or the relaxation of morals."[36] Guadet had seized this notion of cultural determinism from Hippolyte Taine, the professor of the history of art and aesthetics at the Ecole from 1864 to 1883, and on this broad canvas he painted the image of modern architecture.

It was Taine and Guadet whom Paul Cret quoted most frequently in his own discussion of modernity. Taine supplied the controlling notion of the spirit, or "'moral temperature,'" of a time.[37] Guadet provided the "science of design" needed to translate that spirit into architecture, allowing Cret "to try to do a piece of work as good as I can, letting the solution of a modern problem develop into a modern building . . . ."[38] Cret's confidence in the ability of the modern world to create its own style was absolute; in 1923 he proclaimed to a gathering of architects in Philadelphia, "Our architecture is modern and cannot be anything else."[39]

The cultural forces that would define modernism were set forth by Cret in 1922, in the essay on "Modern Architecture" that he wrote for a book on the fine arts edited by the American Institute of Architects. The chairman of the editorial committee, Clarence Zantzinger, was one of the architects of the Philadelphia Museum of Art. In his chapter, Cret explained in familiar terms the Beaux-Arts system and its way of generating solutions from modern programs, and he went on to detail a host of the distinctive features of these programs, including new technology and a new universality of problems that was making architecture less regional and more international. But the most important new factor was a changed clientele. As Cret explained, "Our architecture is concerned primarily with satisfying the needs of its new master, the democracy, by producing administration buildings, hotels, railroad terminals, commercial buildings, hospitals." Therefore he called modern architecture "this art of the democracy."[40]

Cret's position in these matters had been clearly defined by 1927, when he tested his modernism against that of Le Corbusier. It was in that year that the latter's *Towards a New Architecture* was published in English, and it may have been in response to friendly questioning about the book that Cret agreed to speak about it to the T-Square Club on November 19. He must have been astonished at what he read, and although he claimed that he spoke "as a scientist" and with scientific objectivity,[41] his audience must have been dumbstruck both by his generous exposition of Le Corbusier's ideas and by their congruity with Cret's own thinking. Here indeed was proof that the Beaux-Arts path to modernism was to be taken seriously.

Cret commenced his lecture by listing the "3 rappels," or the three reminders for architects that Le Corbusier posited at the start of his argument. These were mass, surface, and plan, but Le Corbusier had made it plain that it was plan that governed the other two. It was "the generator," just, of course, as the plan generated elevations and massing in the Beaux-Arts system. With these reminders in place, Le Corbusier (as interpreted by Cret) maintained that architects need not be preoccupied with questions of style, again striking close to the position of those younger classicists who followed Guadet. And while Cret noted Le Corbusier's affection for steamships, airplanes, and automobiles and his famous pronouncement that a house was "a machine to live in," he was perceptive enough to note that Le Corbusier held that "architecture is more than the simple utilitarianism . . . . It is . . . plastic . . . . It begins where calculations of the engineer end."[42] This last theme, taken up again by Cret in an article published eight months later, was sufficient lubrication to permit the almost frictionless meshing of classicism and modernism.[43] Cret could also agree with Le Corbusier in censuring ornament—although Cret's position was less extreme—and in arguing that good proportions must replace detail work as the basis of modern design. This, too, he discussed later in a published article.[44] Cret seemed to hold up the example of Le Corbusier as conclusive proof that the Beaux-Arts system was modern, or at least compatible with modernity.

The parallel positions put forward by the two French-speaking architects were, of course, products of their common attachment to the doctrine of the Ecole des Beaux-Arts. Le Corbusier had lost few opportunities to denigrate its teachings, but he remained enmeshed in the generously broad structure of its system. An admirer of Saint Peter's and the Parthenon, a believer in the need to pose the problem properly before turning to the drafting board, and a proponent of a universal architecture that abolished national and regional variation, he espoused many of the strongest principles of the Ecole. Where he differed, of course, was in the vocabulary in which solutions were to be conceived. For him, the proscription of historical styles was absolute, and in place of the familiar forms of classicism he erected a philosophy of communication through abstract means. Here Cret could not follow with confidence.

Paul Cret would advance no further toward Le Corbusier's abstraction than to share the notion of "empathy." This he probably encountered in Geoffrey Scott's *Architecture of Humanism* (1914), a work he praised.[45] Scott offered a brilliant dissection of the internal inconsistencies of the romantic and materialist architectural thought of the nineteenth century, and in its place he introduced the concept of empathy, borrowed from German aesthetic theory.[46] This concept suggested that architects created designs, and that viewers understood them, by establishing an analogy between their own bodies and architecture. Buildings were perceived as creatures, struggling with environmental forces just as humans did. Or, in Scott's words:

We have transcribed ourselves into terms of architecture. . . . We transcribe architecture into terms of ourselves.

This is the humanism of architecture. The tendency to project the image of our functions into concrete forms is the basis, for architecture, of creative design. The tendency to recognise, in concrete forms, the image of those functions is the true basis, in its turn, of critical appreciation [Scott's emphasis].[47]

Such creaturely buildings need not rely on historical allusion to convey their messages. They could proceed directly to the consciousness of the beholder, and so Scott could write that "architecture, simply and immediately perceived, is a combination, revealed through light and shade, of spaces, of masses, and of lines."[48] That this was virtually—albeit intentionally—a prescription for abstraction is apparent if Scott's words are compared to Le Corbusier's famous definition of architecture as "the masterly, correct and magnificent play of masses brought together in light."[49] Le Corbusier in fact based his theory of abstraction at least in part on what sounds like an empathic reaction: "If we are brought up short by the Parthenon, it is because a chord inside us is struck when we see it; the axis is touched." He added in a caption, "There are no symbols attached to these forms [of the Parthenon]: [but] they provoke definite sensations; there is no need of a key in order to understand them."[50]

But Cret did not follow empathy all the way into this symbolless realm. He did write and speak of the "Physiognomy of Modern Architecture," probably with an awareness of the implications of this phrase for empathic interpretation, but he was no abstractionist.[51] For him, empathy was no more than the traditional analogies that could be drawn between human proportions and the proportions of the classical orders. It explained the continuing intelligibility of those forms and why modern architecture could resemble that of the past. One need not seek out a new vocabulary of abstraction, for twentieth-century demands were sufficient to convert classicism into the language of a modern, democratic society.

Fiske Kimball and Paul Cret were spokesmen for two powerful forces in American architectural life, the one committed to the power of the eye and the geometrical language of form, the other in love with the beauty of system and the evolutionary strength of historical forces. Both understood that classicism had become modern in twentieth-century America, although they understood that process differently. For Kimball, the modern revolution had occurred within art itself, in the debate over visual alternatives that had split the artistic world between formalists and romantics at the end of the nineteenth century. For Cret, modernity had come when the Beaux-Arts system responded automatically to the titanic forces that had reshaped an entire civilization. But both agreed, like the avant-gardists of Europe, that the new state of architecture was universal. If one followed Kimball, architecture had adopted an international formal vocabulary. If one sided with Cret, its universality was the natural outgrowth of a world culture that had become increasingly homogeneous. That polarity—and the modern vision that subsumed it—defined the artistic arena in which the parkway was designed.

The Benjamin Franklin Parkway

Modern classicism in America in general and in Philadelphia in particular was more than a matter of architecture. It was an ally of the "city beautiful" movement in city planning, whose model of an orderly, classical metropolis, crisscrossed by boulevards and dominated by stately groups of public buildings, was America's first important contribution to urban design. Such was the vision of the future conjured up in 1903 by Charles Mulford Robinson, one of the movement's greatest polemicists:

There is a promise in the sky of a new day. The darkness rolls away, and the buildings that had been shadows stand forth distinctly in the gray air. The tall façades glow as the sun rises; their windows shine as topaz; their pennants of steam, tugging flutteringly from high chimneys, are changed to silvery plumes. Whatever was dingy, coarse, and ugly, is either transformed or hidden in shadow. The streets, bathed in the fresh morning light, fairly sparkle, their pavements from upper windows appearing smooth and clean. There seems to be a new city for the work of the new day.[1]

Even with such shining imagery, city planning had down-to-earth political implications, and the "city beautiful" was a creature of the Progressive Era of the early twentieth century. In the complex politics of the day, the movement won natural friends among the reformers, but they were often burdened with scruples that did not make them reliable patrons of the arts. On the other hand, in the melee between progressive and organization forces, corruptible machine politicians often saw the wisdom of embracing popular public works programs. Such was the case for the "city beautiful" movement in Philadelphia, where the fate of the Benjamin Franklin Parkway was determined by a confusing battle between confident bosses and well-meaning but often powerless idealists. In the end, it was only realized because of cooperation from the forces of corruption. Indeed, Lincoln Steffens, who attached the epithet "corrupt and contented" to Philadelphia in 1903, declared that the "City Beautiful clubs" that boosted the parkway had sold out to the machine.[2]

A Battleground

The "city beautiful" movement, around which this conflict swirled, had its fountainhead in Chicago in the World's Columbian Exposition of 1893 (see fig. 4).[3] The fairground, designed by Daniel H. Burnham and a national team of architects, not only served as a showcase for classical architecture but also gave Americans a vision of what an entire planned city could be like, with uniform cornice heights and carefully contrived vistas. It was the most memorable public event in the history of American architecture. As Fiske Kimball wrote in 1927:

The cumulative impression of the classic phantasm was overwhelming. The throng of visitors, many of whom were seeing large buildings for the first time, was deeply stirred by the ordered magnificence and harmony of the Court of Honor. The example of unified effort and effect, associated with the classic forms in which it had been achieved, was stamped on the memory of the whole nation.[4]

It was this sight that had inspired Robinson's picture of the metropolis of the future, and it had been inspired in turn by Paris as it looked in the late nineteenth century. The broad, carefully controlled boulevards that Baron Haussmann had created for the Second Empire were still fresh, and, as rendered in paint by the Impressionists, they seemed to epitomize the urban environment of a great modern civilization. Their symbolism was generically about power, public life, mobility, and leisure, but it was no more specific than that. The boulevards could thus serve as the essential but neutral infrastructure for the Commune and Third Republic just as faithfully as they had served Napoleon III. Paris was thus recognized as an unprejudiced stage for the enactment of modern life.

It was around this neutral, modern imagery that many of the strongest forces in American political life would battle. Reformers naturally strove to capitalize on the "city beautiful" movement and realize its visions. They succeeded in some instances, including Cleveland, where reform mayor Tom Johnson was closely associated with the Cleveland Group Plan of Daniel Burnham and Arnold W. Brunner. Presented in 1903 and largely completed, the Cleveland plan opened up a great public space and surrounded it with civic buildings.[5] The same could be seen in Washington, D.C., where the Senate Park Commission Plan (called the "McMillan Plan" after its patron, Senator James McMillan) cleared Pierre L'Enfant's Mall of a century of picturesque but thoughtless obstruction. The report was prepared in 1901–2 by Burnham, McKim, Frederick Law Olmsted, Jr., and Augustus Saint-Gaudens, and it was endorsed and supported by President Theodore Roosevelt and the Progressives.[6]

But in Philadelphia, the battle lines over the "city beautiful" were determined differently. Never able to secure a firm foothold in government, the reformers who wanted to build the parkway, like everyone else in the city, were dependent on the longest-lived political machine in the nation.[7] Their nemesis was the Republican Party's alliance of contractors, public transportation interests, utilities, and the Pennsylvania Railroad that had seized the city just after the Civil War and held it in a stranglehold for almost eighty years. The grip was relaxed for only a few, brief episodes of reform. Republican city bosses enjoyed the reliable support of new immigrant voters and the more fickle sustenance of state bosses like Matthew Quay and his successor Boies Penrose, both of whom were elected to the United States Senate. The successive city leaders were "King" James McManes, David Martin, Israel Durham, James "Sunny Jim" McNichol, and the Vare brothers (George, Edwin, and William). None was ever elected mayor, but this did not seem strange to Philadelphians, whose "contentment" so infuriated Lincoln Steffens. So long as it worked, they were usually willing to accept William Vare's rosy description of the modern machine:

I firmly believe in the principle of organized politics. I am satisfied that our present day development makes organization as necessary

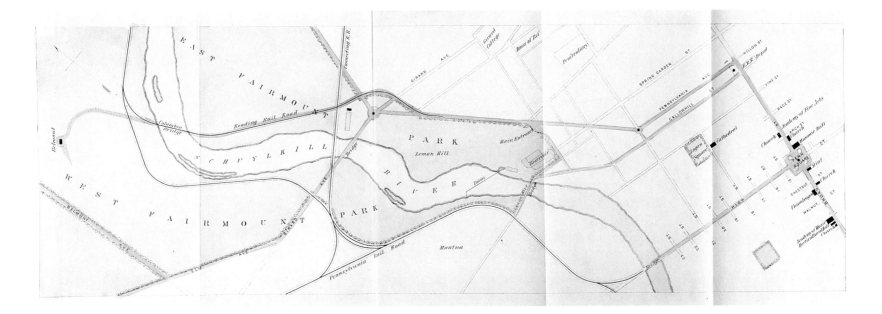

Fig. 8. John Penington & Son, publishers, *Proposed Boulevards*. Plan. From *Broad Street, Penn Square, and the Park* (Philadelphia, 1871). Collection of Mrs. Joseph Carson, Philadelphia

for public affairs as it is for industry, for labor and for society generally. Organization in politics only reflects the trend of modern times and it should be accepted as a present day condition, not for evil, but for possible public good.[8]

Such a system could build a parkway, if it wanted to.

A Road to the Park

The agitation for a boulevard connecting the center of William Penn's city with Fairmount Park gathered momentum slowly. It began as a component of the movement to establish the park itself, which had been consolidated in 1858 and as such was part of the general park movement that swept America in the second half of the nineteenth century. But in the 1890s the discussion of the parkway was broadened to encompass the full range of city planning interests that were born out of the Columbian Exposition, and every successive phase of the campaign was tinged by the colors of the most recent controversies in urban design.[9]

The earliest expressions of interest in a park boulevard came from individuals. Such was the source of the first image of such a roadway, presented in an anonymous pamphlet published in 1871 by John Penington & Son (fig. 8). With a refrain that would be picked up by proponents of the project for the next fifty years, its author pointed to the boulevards of Paris and demanded,

If the great park, with which we have undertaken to adorn the city, is to be a place of general resort and to benefit all of our citizens, it must be brought within reach of all. It must be connected with Broad Street and with the centre of the city by as short a route as possible; and the avenues which lead to it must be made elegant and attractive; in short, must be made part of the park.[10]

Accordingly, he proposed building two boulevards. One, called "Pennsylvania Avenue," was to replace the Reading Railroad tracks that ran westward from Broad Street, just north of Callowhill Street, and then turn northwestward to the east park entrance at Fairmount. The other was to make use of Callowhill Street itself as a route to the western part of the park, on the opposite bank of the Schuylkill River. Neither boulevard had the present-day site of City Hall as a terminus, for the author strenuously opposed what was then only a proposal to erect the new building on Penn Square, at the junction of Broad and Market streets. He wanted the square to be kept open, on the model of the Place de la Concorde in Paris.

Much of the same underlying purpose could be detected thirteen years later in the proposal made by Charles K. Landis (1835–1900), the utopian founder and developer of Vineland, New Jersey. However, Landis's poster map, imprinted with the instruction "Please hang this up," now showed a "grand avenue" that led directly from Penn Square to the reservoir on Fairmount (fig. 9). Two factors figured in this realignment. There was first, the experience of the Centennial Exposition of 1876, which had attracted hundreds of thousands of visitors to the fairgrounds in Fairmount Park and demonstrated the need for the most direct possible route to the park from downtown. And, since the Penington pamphlet, the site of City Hall had been fixed and work had finally commenced. The projected tower offered itself as an attractive terminus for a great boulevard. For Landis, these considerations justified the enormous expense of condemnation and demolition that his plan would entail.

The Windrim Plan

In 1887, the state legislature gave the city a new charter, increasing the power of the mayor by giving him direct authority over the administrative departments that had formerly answered to the city's cumbrous bicameral legislature. This change was engineered by the reformers, notably the Committee of One Hundred, and their dreams were partly fulfilled during the brief respite from machine rule that Philadelphia enjoyed under mayors Edwin H. Fitler and Edwin S. Stuart (1887–95). It was during the "reign of the Edwins," with the example of the Chicago fair shining in the west, that the boulevard scheme sud-

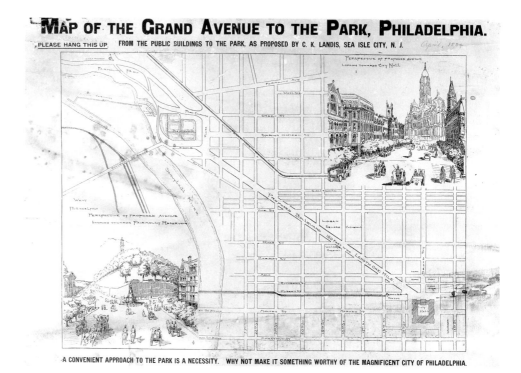

denly seized the attention of the city's leaders. But in the end the project, like the two honorable mayors, was pulled into the quagmire of Philadelphia politics and finally killed by the ethical doubts of the reformers themselves.

This first serious campaign for a parkway began in June 1891, when a group of prominent citizens gathered to discuss the need for a direct connection to the park and to begin a petition drive.[11] With about five hundred signatures, their petition was introduced into Common Council on June 11 by Thomas Hicks, councilman for the Thirty-Fourth Ward and legislative leader of the ensuing efforts.[12] The matter was then referred to committee and to the Bureau of Surveys, and from them came a favorable report that paved the way for legislation, introduced by Hicks on October 8. But there was insufficient support for the measure among his fellow councilmen, and he was

Fig. 9. Charles K. Landis (1835–1900), *Map of the Grand Avenue to the Park*. Plan and two perspectives, April 29, 1884. Lithograph with letterpress text, 18¹/₁₆ x 21¼" (45.9 x 54 cm). Inscribed: C. K. LANDIS, SEA ISLE CITY, N. J. April, 1884. Collection of Mrs. Joseph Carson, Philadelphia

therefore glad to see it sent to the Department of Public Works for a full study.

The director of public works was James H. Windrim (1840–1919), best known as the architect of the Masonic Temple at Broad and Filbert streets (1867–73). In 1891 he had just returned from service as the supervising architect of the United States Treasury in Washington in order to take up his position in the cabinet of Mayor Stuart, the respected owner of Leary's bookstore. Windrim produced a design for a boulevard 160 feet wide that led from Penn Square to the south flank of Fairmount, close to the end of the Spring Garden Street Bridge (fig. 10). With its eastern end centered on City Hall tower, the tree-lined roadway passed north of the craggy mass of the Pennsylvania Railroad's Broad Street Station and then cut northwestward to cross Logan Square on a diagonal that left undisturbed the Cathedral of Saints Peter and Paul on the east side of the square. West of Logan Square, the route proceeded undeflected through the brick mills and houses that lay between the square and the park. The mayor presented this plan to Councils on February 25, 1892.

Beating back complaints from some of the owners of factories in the proposed path of the parkway, Hicks won passage for a bill that embodied the Windrim design from Common Council on March 29. Select Council passed the measure unanimously, with almost no discussion, and the mayor signed the ordinance on April 12. After confirmation by the Bureau of Surveys, the parkway was, for the first time, an established fact—inscribed on the official maps of the city. But despite this success, Stuart and Windrim's plan did not enjoy deep support from the organization politicians who controlled Councils. Abetted by the Panic of 1893, which was blamed by many on the foes of the Republican establishment, they kept the question of funding the new street off the public agenda for two years.

It was not until April 2, 1894, that Stuart could ask to open the park boulevard. A bill to condemn all of the required properties west of Logan Square was introduced, and Hicks and his allies were able to obtain the agreement of Councils in late June. Victory seemed at hand, although the finances of the project were shaky, relying not on appropriations but on the mayor's use of mandamus orders to redirect funds that were already appropriated.

The 1894 campaign for the boulevard enjoyed the support of the city's Republican newspapers and the business community, all of whom had come to see that the project would help the machine in the long run, even if a reformer like Stuart took credit for its initiation. Including the parkway on its agenda for a "New Philadelphia," the *Inquirer* led the fight with a long series of ardent editorials that decried the "old fogy element" who could not imagine anything but an old-fashioned city with brick houses "of oblong measurement, with marble door steps and white shutters."[13] Its rhapsodic celebration of "the people's avenue" borrowed heavily from lawyer James M. Beck, a lifelong proponent of the project who helped to establish that there was more at stake than a convenient route to the park. "Apart from the fact that it will . . .

Fig. 10. James H. Windrim (1840–1919), *Park Boulevard from City Hall to Fairmount Park*. Bird's-eye perspective from southeast, February 24, 1892. J. Hutchinson, delineator. Photograph of lost drawing. Inscribed: *Recommended February 24, 1892,—by—JAS. H. WINDRIM, Director of Public Works J. Hutchinson 1892*. Free Library of Philadelphia, Print and Picture Department

break the regularity of our streets," Beck wrote in the *Inquirer*, "which is destructive of architectural effect and has produced a monotony of appearance that has added nothing to the reputation of our city for beauty, . . . it will give us a magnificent driveway to the Park, [and] it will further create by its intersection with Broad and Penn Square, one of the most imposing plazas in the world." Moreover, the fruits of this beautification would be tangible, for Beck and the *Inquirer* argued that, as Paris had shown, beauty was an investment, attracting those who would fill the coffers of the city's merchants. Beck predicted "that that American city which first appreciates the utility of mere beauty will ultimately lead our Western civilization."[14]

Mayor Stuart must have watched these events with pleasure that turned to alarm. While his support for the boulevard was sincere, so was his commitment to sound management, and the use of mandamuses to pay for the project had dangerous implications. Moreover, the city was pressed by the need to rebuild its water supply system and improve the Delaware River piers. These, unlike the boulevard, were the kind of "good government" projects that he could support even in the financially difficult period that followed the Panic. On July 12, to the accompaniment of derisive hoots from the *Inquirer*, Stuart announced that he would veto the parkway legislation.[15] Far from overriding his veto, Councils now stampeded to remove the boulevard from the map entirely, lest the threat of condemnation lie like an incubus upon property owners. On December 14, 1894, it was stricken from the official surveys.

During the next legislative season, Councilman William G. Huey, one of Hicks's allies, promoted a more modest scheme that revived part of the Penington formula of 1871. Striking out due west from North Broad Street, his design would enlarge tiny Carlton Street, connect it to a roofed-over Reading Railroad line at Twenty-Second Street, and then proceed northwestward atop the railway to the park. The architects Clarence Schermerhorn and

Henry Reinhold, who had designed several houses for Huey in suburban Bala, worked out the details of the proposal, but it found no support among that majority who had endorsed at least the principle of the more ambitious Windrim-Stuart plan.[16]

Organizations Allied for a Parkway

Five years passed before an effort to restore the parkway to the city map could be mounted. But in 1900–1905, with the McMillan Plan for Washington as the backdrop, that restoration was accomplished. More important still, there came together a group of civic improvement organizations that were committed to the project, and it was they that would keep it before the public eye until it was completed.

Much of the credit for this success belongs to Albert Kelsey (1870–1950), an architect whose diverse background made him equally at home in the various camps of American architecture. As a founder and first president (in 1899) of the Architectural League of America, he had helped to fashion a volatile alliance between midwestern architects, shaped by the unconventional thinking of John Wellborn Root and Louis Sullivan, and eastern architectural associations like the T-Square Club of Philadelphia, where the method of the Ecole des Beaux-Arts was revered. What united these forces was their enmity toward the American Institute of Architects, the fortress of the architectural establishment and the home of what Kimball would call the "American classic." For a while, at least, this bond was sufficient. Alliance-building on behalf of the Philadelphia parkway was also difficult.

Kelsey launched his campaign with a speech entitled "A Rational Beauty for American Cities," delivered on January 27, 1900, at the Drexel Institute in Philadelphia. In it, he called for regional planning in order "to re-organize the crude growths of American municipalities."[17] More concrete objectives were added ten days later, when Kelsey helped to organize a meeting of those interested in urban reform at the home of local industrialist Daniel Baugh, a founder of the Art Club of Philadel-

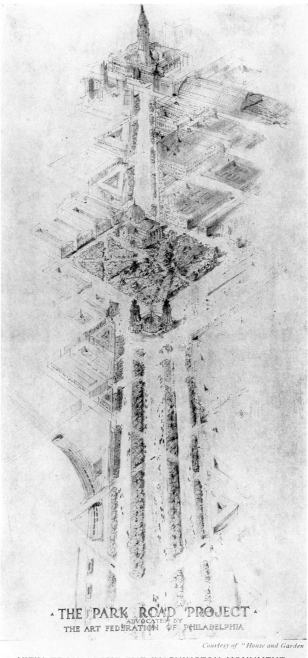

· THE PARK ROAD PROJECT ·
ADVOCATED BY
THE ART FEDERATION OF PHILADELPHIA

Courtesy of "House and Garden"

VIEW FROM ABOVE THE WASHINGTON MONUMENT

phia in 1887 and an active supporter of The University Museum of the University of Pennsylvania. They in turn invited representatives from eighteen cultural organizations to meet on April 10 at the Art Club. There, on the motion of architect Walter Cope, they created the "Art Federation of Philadelphia," with Baugh as president, Cope and James Beck as two of the vice-presidents, and Kelsey on the executive committee. All of the energy of the new organization was poured into the immediate formation of a boulevard committee headed by Beck and with Kelsey as chairman of a subcommittee of "experts."[18]

Over the next two years, the boulevard committee met more than a dozen times, in the end adopting the proposal put forward by Wilson Eyre, Jr., of the technical committee that the axis of the parkway should be aligned on the dome of the Catholic cathedral. The roadway would circle the cathedral, creating an enlarged Logan Square in the process, before continuing northwestward on an axis different from that used east of the square. Its western terminus was to be the equestrian statue of Washington that had been erected by the Society of the Cincinnati at the main entrance to the park, just north of the Fairmount reservoir (fig. 11). Kelsey designed a twin-towered Soldiers and Sailors Monument for the northwest corner of Logan Square, intended to frame views of the cathedral and City Hall tower for those coming down the boulevard from the park.

Elegant in conception, the Eyre-Kelsey proposal made maximum use of existing buildings and sculpture. But its broken axis, occluded at midpoint by the cathedral and terminated at the west by a smallish statue rather than the bulk of Fairmount, must have disappointed many of those who supported the parkway idea. In February 1902, at the behest of some of these citizens, the architect William J. McAuley designed a boulevard that ran ramrod straight from a plaza north of City Hall to the foot of Fairmount, passing just south of the cathedral en route.[19] Later in the spring, the McAuley supporters and the Art Federation began to confer, and, after a handful of meetings, they created the "Parkway Association." John H. Converse (a partner in the city's Baldwin Locomotive Works) was president, John G. Johnson (a lawyer and painting collector) and James Beck were among the vice-presidents, and the executive board included Alexander J. Cassatt (president of the Pennsylvania Railroad), Edward T. Stotesbury (a major partner in the Drexel and Morgan banking interests), and Peter A. B. Widener (a streetcar magnate and a great art collector). Samuel H. Ashridge, the machine's notorious "boodle mayor," was also among the founders, and on Beck's motion, they unanimously adopted the McAuley plan on June 12, 1902. Over a dozen editorials supporting their action appeared in the next few weeks. An invincible alliance had been created between powerful citizens and corrupt politicians.[20]

That fall, Kelsey, the secretary of the Parkway Association, compiled a booklet that detailed its story and assembled an array of stirring endorsements.[21] He illustrated the proposed plan, as he had redrawn it, and presented the same range of arguments that had been advanced to support the scheme in the 1890s (fig. 12). Inspirational photographs showed the great boulevards and avenues of Paris, Berlin, Mexico City, and Washington, D.C., and Beck introduced the brochure with the words, "The Boulevard project will not die."[22] On March 28, 1903, four months after its publication, Mayor Ashridge was able to sign an ordinance that restored the boulevard to the city map.

In their campaigns for the parkway, the Art Federation and the Parkway Association had been staunchly supported by two other municipal organizations of great importance for the continuing story of the project: the Fairmount Park Art Association and the City Parks Association of Philadelphia. As their names suggest, both were founded to promote the late-nineteenth-century movement to build and sustain urban parks, but in the twentieth century both accepted a wider range of challenges as their rightful domain. The new park boulevard was part of this new territory.

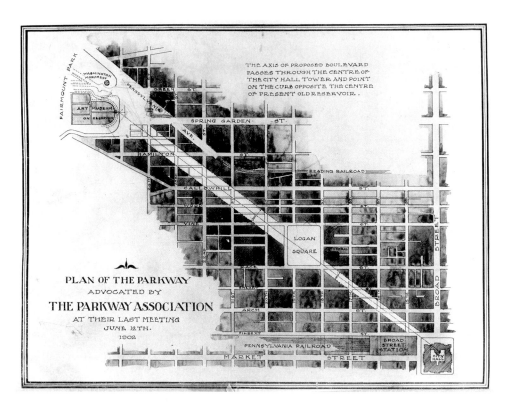

The older of the two, the Fairmount Park Art Association, had been created in 1871 to secure sculpture for the park and to beautify it in other ways. But starting in 1900, it increasingly turned its attention to some of the other problems of the city. It was then that Leslie W. Miller, principal of the industrial art school of the Pennsylvania Museum, was appointed to the important post of secretary. In this position he was responsible for the day-to-day affairs of the association, and for the next twenty years, under presidents like James Beck, John Converse, and Edward Stotesbury, he guided its unswerving and influential support for the parkway and related work. The major speakers chosen for the annual meetings held during the first years of Miller's tenure set the stage for these activities: Albert Kelsey ("A Rational Beauty for American Cities," 1900), Walter Cope ("The Relation of Natural

Fig. 12. Albert Kelsey, *Parkway Plan as Prepared for the Parkway Association*. Plan, 1902. Inscribed: *JUNE 12TH. 1902*. From Albert Kelsey, ed. and comp., *The Proposed Parkway for Philadelphia . . .* (Philadelphia, 1902), p. 6. University of Pennsylvania, Fine Arts Library, Philadelphia

to Artificial Beauty in Landscape," 1901), Kelsey ("Parkways and Monumental Thoroughfares," followed by Beck's "A Plea for the Parkway," 1902), Beck and Mayor John Weaver (separate remarks on the parkway, 1903), Frederick Law Olmsted, Jr. ("Progress in the Development of Park Systems—The Washington Example," 1904), and Frank Miles Day ("City Planning," 1905).[23]

The City Parks Association was slightly younger, having been founded in 1888, and, after two decades of work limited to the creation of additional parks, it too appointed an activist secretary in 1900, Andrew Wright Crawford. Aided by the architect Frank Miles Day, Crawford steered the association toward the broader issues of city planning. The first fruit of this was a *Special Report on the City Plan*, published in April 1902, in which Crawford made the case against extending the "baneful influence" of Philadelphia's gridiron street system into the surrounding hilly countryside.[24] It would be far better, he argued, to create diagonal roads, like the existing Ridge and Passyunk avenues or the proposed system of radiating boulevards that Day had designed at his behest for South Philadelphia. The Fairmount parkway, then being hammered out by the Art Federation and the Parkway Association, was also praised, and in the City Parks Association's next annual report Crawford cited Kelsey's pamphlet about it with enthusiasm. He also boosted the Northeastern (now Roosevelt) Boulevard, which, like the parkway, had recently been placed on the city map by Councils.[25]

Crawford and the City Parks Association made a specialty of arguing the economic case for such projects. Development costs, they asserted, would be more than offset by increased tax revenues from the improved properties. It was inaction that would be costly: "If Philadelphia remains rectangular, ugly, uninteresting, it will lose the millions of money that annually pass its doors."[26]

On many issues the interests of the City Parks Association and the Fairmount Park Art Association coincided exactly, and in January 1904, Miller and Crawford were among those who collaborated in creating the "Organizations Allied for the Acquisition of a Comprehensive Park System."[27] With Miller as chairman and Crawford as secretary, the alliance enlisted dozens of local civic organizations, schools, and government departments, and campaigned tirelessly for the conversion of virtually all of the region's creek and river valleys into parkland. Using Boston's "emerald necklace" of parks as their model for this kind of regional planning, in 1905 Crawford and Day prepared a comparative survey of American metropolitan park systems in which the Boston example and the system proposed for Washington were highly praised.[28]

With such prodding the machine moved quickly, and it seemed that Philadelphia's own parkway would soon join those of other cities. On October 13, 1906, Mayor John Weaver, who had experimented briefly with reform but was now back in the good graces of the organization, signed an ordinance to acquire all the needed properties west of Logan Square. Unfortunately, the victory was not absolute, for some months earlier Councils had bowed to political interests and approved a modification of the Parkway Association plan, again deflecting the axis of the avenue northward. As in the Eyre-Kelsey plan for the Art Federation, the western terminus was once more the Washington monument, and by breaking the axis of the roadway as it passed through Logan Square it made economical use of Pennsylvania Avenue, which the Reading Railroad had built for itself over its tracks in the 1890s. It was along this route that the demolition began on February 22, 1907, when the first brick was ceremonially removed from the chimney of a modest three-story house at 422 North Twenty-Second Street. The building was gone before the end of the day (fig. 13).

Mayor John Reyburn

Thus begun, the parkway was only a few weeks old when Mayor John E. Reyburn took office on April 1, 1907, and he quickly made the project his own. The new mayor had resigned from his fifth term in the United States House of Representatives to take up this position, and he returned to Philadelphia full of admiration for the proposals for Washington that he had seen in the McMillan Plan. He was thus very susceptible to the arguments that he now heard about the defects of the selected route. He immediately ordered that the project be restudied, and in the end the axis was adjusted. Reyburn's eagerness to promote the parkway and the other parts of a great works program may have also been related to his close connections with Philadelphia's great contractor bosses, "Sunny Jim" McNichol and the Vare brothers. After Reyburn left office, it was discovered that McNichol had gotten the city to redesign the Northeastern Boulevard in a way that maximized the profits of his construction company.

Reyburn's particular interest in the parkway had been kindled a few days after his inauguration when Peter A. B. Widener, the mighty developer of streetcar suburbs and art collector, invited him to call on him at his home, Lynnewood Hall, in suburban Elkins Park. Widener had been agitating for a new city art museum since 1893, and he now impressed upon the mayor the great possibility afforded by aiming the parkway directly at Fairmount, whose summit might be crowned by the new gallery. Indeed, he promised to build such a museum for the city, if only the parkway could be realigned.[29] The expectant mayor toured the parkway site on April 5, and, together with Council President McCurdy, Reyburn began to see what could be done to satisfy Widener's demands.

It was at precisely this point that the Fairmount Park Art Association entered the scene. Like Widener, it strongly supported the realignment of the boulevard, but, lacking the clout of Widener's wealth and position, the Art Association chose to bolster its case by commissioning a comprehensive plan for the development of the parkway from a group of architectural experts. Chosen on April 26, just three weeks after Reyburn's encounter with Widener, this team created a picture of the opportunities that were made possible by Widener's promised support. It also brought together most of those who would oversee the later realization of the parkway and its buildings: Paul

Fig. 13. 422 North Twenty-Second Street after partial demolition, February 22, 1907. City Archives of Philadelphia, 116.01, 2449

Cret, Clarence Zantzinger and his partners, and Horace Trumbauer.[30]

When named to the panel in 1907, Cret had only been in America for three and one-half years, but his intelligence, charm, and fluent English had already made him a kind of native son. Enormously respected by the local architectural community, he was working with Albert Kelsey in the competition for the headquarters building of the International Bureau of American Republics (now the Organization of American States) in Washington. Two months after Cret was appointed by the Fairmount Park Art Association, he learned that he and Kelsey had won the Washington commission.[31] Although Cret's relationship with Kelsey was sometimes stormy, with his partner driven to complain that he bore an unfair portion of the work,[32] the peripatetic Frenchman must have found Kelsey to be a priceless archive of information about the parkway project.

Clarence Zantzinger (1872–1954) was a *diplômé* of the Ecole des Beaux-Arts in 1901, and he may have known Cret in Paris. They had certainly been drawn together by various circumstances in Philadelphia. In 1905, they and Zantzinger's partner Charles Borie had collaborated on a study of the beautification of the banks of the Schuylkill, apparently undertaken for either the Fairmount Park Art Association or the City Parks Association. Cret took responsibility for the west bank.[33] It was Cret's custom to form partnerships with Americans for his major commissions, and, after his rather unhappy experience with Kelsey, Zantzinger was his usual choice. They worked together on the Indianapolis Public Library (1914–18), the Detroit Institute of Arts (1919–27), and the unsuccessful competition bids for the Nebraska capitol in Lincoln (1919) and the Liberty Memorial in Kansas City (1920).

Cret was not always entirely satisfied with his collaborator's work, which sometimes seemed dry and lifeless by French standards. During World War I, which he spent in the French army, he even complained to his wife about the "badly overcooked rationalisms" with which Zantzinger was doctoring the Indianapolis library design.[34] But at that time he also suspected Zantzinger of German sympathies. His own students apart, however, Zantzinger probably enjoyed more of Cret's respect than any other Philadelphian.

The same sympathy extended to Zantzinger's partners, Charles L. Borie, Jr. (1870–1943), and Milton B. Medary, Jr. (1874–1929). A civil engineering student at the University of Pennsylvania, Borie had worked in his father's banking office until 1902, when Wilson Eyre's work for the senior Borie inspired him to try his own hand in architecture. Zantzinger accepted Borie as a business partner, but his design talents soon blossomed. He was also very well connected socially, and, like Zantzinger, he played a large role in the various organizations that promoted municipal improvements. Indeed, Borie was made a trustee of the Fairmount Park Art Association soon after Zantzinger was appointed to the team of architects. He played a large part in making the 1907 design.

Milton Medary was practicing as an independent architect in 1907 and did not participate in the report made for the Fairmount Park Art Association. When he did join Zantzinger and Borie in 1910, however, he was immediately brought into their ongoing work on the parkway. He had studied architecture briefly at Pennsylvania, and although Cret sometimes denigrated his lack of training, he regarded him fondly.[35]

A gulf separated the art association's third appointee—Horace Trumbauer (1868–1938)—from Cret and the Zantzinger partnership. The latter had university associations and Beaux-Arts sympathies, whereas Trumbauer had been trained by the old-fashioned apprenticeship method in the architectural office of G. W. and W. D. Hewitt. They had also either inherited or won acceptance by Philadelphia's old elite, while he served its brashest *nouveaux riches*, P.A.B. Widener and William Elkins, the utility monopolists turned art collectors, for whom he built great houses in Elkins Park. Trumbauer's architectural styles were as varied as the needs of his clients, and he hired the talent necessary to produce whatever was needed. This chameleonism earned him the deep contempt of Cret, who saw combined in Trumbauer all of the worst features of American architectural practice. To his wife Cret confided that his own artistic stubbornness, while sometimes trying, was essential for any architect who was to be more than "a simple Trumbauer."[36] Nevertheless, it was Trumbauer's open way of doing business that led him to employ talented designers like Julian Abele (1881–1950), the first black graduate in architecture from the University of Pennsylvania. Trumbauer hired Abele, an architect with some French experience, around 1906, and he became one of the chief designers in the office in 1909. His hand may be seen in some of the parkway buildings.

Such was the team of experts that the Fairmount Park Art Association assembled in April 1907. Cret, Borie, and Zantzinger had worked together before on similar projects and thus in a sense represented the architectural and political reformers' long-standing interest in the boulevard. Trumbauer, on the other hand, represented P.A.B. Widener's vital personal interests. Together, they also represented the two brands of classical architecture then being practiced in America. But in 1907 none of these differences were detectable, because everyone soon agreed about the proper route of the parkway.

Cret and Trumbauer accepted their appointments to the parkway design panel immediately, but Zantzinger was out of town and did not reply until May 20.[37] Leslie W. Miller, secretary of the association, reassured him then that little had been done in his absence and that Borie could fill him in easily, since, as a trustee of the art association, he was "the author of the whole movement, and can tell you much better than anyone else."[38] Zantzinger later recalled that it was his partner who had pushed from the start for a realignment of the axis onto Fairmount and that

it was he who located the Philadelphia Museum of Art on Fairmount as the focal point of this axis, and he who conceived the notion of creating an art educational center for Philadelphia by grouping about the foot of Fairmount the art teaching institutions of the city. These institutions in his thought will eventually surround a plaza which, while creating a proper foreground for the museum on the height, at the same time serves as a physical terminus for the Parkway and other radiating avenues. The opportunity is, perhaps, unique in any city in the world and it was he who saw it, and he that conceived of thus creating about the foot of an acropolis devoted to the presentation of works of art the institutions in which artists should be locally trained.[39]

Borie's idea was quickly put into shape during the month that elapsed before Cret sailed for his summer holiday in France. It formed the substance of Zantzinger's preliminary report to the association of July 3, 1907,[40] and, when

Cret returned, he prepared a bird's-eye view of the shifted axis with a cluster of institutions gathered at the foot of Fairmount (fig. 14). Stretching away from the hill to the city, the boulevard was closely lined by large buildings, giving it a distinctly urban, Parisian character. As Zantzinger recorded, "it is not an extension of Fairmount Park which is being created. It is an avenue in the city giving access to Fairmount Park . . . ."[41]

Fig. 14. Paul P. Cret (1876–1945), Horace Trumbauer (1868–1938), and Zantzinger and Borie, *Parkway Plan as Prepared for the Fairmount Park Art Association*. Bird's-eye perspective from east, 1907. Paul P. Cret, delineator. Lithograph, 34 x 31¾″ (86.4 x 80.6 cm). Inscribed: *P.P.C. HORACE TRUMBAUER C. C. ZANTZINGER PAUL P. CRET*. Philadelphia Museum of Art, Archives, 90.1

Fig. 15. The future route of the parkway seen from City Hall tower, with the short stretch of the "temporary parkway" visible at top center; May 24, 1909. City Archives of Philadelphia, 116, 3384

In early July 1907, while Cret was incapacitated in France by a long illness, the others met with Mayor Reyburn. Already committed to shifting the parkway, the mayor was pleased with their recommendations, and, as Zantzinger reported to Cret, he asked for the Department of Public Works to estimate the costs of the project.[42] It was then that a major difficulty emerged, for the more southerly routing was found to add about $2 million to the cost of the project, traversing, as it did, industrial properties that would be more expensive to acquire. In the fall, City Council President McCurdy sought to overcome this problem with an ordinance for a parkway that, while still focused on the prospective museum site, managed to skirt the most expensive land by again breaking the axis at Logan Square.[43]

Despite its cost, the architects remained determined to preserve the straight axis, and on November 11, Borie, Miller, and Andrew Wright Crawford (who, as secretary of the City Parks Association, had joined with the Fairmount Park Art Association in supporting the project) met again with the mayor.[44] The financial situation was, they discovered, genuinely serious, and so they attempted to piece together a compromise. It consisted of a straight, single-axis boulevard from City Hall to the park that skirted the most expensive, south-lying real estate. But in order to provide an elevated building site for the museum at the end of this more northerly axis, an artificial extension was to be built northward from the Fairmount hilltop. It appeared that even this would be cheaper than the condemnation of certain property.

Zantzinger included the compromise plan in his final report to the Fairmount Park Art Association on December 12, 1907, but the architects also presented their original scheme. The comparison of the two made the hill-building alternative look ludicrous, and Mayor Reyburn graciously conceded that the commission knew "'more about it than I do, therefore I will be guided by their advice.'"[45]

For more than a year, the mayor campaigned for the support he needed to drive the parkway axis straight through the expensive properties that lay between Logan Square and Fairmount (figs. 15–16). In April 1908 he won approval from the voters for a loan of $1 million for the boulevard, and on November 25 he conducted a celebrated afternoon tour for councilmen and representatives of the various public institutions that he hoped to interest in Borie's cultural center. Together with Miller and Borie, he led them along the proposed parkway route and to the top of Fairmount, where they enjoyed the panoramic view. They then repaired to his house at Nineteenth and Spring Garden streets for refreshments, and as they

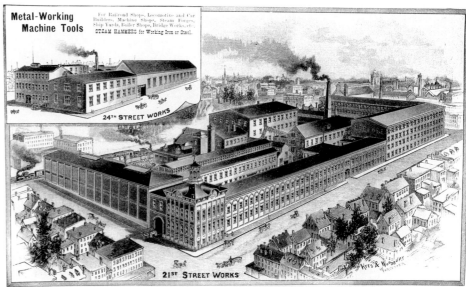

walked along the mayor pointed back to the reservoir and proclaimed, "'That's where the City Museum will be!'" A councilman was overheard to say, "'Oh, let the old fool ramble on. It can't happen!'" But among those in the mayor's party was Eli Kirk Price, a grandson of one of the first great advocates of Fairmount Park and the president of the City Parks Association and vice-president of the Fairmount Park Commission. Price was converted to Reyburn's vision that afternoon, and the parkway had thus won its staunchest supporter.[46]

Finally, after months of intense lobbying, Councils placed the Cret-Zantzinger-Borie plan on the official city map on June 8, 1909, and that fall the mayor built wooden pergolas along the "temporary parkway," as the abandoned route, where demolition had begun, was euphemistically labeled (fig. 17). These were designed to give some impression of the effect that unified facades would ultimately create, but Reyburn surely realized that more substantive progress would require yet broader sup-

Fig. 16. *Bement, Miles & Co., Twenty-First and Callowhill Streets.* Bird's-eye perspective from north, 1892. Engraving, 6¼ x 9¾" (15.9 x 24.8 cm). Inscribed: KEYS & WOODBURY WORCESTER. The Historical Society of Pennsylvania, Philadelphia. Campbell Collection, vol. 90, p. 135

port. To that end, on October 7 he assembled a very large group of prominent bankers and businessmen who, together with his department heads, agreed to serve on a "Comprehensive Plans Committee." His model may have been the *Plan of Chicago*, the wide-ranging document prepared by Daniel Burnham and Edward H. Bennett for the Commercial Club of that city and just published on July 4.[47] But Reyburn's committee was also clearly guided by the local example of regional planning set by the City Parks Association, which campaigned forcefully for the committee.[48]

Although the committee established the Fairmount parkway as the centerpiece of its deliberations, it also divided itself into working groups, many of which considered such issues as port facilities, Latin-American trade, and railroads. They labored at this for more than a year while the mayor, now strongly seconded by Price, strove to lure the city's schools and other cultural institutions into moving to the parkway. Condemnation and demolition, meanwhile, proceeded on the new alignment as rapidly as the relatively small appropriations would allow.

The timing of the report of the committee was carefully scheduled to prepare the scene for the Third Annual City Planning Conference, to be held in Philadelphia in May 1911. To accompany the report, the Department of Public Works constructed a thirty-foot model of the parkway, and William E. Groben (1883–1961), a talented young Ecole-trained architect in the department, prepared drawings of the proposed art museum and the institutions that were to gather around it (figs. 18–19). A first glimpse of these materials was afforded when the Comprehensive Plans Committee reported to the mayor on February 24, 1911, and they excited universal admiration. Frederick Law Olmsted, Jr., president of the City Planning Conference held the year before, explained that it was Reyburn's work that had attracted the 1911 convention to Philadelphia: "'Your city,' he said, 'is the farthest advanced in the country . . . in city planning.'"[49]

The conference, which was held on May 15–17, 1911, attracted two hundred delegates from more than one hundred cities in Canada, Britain, and the United States.[50] Mayor Reyburn played the proud host for lavish dinners and tours of his city, and those in attendance heard lectures by Olmsted, Ernest Flagg, Raymond Unwin, and Frank Miles Day, among others. The public thronged to exhibitions that lined the corridors and filled the public rooms on the second and third floors of City Hall, with twenty thousand reportedly visiting on the first day. They could see Groben's drawings and the great model of the parkway and compare them with equally lavish presentations of the *Plan of Chicago* and the McMillan Plan for Washington. As the *Public Ledger* editorialized, the exhibited works offered a clear lesson:

They show . . . in a superlative degree that [a] combination of art and good taste in architectural designing and landscape gardening is the dominant note in all modern municipal progress, a trend which practically took its start — so far as America is concerned — from the Chicago Exposition in 1894 [sic], and which has revolutionized the external aspects of the public works of the nation.[51]

The exhibition remained open for a month after the conference, with frequent noontime lectures by local experts, and when it was over a vision of the parkway had become public property.

Fig. 17. Construction of pergolas on the temporary parkway, September 25, 1909. City Archives of Philadelphia, 116.01, 3587

In the June 1911 election, the voters approved another $1 million loan for the parkway, and Reyburn, in his last months in office, pushed to demolish as much as possible. Large tracts of open land were now visible west of Logan Square, and some lots had also been cleared for a public plaza north of City Hall. On June 12 the Fairmount Park Commission appointed the team of Borie, Trumbauer, and Zantzinger to design an art museum, followed on July 8 by a vote in Councils to make the Comprehensive Plans Committee permanent. John Reyburn's legacy seemed to be complete, his accomplishment summarized in the *Public Ledger*'s pronouncement: "The recent agitation for 'city planning' is not a fad."[52]

Completion

Reyburn was succeeded as mayor by Rudolph Blankenburg, the perennial "old war horse of reform" whose election in 1911 was the first significant success for Progressive Era politics in Philadelphia. The "Old Dutch Cleanser" had run on a platform supporting the continuation of Reyburn's city planning work, but he promised to entrust the project to honest hands. This seemed to have been guaranteed when, following his election, Blankenburg institutionalized the Comprehensive Plans Committee and appointed Morris Llewellyn Cooke as his director of public works. A protégé of efficiency expert Frederick Taylor, Cooke reformed the bidding and contracting practices of his department and fired more than a thousand workers in his four years on the job. But he and Blankenburg repeatedly failed to obtain the appropriations they needed from the machine-controlled City Councils, and when funding finally was approved, the result was sometimes astonishing. Such was the case in 1915 when money was at last provided for the Broad Street subway and "Sunny Jim" McNichol tendered the bona fide lowest bid.[53]

The parkway languished during the four years of Blankenburg's administration, and at the end of his term his own house still stood undisturbed on the west side of quiet Logan Square (fig. 20). However, during those years

Fig. 18. Department of Public Works, City of Philadelphia, *The Parkway as Shown on the Comprehensive Plan.* Model from southeast and plan of Fairmount Plaza, May 1911. Photograph of lost originals. City Archives of Philadelphia, 117.01, 4750

Fig. 19. Department of Public Works, City of Philadelphia, *Fairmount Plaza and the Art Museum.* Perspective from south, 1911. William E. Groben (1883–1961), delineator. Photograph of lost watercolor. Inscribed: *William E. Groben, Architect—Department of Public Works. 1911.* City Archives of Philadelphia, 117.01, 4762

the state legislature had taken action that was profoundly important for the shape assumed by the project when it did resume: In May 1915 the representatives gave all cities the important right to control construction within two hundred feet of park land, and the Philadelphia City Councils responded by voting to annex the parkway to Fairmount Park. This would give protective jurisdiction over the impending development to the Fairmount Park Commission, an arm of city government that had been created in 1867 to oversee the city's growing park system. Although appointed by the mayor and funded by Councils, the commission was notably autonomous (it even had its own police force), and it was this independence that apparently prompted Blankenburg to veto the bill that would have placed the parkway under their authority. His veto was overridden, but the Fairmount Park Commission waited until Mayor Thomas B. Smith took office in 1916 before it exercised its new powers and drafted separate height and land use regulations for the Fairmount–Logan Square and Logan Square–City Hall components of the parkway. These controls, effectively the city's first zoning, were adopted by the commission on December 13, 1916.[54]

Smith's election restored machine rule to City Hall, and while in office he was twice indicted for election offenses. But his friendship with contractors did foster a favorable attitude toward all public works projects. While it was Reyburn who permanently put the parkway on the map, it was Smith who placed it on the ground. During his first year as mayor he secured an extraordinary loan of $9 million for its construction, and on July 24, 1916, he signed an ordinance to open the boulevard for its entire length. Work leapt ahead, and by the time America entered the war in Europe on April 6, 1917, there were acres of rubble in which the marines could practice battlefield maneuvers.[55] That fall, a contract for $202,000 was awarded to the McNichol Paving and Construction Company to complete the roadway between Logan Square and the park.[56]

Wartime posed remarkably few obstacles for the rapid execution of the project. Two factory buildings engaged in war work were allowed to stand on the periphery of the site for the duration of the conflict, and the Medico-Chirurgical Hospital, which lay across the route of the parkway between Seventeenth and Eighteenth streets, was also spared; it first served as a navy hospital and was then pressed into use during the influenza epidemic of 1918 (fig. 21). Everything else was demolished by the end of the summer of 1918, and on October 26, with a temporary road laid around the hospital, the parkway was declared fully open. It was ready to receive the heroes from Europe, where the official armistice was still several weeks away.

The Fairmount Park Commission, vested with its new powers, watched this giddy progress with some apprehension. The official plan had been adopted in 1909, and it in turn was based on the Cret-Zantzinger-Trumbauer report of 1907—all of this occurring long before the parkway had come under its jurisdiction. On March 3, 1917, at the urging of its president, Edward T. Stotesbury, the commission hired a consultant to look again at the design of the proposed roadways and the siting of buildings. Their selection fell on Jacques Gréber (1882–1962), a French landscape architect and city planner who had first visited America in 1910 and was then in Philadelphia designing the grounds for Whitemarsh Hall, the great Palladian house that Trumbauer was building for Stotesbury on the outskirts of the city. A product of the Ecole des Beaux-Arts, Gréber was to have a distinguished career as one of that generation of planners who took the lessons of French academic design for one last time both into the provinces and across the globe.[57] He made master plans for Paris's fortification zone (1919) as well as for Lille (1920), Marseilles (1930–33), Ottawa (1939, 1945–51), and Rouen (1942, 1945). In 1928 he was appointed to the committee that reviewed the planning proposals made by all French cities, and he served as chief architect of the Exposition Internationale in Paris in 1937. But all this lay

in the future when Gréber received his Philadelphia assignment in 1917. It was here that he made his reputation.

A month after Gréber's appointment, America joined the war and he returned to France, but the hostilities did not interrupt his work for Philadelphia. That fall his Paris office began to turn out a vast series of plans, rendered elevations, and sections of the parkway and its buildings, and Gréber himself came back to Philadelphia in November 1917 with a sheaf of huge drawings (figs. 22, 23, 53), which he augmented with his own lively crayon sketches, made in Philadelphia (fig. 24). This material was presented to the Art Jury, the panel appointed by the mayor to review the design of public buildings, and they granted their approval on January 25, 1918. At the annual meeting of the Fairmount Park Art Association on January 30, 1918, the drawings were publicly exhibited for the first time, and, at Charles Borie's suggestion, the association undertook to publish them in the form of a booklet.[58]

On February 14, 1918, Gréber won an even larger commission from the Fairmount Park Commission: a contract for $40,000 for detailed scale drawings of the park-

Fig. 20. Logan Square in the snow, looking north, December 16, 1915. The Franklin Institute Science Museum, Philadelphia

Fig. 21. The parkway from City Hall tower, with the Medico-Chirurgical Hospital still standing in the future roadway; March 18, 1918. City Archives of Philadelphia, 116, 14806

way drives and the landscaping around the museum.[59] He returned again to Paris but was back in America in November, on the eve of the armistice. At the behest of Joseph Widener, for whom he had reconfigured the gardens at Lynnewood Hall, he now designed a victory arch to greet the troops on South Broad Street.[60] However, the project, sketched out in office space borrowed from Trumbauer, was never realized.

Leaving Philadelphia at peace on December 21, Gréber launched a final great campaign of drawing in Paris during the first months of 1919 (figs. 26, 63); this work was approved by the Fairmount Park Commission on March 12. Gréber came again to Philadelphia in July, leading a delegation of French architects who were gather-

ing ideas for postwar reconstruction, but save for a small contract for very large-scale details of landscape features in 1922, his landscaping work on the parkway was over.[61] More than one hundred drawings had been prepared.

The starting point for Gréber's labors was clearly the Cret-Zantzinger-Trumbauer design of 1907, in large part because the great, triple roadway west of Logan Square had already been built as shown on their plan before he arrived. But Gréber was nevertheless able to change one of the fundamental characteristics of the earlier scheme, converting the parkway from an urban boulevard into a green wedge of park, reaching inward toward the congested center of the city. He now extended Pennsylvania Avenue eastward all the way to Logan Square on a converging course with the main roadway, and to balance it he created a secondary avenue on the other side of the main carriageways. Together they defined a triangle of parkland, for rather than line the boulevard with buildings, Gréber scattered only a few structures through the landscape. In addition to the art schools that he showed gathered around the plaza at the foot of Fairmount, the most notable of these buildings was a proposed Episcopal cathedral, shown on the present Rodin Museum site at Twenty-Second Street in his 1917–18 drawings but shifted to the other side of the parkway in 1919. Making note himself of the new image in which the project was cast, Gréber observed that it included both "'the creation of a real civic center'" in the buildings at Fairmount and around Logan Square, and "'the opening of the very heart of the city to the sanitary breezes of Fairmount Park.'"[62]

Gréber's design also nicely smoothed some of the awkwardnesses of the earlier plan. Fairmount Plaza, heretofore a great, windswept expanse of paving, now had the monument of Washington moved to its center, to be placed between a pair of new fountains. Logan Square, enlarged westward to Twentieth Street, was now converted wholeheartedly into Logan "Circle." On its north side he showed a pair of structures that were detailed like the eighteenth-century buildings on the north side of the

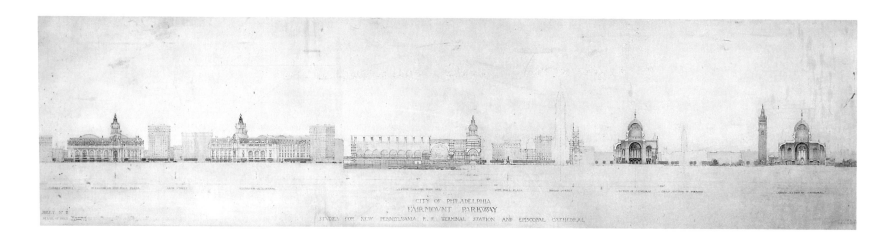

Fig. 22. Jacques Gréber (1882–1962), *The New Pennsylvania Railroad Station and Episcopal Cathedral*. Elevations and sections, October 25, 1917. Gréber office, delineators. Brown line and watercolor, 26¾ x 107¾″ (68 x 273.7 cm). Inscribed: *J. GRÉBER, S.A.D.G. PARIS, x 25th 1917*. Philadelphia Museum of Art, Archives, 90.7

Fig. 22, detail

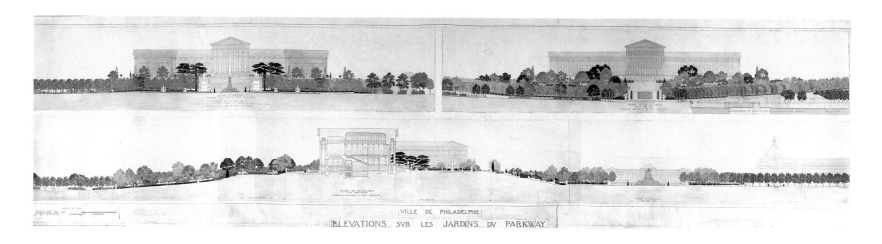

Fig. 23. Jacques Gréber, *The Art Museum and the Pennsylvania Academy of the Fine Arts.* Elevations and section, fall 1917. Gréber office, delineators. Watercolor, gouache, metallic paint, and ink on paper; 38¼ x 155″ (97.2 x 393.7 cm). Inscribed: *Jacques Gréber* **TRUMBAUER, ZANTZINGER ET BORIE, ARCHITECTES**. Philadelphia Museum of Art, Archives, 90.8

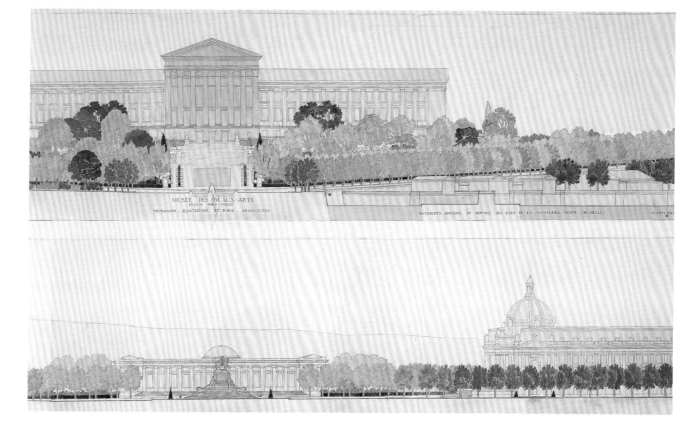

Fig. 23, detail

Place de la Concorde in Paris; these were realized as the present Free Library and Municipal Court. Gréber was, of course, conscious of this reference to Paris and of the entire project's resemblance to the Champs Elysées, which he alluded to gracefully:

"I am glad to say that, if by this work the city of Paris may be enabled to bring to its sister in America the inspiration of what makes Paris so attractive to visitors, it will be the first opportunity of Paris to pay a little of the great debt of thankfulness for what Philadelphia and its citizens have done for France during the last three years."[63]

Cret, from his vantage in the French army, naturally harbored resentments as he watched Gréber at work. With his nation at war, he saw his countryman commuting back and forth across the Atlantic to Cret's adopted city, allying himself with Trumbauer, Cret's frequent nemesis, and pushing himself into the forefront of a project that Cret considered his own. His resentments were further inflamed early in 1918 when Kelsey sent him newspaper clippings that illustrated what Gréber was proposing. Kelsey gave the work a mixed review,[64] but Cret, to his wife, was scathing:

Gréber cuts for himself a coat from the fabric that I have woven. His project does not bring a single new idea to the beautification and improvement of Philadelphia. It takes up all of the principles that we already established, overloading them with a very academic sauce (whose least defect is being unrealizable), and presents them pleasantly enough in a series of drawings made in Paris by a band of students at the Ecole.[65]

In December 1918 Kelsey wrote again, enclosing a clipping of an interview in which Gréber announced that he was about to return to France, where he would do what he could to get Cret released from the service as soon as possible. Kelsey seemed to take some small pleasure at the pain that this arrogant assertion would cause his erstwhile collaborator, and he went on:

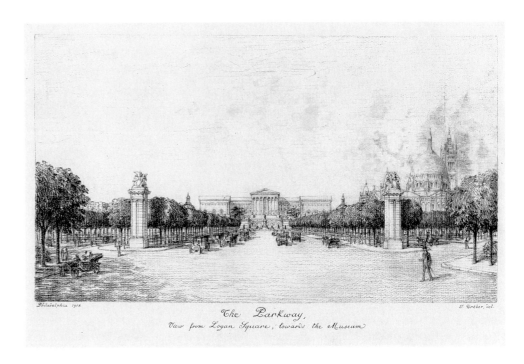

Without venturing to comment on Greber's interview I will tell you this: A year ago I was lunching at the Art Club & turning to see who was at the next table I saw Greber & Trumbauer, & heard the latter say: "you make the balls & I'll throw them": Then Greber said something about Cret—"he's a very good designer." "No," Trumbauer scoffed—& I heard no more—.[66]

Cret was now seriously worried—or at least annoyed—for he could not have known that at the time of the overheard conversation Gréber was using Trumbauer's office to work on the garden design for Whitemarsh Hall and that their ambiguous words were probably directed at that project. Not realizing this, on January 10, 1919, Cret wrote to Eli Kirk Price, vice-president of the Fairmount Park Commission, who replied with praise and courtesy. Most important, he reassured Cret that Gréber's work "was limited to the preparation of plans for the landscape gardening required for the development of the

Fig. 24. Jacques Gréber, *The Parkway, Looking from Logan Square Toward the Art Museum.* Perspective, 1918. Crayon on paper, mounted on card; 19⅜ x 26¾" (49.2 x 67.9 cm). Inscribed: *Philadelphia 1918 J. Gréber, del.* The Commissioners of Fairmount Park, Philadelphia

Parkway in accordance with your original designs and especially for the treatment of the grounds surrounding the Art Museum, for which no plan had ever been prepared."[67] This was not strictly true, but it was a small offense to lie diplomatically in order to ease the traumas induced by separation and war. Indeed, Cret and Gréber were reconciled in time, and they collaborated congenially enough on the Rodin Museum and other later planning projects.

Cret's distant misgivings counted for little in any case, and the Art Jury strongly recommended that Councils place Gréber's design on the city plan. But this was never done, perhaps because Gréber's proposal only seemed to be a minor adjustment to the already recorded design. Many of its salient features were built anyway under the direction of the Fairmount Park Commission: For example, the plaza below Fairmount was redesigned with the Washington statue at its center, and Logan Circle

was cast in the form that, save for its perforation by the Vine Street Expressway, is found today. More important, Gréber's vision of a wedge of park replaced the concept of a boulevard; indeed it became even more of a park because many of the potential tenants found it impossible to build the projected new buildings.

Jacques Gréber revisited Philadelphia on many occasions during his career. In 1926–29 his work on the Rodin Museum brought him across the Atlantic frequently, and in 1930 he served as a consultant for the city's newly created City Planning Commission. On these visits he would have seen the new parkway complete. To be sure, the memorial oak trees—honoring those sacrificed in the First World War—had not yet filled in. But some 1,300 properties had been demolished at a cost nearing $35 million, and since 1928 Fairmount had been crowned by a great, yellow temple of art (fig. 25). Charles Mulford Robinson's "promise . . . of a new day" had been fulfilled.

Fig. 25. The parkway, with the soon-to-open art museum framed by the Soldiers and Sailors Monument, February 17, 1928. City Archives of Philadelphia, 116.01, 25260

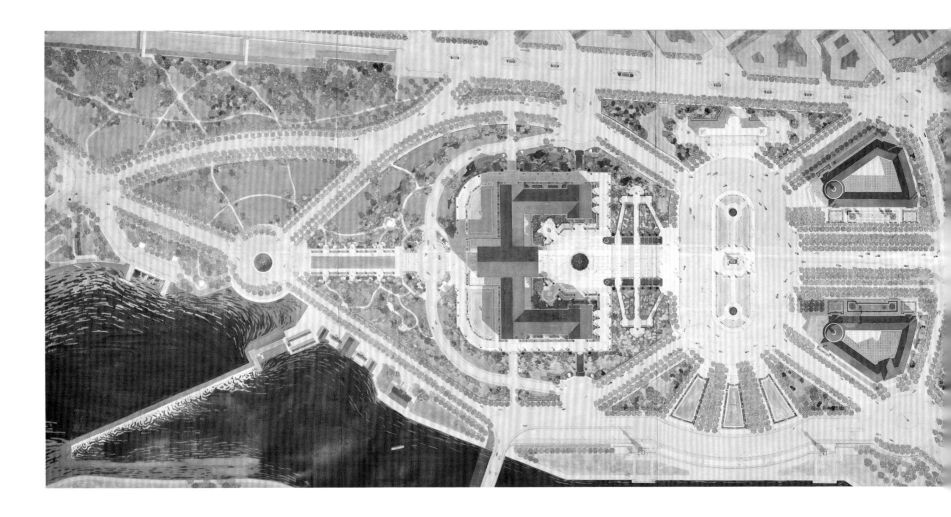

Fig. 26. Jacques Gréber, *The Parkway from Fairmount to Logan Square*. Plan, c. February 1919. Gréber office, delineators. Watercolor and ink on two sheets of paper, 55⅜ x 219⅜″ (140.6 x 557.2 cm) (overall). Philadelphia Museum of Art, Archives, 90.9a,b

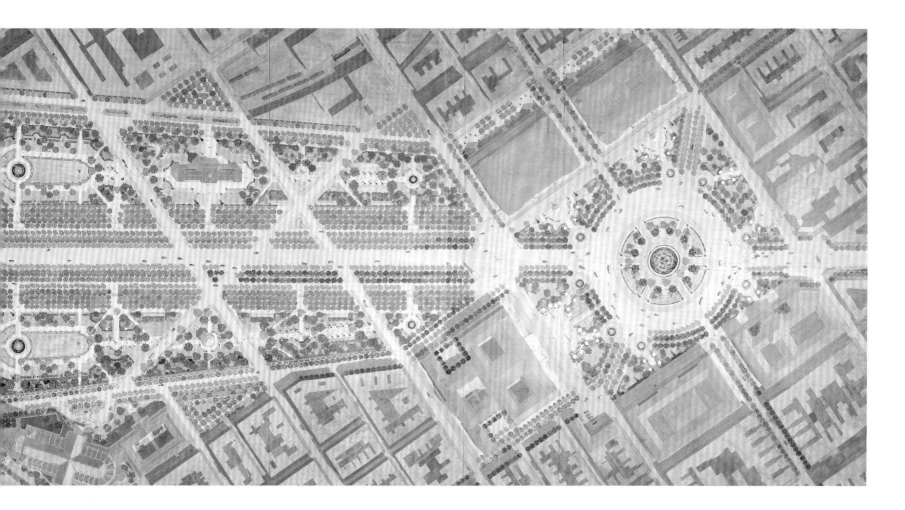

The Museum of Art:
"A Philadelphian Acropolis"

Hugh Ferriss's imaginative rendering of masses of people gathered before the steps of the new
art museum, 1925 (fig. 56, detail)

When the Pennsylvania Museum welcomed the public to its new home on Fairmount in March 1928, it had been almost thirty-four years to the day since P.A.B. Widener had persuaded the Fairmount Park Commission to construct a new building. Even at its opening, however, only twenty exhibition galleries had been completed, and the ordeal of finishing just this small part of the vast structure had already alienated many of those whom it had been designed to please. John G. Johnson had added a codicil to his will shortly before his death in 1917 that was designed to keep his exceptional art collection in a home of its own, and in 1920 Widener's son and heir had let it be known that his father's paintings would never hang inside the new museum. But out of this story of delay and bitterness emerged a building and an institution of unusual strengths that is also a mirror of the vitality with which American architecture faced the new century.[1]

The construction of a new museum was first mooted in 1893, when the city received the paintings assembled by W. P. Wilstach, a Philadelphia leather manufacturer. His collection also came with an endowment of over $500,000. The Fairmount Park Commission, to whom the city entrusted both the paintings and the funds, immediately launched a purchasing campaign that was guided in turn by commissioners P.A.B. Widener and John G. Johnson—the city's greatest collectors and, it was hoped from the start, future contributors to the city's art collection. The prospect of joining New York and Boston in the first rank of American museums was immediately apparent.

The new pictures were placed in Memorial Hall, built in Fairmount Park as part of the great Centennial Exhibition of 1876 (fig. 27).[2] There they joined the heterogeneous holdings of the Pennsylvania Museum, chartered after the fair to maintain a collection of hand- and machine-made artifacts and to administer a school of industrial and applied arts. Modeled on the Victoria and Albert Museum and its associated school in London, the Pennsylvania Museum had scarcely been an "art" museum at all before 1893, but the arrival of the Wilstach Collection and the attentions of Widener and Johnson began to redirect its development. The metamorphosis was made complete in 1938, when the institution, now housed in its temple on Fairmount, officially renamed itself the Philadelphia Museum of Art, the name most people had attached to it ever since the move into the new building ten years earlier. After World War II the museum also detached itself from its schools, today the independent Philadelphia University of the Arts and the Philadelphia College of Textiles and Science.

Memorial Hall, although designed by Hermann J. Schwarzmann (1846–1891) to serve as the art gallery of the centennial, functioned badly as a modern art museum. The Wilstach paintings had to be hung on freestanding wall panels beneath the unsatisfactory skylights of the cavernous west gallery, and the building was soon strained by robust attendance figures, with 379,419 visitors coming through the doors in 1894.[3] Calls were promptly made to enlarge and improve the building, and these were repeated at regular intervals for the next decade. But the Fairmount Park Commission, its owner, only reluctantly provided additional galleries in 1901–3 by enclosing the two courtyards on either side of the south entrance. John G. Johnson complained in 1900 that to tinker with the old building "'would be to throw good money after bad. . . . The building is an architectural botch as a repository for good pictures . . . .'"[4] In this he was strongly seconded by Widener.

A Competition for Lemon Hill

It was P.A.B. Widener's vision of an entirely new building, closer to the city but still in the park, that was eventually realized on Fairmount. He let his feelings be known on this subject in 1893, and on March 10, 1894, he convinced the Fairmount Park Commission to forgo making improvements to Lemon Hill, the Federal period mansion that stands on a hilltop above the Schuylkill near Boathouse Row. Lemon Hill, he argued, was the proper site

for a new museum, and he made them agree instead to ask the City Councils for $25,000 with which to obtain a design.[5] One month later the commission's Committee on Memorial Hall (on which Widener served) reported unfavorably on the proposal to enlarge the 1876 gallery, seconding Widener's plan for a new museum. Consultation with the Park Committee of Councils had begun.[6]

The year 1894 saw Mayor Stuart's efforts to open the parkway wither and die, but the museum plan proceeded with increasing momentum. On June 4 the Park Commission approved the first purchases out of the Wilstach bequest—Eugène Delacroix's *Interior of a Dominican Convent in Madrid (The Respectable Apology)*[7] and Félix Ziem's *Mills in Holland*.[8] Justice Samuel Thompson, chairman of the Memorial Hall committee, crowed that they were thus beginning to "lay the substantial foundations of a gallery that will make Philadelphia one of the greatest of the great art cities of the world."[9] On March 9, 1895, with $25,000 in prize money made available by the city, the commission voted to conduct an open competition for the design of a museum on Lemon Hill. Good

Fig. 27. Hermann J. Schwarzmann (1846–1891), *Memorial Hall*. The large east gallery, used to display tapestries and pottery; the Wilstach Collection occupied the identical west gallery. From *The Fortieth Annual Report of the Trustees of the Pennsylvania Museum and School of Industrial Art* (Philadelphia, 1916)

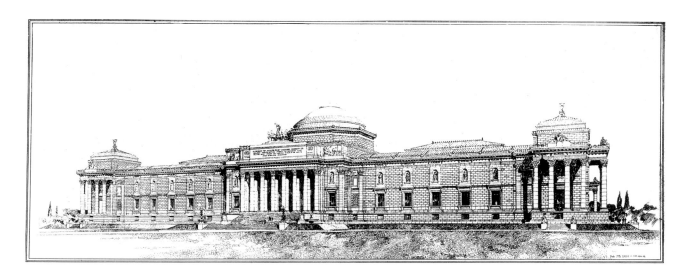

news bred more of the same, and in April they learned that the trustees of the Franklin Fund, set up by Benjamin Franklin in his will to benefit his adopted city, would assign $158,000 to the project if Franklin's name were attached to the building and if the city made an adequate supplemental appropriation. The commission voted on May 11, 1895, to build the gallery in parts, naming each section for its benefactor.[10]

Meanwhile, the competing architects had begun to work on their entries, and on June 27 a delegation of them met with the Memorial Hall committee (assigned the task of overseeing the contest) to discuss the terms of the event. They were understandably anxious, for competitions in the nineteenth century were characteristically mismanaged affairs with little protection for entrants and few pleasures even for winners. As a result of this sorry history, the American Institute of Architects had drafted a set of recommended guidelines, and it was to press for the adoption of two of these that the architects met with the commissioners. First, they asked that a panel of architectural experts be assembled to judge the designs, rescuing them from the inexperience and possible prejudices of the commission itself. They even recommended a list of

jurors designed to lift the competition out of its parochial context: Warren Laird (head of the new architecture school at the University of Pennsylvania), William Robert Ware and Francis Chandler (similarly positioned at Columbia and MIT, respectively), Richard Morris Hunt (the dean of the profession), Daniel Burnham of Chicago, Howard Walker (director of the Museum of Fine Arts in Boston), and Robert D. Andrews (a protégé of the architect H. H. Richardson). The competitors' second request was that the contest winner be guaranteed the commission for designing the actual building. The committee clearly understood the sense and sensitivity of these issues, but they were reluctant to cede their powers. They pledged only to employ "a number of skilled advisors," without naming them, and to "advise" that the winning architect be hired. The petitioners must have come away disappointed, and in the end none of the best of the young Philadelphia designers submitted entries. Frank Miles Day, Wilson Eyre, and the partners Walter Cope and John Stewardson all stood on the sidelines as architects from out of town contested over the Lemon Hill proposal.[11]

In October 1895, just before the submissions were due, the Fairmount Park Commission fulfilled its commitment to the entrants by naming a most distinguished panel of five expert jurors. At Widener's suggestion, these included two of the architects put forward by the competitors, William Robert Ware and Daniel Burnham, plus Stanford White of the New York firm of McKim, Mead, and White. To represent Philadelphia interests, the commission also appointed Joseph M. Wilson, a noted architect and engineer, and John G. Johnson, who had just been made a Fairmount Park commissioner.[12] The judges met with the Memorial Hall committee on October 31, when they viewed the sixty-seven designs for the first time, and they returned to Philadelphia to meet on December 2, 1895. The next day they named the winning team, Henry Bacon and James Brite of New York, and their unanimous recommendation was unanimously accepted by the commission. There was now a picture of a museum to attach to the dream (fig. 28).

Henry Bacon (1866–1924) seems to have been responsible for most of the winning design, for his partner was hospitalized with appendicitis in the midst of the work.[13] The presentation perspective was made in pen and ink, his favorite medium, and it shows a building that is full of reminiscences of his recent work in the office of McKim, Mead, and White, where he remained until 1897. The severe central block, with its shallow, Roman dome rising on an octagonal drum behind an unpedimented portico, was directly borrowed from McKim's Low Memorial Library at Columbia University, designed the year before. Bacon may have been responsible for a fine perspective made of the library, and his signed drawings, executed in the summer of 1895 while preparing for the Philadelphia competition, show that he was at work on another related design, the Brooklyn Museum. This was also a commission assigned to McKim within the office, as plainly demonstrated by its grave synthesis of antiquity and geometry. The pilasters carried across the face of the Brooklyn design were replaced by Bacon in the Philadelphia proposal with concatenated windows and niches, and, in another departure from the Brooklyn

Museum, at Philadelphia he pulled the columns of his corner pavilions away from the body of the building to enliven its perimeter. Nevertheless, in overall massing Bacon had clearly subscribed to McKim's museum formula. The Philadelphia plan, too, followed the Brooklyn precedent, with long galleries arranged around great, glass-roofed courtyards (four in Brooklyn, two in Philadelphia) and a dome rising in the center of the composition. The architectural style that Kimball would call the "American classic" was ready to take root on Fairmount.

The judges defended their recommendations for more than an hour under the questioning of the commissioners, placing Bacon's design and those of the three other premiated entrants in the critical context of their time. Their prejudices were strongly in favor of the McKim brand of classicism, and when the names of the anonymous entries were revealed, it turned out that three of the winners had passed through his office. Diversions from McKim's norms toward the style of the Ecole des Beaux-Arts were noted and censured. For example, the fourth-place entry by John Galen Howard, who had trained at the Ecole before coming to McKim, Mead, and White, was criticized by Burnham, the spokesman of the jury, for a florid French style unsuited to "severer or more serious work." Marcel Perouse de Monclos of Paris, the only "outsider," placed third with a design whose ingenious radial plan was wonderingly admired, but the judges could not award the final palm to a designer who had so totally "'let himself loose . . . .'" By contrast, Austin W. Lord (who had also worked on the Columbia University and Brooklyn Museum designs for McKim) had evidently been able to purge himself of his Parisian memories, and it was to his entry, the judges admitted, that they first intended to give the first prize. Its exterior was "monumental," and the plan was of the type "now generally accepted as the proper one for an extensive art museum" (that is, like Brooklyn). But in studying it further, the jurors had realized that the dome would cast long shadows across the skylights and that the design could not be easily erected in sections, as was intended. The part that would naturally be built first could not be a complete museum, and White commented that it would take the treasury of the French government, headed by Napoleon, to pay for the entire scheme.[14]

The jurors then determined that Bacon's design had the strengths of Lord's entry without its defects. It too was "architecturally rich in appearance," and it possessed the normative plan, but so arranged to permit piecemeal construction and to keep shadows off the skylights. Perhaps most decisive was the jury's conclusion that Bacon was fully qualified to correct the small defects that were detectable in the placement of staircases in the rotunda and in the detailing of wall surfaces (probably judged too busy). White asserted confidently that "the designer shows that he is capable of carrying out any work," whereas he considered that Austin Lord, although six years older than Bacon, would lack "the power to carry out the work in execution." Swayed by this reasoning, the commission voted to award the first prize of $6,000 to Bacon and Brite.[15]

That none of the premiums went to the twenty-two Philadelphians who had entered the contest was quickly commented on. The fact that Bacon had both worked for Stanford White's firm and, it was learned, assisted Charles Atwood in the design office of the Columbian Exposition under Burnham's supervision roused suspicions of favoritism. Although the entries were anonymous, many were sure that the judges had recognized the drawing styles of the entrants. The *Inquirer* interviewed several of the disgruntled local designers and published their complaints and their entries on the Sunday after the awards were made.[16] Most poignant were the comments of former Director of Public Works James H. Windrim, whose parkway had just disappeared from the city plan. He had heard from one of the jurors that the design submitted by his son John had been judged head to head against Bacon's for half a day. Why, he wondered, did it not deserve at least the second prize? And Thomas P.

Lonsdale spoke for many when he complained, "'It seems that New York and Chicago get everything in the way of awards, while Philadelphia is left to plod along . . . .'" This angry chorus climaxed when William Bleddyn Powell, the city architect (then overseeing the completion of the scandal-dogged City Hall), wrote directly to the commission to attack the judges' apparent prejudices. The enraged commissioners, led by Widener, considered returning the libelous document to its author, but decided in the end merely to table it.[17]

Gradually, the competition came to be seen with less heat. The commissioners individually expressed their satisfaction with the fairness of the awards and the credibility of the jury's report, and a number of the prominent architects who had declined to enter now defended the decision of the judges. Frank Miles Day, John Stewardson, and Wilson Eyre all argued against upsetting the decision, and Day and Eyre pointed out that the lack of guaranteed employment for the winner had kept the best local men from entering. In Eyre's view, those Philadelphians who did compete "'went into the plan with their eyes open and they have nobody to blame but themselves.'"[18] On December 13, 1895, the Memorial Hall committee agreed to ask Bacon and Brite about their terms and fees for overseeing the construction of the museum, and the architects soon replied at length.[19]

But suspicions of favoritism and local pride continued to work against the employment of the young architects from New York, and the parkway project itself languished. Mayor Charles Warwick showed little interest in either reviving the boulevard scheme of his predecessor or pursuing Councilman Huey's less ambitious "concourse" proposal, and when the Fairmount Park Commission's Memorial Hall committee finally read Bacon and Brite's letter into the minutes in May 1896, they deferred its discussion until a later date.[20] Although the voters approved $200,000 for housing the city's art in the loan referendum of 1897, the funds were never appropriated by City Councils, and the perennial suggestion to enlarge Memorial

Hall was raised again. So dilatory were the city authorities that on March 13, 1907, the Board of City Trusts withdrew the promised support of the Franklin Fund, offered to the museum project a dozen years earlier.[21]

Beginning Again: Widener and Fairmount

Nevertheless, forces were combining in the first years of the new century that would revive the campaign for a new museum. The agitation of 1900–1902 by the Art Federation and the Parkway Association restored the parkway to the city plan early in 1903 and created a broad new basis of support for "city beautiful" improvements. These new supporters saw that the city's plans to stop taking water from the filthy Schuylkill would soon make the river-fed reservoir on the Fairmount hilltop obsolete, thus creating a building site immediately adjacent to the terminus of their planned boulevard. Promptly recognizing the advantages of this location over Lemon Hill, P.A.B. Widener now resumed his efforts on behalf of the art gallery. He gained the ear of Mayor John Weaver and painted a glowing picture of a new museum atop the old reservoir. Such a plan was included in the report of the Department of Public Works in 1903,[22] and on December 16, 1904, Weaver publicly embraced the proposal at the annual meeting of the Fairmount Park Art Association.[23] Next May, apparently at the behest of the Art Association or the City Parks Association, the architectural partners Clarence Zantzinger and Charles Borie joined forces with Paul Cret to present a plan for the improvement of the Schuylkill River banks that included an art gallery atop Fairmount, but one oriented toward the Washington monument rather than the new parkway.[24]

Widener's plan was not, however, immediately endorsed by all of the interested parties. The leading dissenter was John G. Johnson, who was eager to build a new gallery but preferred a downtown site. In October 1906 he urged the Fairmount Park Commission to acquire the lot at Broad and Pine streets from the school of the Pennsylvania Museum for this purpose. There, in a fireproof building, he was sure that the Wilstach collection would soon be joined by "three of the largest private collections in Philadelphia,"[25] namely Widener's, William Elkins's, and his own, then located not far away in his South Broad Street house. When the Fairmount Park Art Association met on December 19, 1906, the announced topic was "the municipal art gallery," and most of the speakers joined the site debate. Samuel Thompson, chairman of the Memorial Hall committee of the Park Commission, admitted that, like Johnson and many of the others who spoke, he preferred the Broad and Pine site. But he had recently discovered that the Wilstach paintings were bound by the terms of their bequest to remain in Fairmount Park, and so it seemed that the matter was settled.[26] Widener, in the meantime, continued to court the mayor, who was now the newly elected John Reyburn, the great parkway proponent. Inviting Reyburn to visit him in early April 1907 at Lynnewood Hall, the huge neo-Palladian house that Horace Trumbauer had built for him in Elkins Park, Widener played his trump card. He told the undoubtedly astonished mayor that if the city provided a site on Fairmount and realigned the parkway on the Fairmount axis, Widener would pay for the museum and place his pictures in it. Reyburn jubilantly reported this news after touring the parkway area on April 5. He told the newspapers that "'nothing stands between the city and Mr. Widener's splendid offer, except the moving of the present lines of the Parkway fifty feet further south and widening the Boulevard to this extent so an uninterrupted view of the new gallery can be had from City Hall.'"[27]

It was widely reported that a museum design by Trumbauer was inspected by Reyburn and Widener during their conference, and although Trumbauer denied this allegation, there is strong circumstantial evidence for its truth. Two years earlier, Trumbauer had engaged Paul Cret to assist him in planning an unspecified "museum of fine arts," at just the time that Widener was intensifying his campaign for Fairmount.[28] Then, when the Fairmount Park Art Association appointed a team of consultants to reconsider the alignment of the parkway on April 26, 1907, hard on the heels of the Widener announcement, they added Trumbauer (known to be Widener's favorite architect) to the team of Cret, Zantzinger, and Borie, who had prepared the earlier Schuylkill report. Indeed, the single-block museum with a central dome that Cret showed in his bird's-eye sketch of the parkway did not resemble the kind of work that he produced independently (see fig. 14). It may well represent the American-style design that he had helped Trumbauer make in 1905 and that Widener had shown to Reyburn in April 1907. Cret's displeasure at the relative gaucheness of its strident geometry and blocky composition may have sparked the dislike that divided him and Trumbauer in later years.

Regardless of Trumbauer's precise role in the affair, Widener had masterfully seized control of the art gallery project. Endorsed by Mayor Reyburn and the Fairmount Park Art Association's consultants, the parkway was rerouted by City Councils according to his wishes, with the museum standing above it on Fairmount. John G. Johnson, whose site preference had been roughly pushed aside, was left to observe, "'All I will say at this time is that the city can never expect, and must never hope, to get an art collection commensurate with its standing until it has a place in which the pictures can be properly housed.'"[29] He refused to say whether the Widener museum would be the home of his pictures, but, for the moment, the question turned out to be irrelevant. Despite the enormous exertions of John Reyburn and the honest efficiency of his successor, Rudolph Blankenburg, construction of the museum had not begun when Widener died on November 6, 1915. His great promise to Reyburn had been tacitly withdrawn long before that.

Eli Kirk Price and the Fairmount Park Commission

Although John Reyburn had failed to act rapidly enough to secure Widener's handsome gift to the city, in his last year in office he did establish the alternate public mechanism that ultimately oversaw the construction of the building. To do so, he capitalized on the growing consensus in support of the art museum project and its Fairmount siting, and he coordinated his efforts to coincide with the publication of his Comprehensive Plan early in 1911.[30] In this he was strongly assisted by his new ally, Eli Kirk Price, the vice-president of the Fairmount Park Commission.

On January 24, 1911, the mayor announced his strategy to the annual meeting of the Fairmount Park Art Association, the staunch supporters of his planning efforts. Averring that the art gallery project "has been close to our hearts, especially for the last three or four years," he went on to promise that he would formally assign the now empty reservoir to the museum and that he would at last seek to appropriate the $200,000 voted by the people in 1897 for the project.[31] This would suffice, he hoped, to prepare the site and acquire a design, all of which was to be conducted by the Fairmount Park Commission. No mention was made of Widener's earlier promises. In March, Reyburn said that he would put the premiated designs from 1895 on display again and ask Cret, Zantzinger, and Trumbauer—the authors of the 1907 report for the Fairmount Park Art Association—"'to confer with me relative to their adaptability to the Fairmount reservoir site.'"[32] But this plan was abandoned after April 10, when Councils approved his appropriation and transferred the site to the Park Commission, because the commissioners had established a committee of their own to secure a museum design. Its members were named on May 12, on the eve of the great City Planning Conference of 1911. They were Widener, commission president Edward T. Stotesbury, Thomas De Witt Cuyler, and George S. Webster (chief engineer of the City Bureau of Surveys), with Eli Kirk Price as chairman.[33]

The Committee on the Art Museum seems to have met officially only twice, and thereafter Price assumed its responsibilities personally. At their first session on June 29, 1911, the commissioners selected a team of architects and asked them to make "a preliminary sketch for the art

Fig. 29. Borie, Trumbauer, and Zantzinger, *Philadelphia Museum of Art*. Southeast elevation with dome, December 1911. Zantzinger, Borie, and Medary office, delineators. Photograph of lost watercolor. Philadelphia Museum of Art, Archives, SF/PHO, Box 1

Fig. 30. Borie, Trumbauer, and Zantzinger, *Philadelphia Musuem of Art*. Southeast elevation without dome, December 1911. Zantzinger, Borie, and Medary office, delineators. Photograph of lost watercolor. Philadelphia Museum of Art, Archives, SF/PHO, Box 1

museum."[34] Their choice fell on Trumbauer, Widener's family architect and later the designer of Whitemarsh Hall for Stotesbury, and the partners Zantzinger and Borie (now joined by Medary, although he was not explicitly mentioned in the record). The commission had thus chosen the same team that had collaborated in 1907 on the parkway study and had been named by Reyburn in March, with one exception: Paul Cret, who had worked on the 1907 project and was on the mayor's list, was now omitted. It may be that Stotesbury and Widener's taste for Trumbauer's "American classic" prevented his appointment. Or Cret may have let it be known after the mayor's announcement that he did not desire to be teamed with Trumbauer again. In any case, even without him the new partnership still contained the seeds of a dispute between the two classicisms, with the Zantzinger office acting as a kind of surrogate for Paul Cret.

Such conflict was immediately revealed. By July 24, 1911, the designers had already prepared sketches for a building that could be erected in parts, and on October 19

Fig. 31. Borie, Trumbauer, and Zantzinger, *Philadelphia Museum of Art*. Perspective from east with dome (detail), December 26, 1911. Horace Trumbauer office, delineators. Blue-line print, 11¾ x 26¼" (29.8 x 66.7 cm). Inscribed: DEC. 26. 1911 C. L. BORIE HORACE TRUMBAUER C. C. ZANTZINGER ASSOCIATE ARCHITECTS. Philadelphia Museum of Art, Archives, 20.5

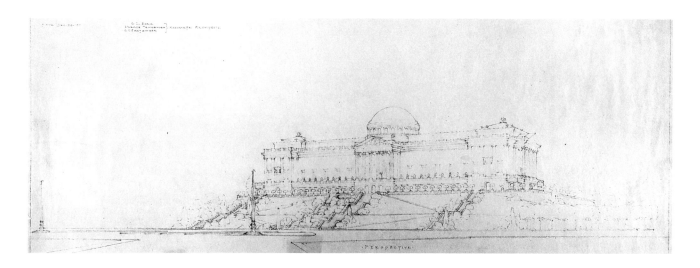

Fig. 32. Borie, Trumbauer, and Zantzinger, *Philadelphia Museum of Art*. Perspective from east without dome (detail), December 26, 1911. Horace Trumbauer office, delineators. Blue-line print, 11½ x 26½" (29.2 x 67.3 cm). Inscribed: DEC. 26. 1911 C. L. BORIE HORACE TRUMBAUER C. C. ZANTZINGER ASSOCIATE ARCHITECTS. Philadelphia Museum of Art, Archives, 20.4

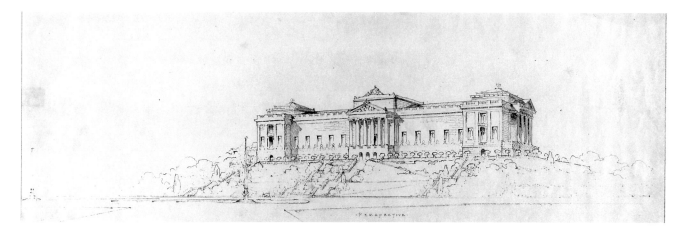

the committee authorized them to produce larger-scale drawings. In late December they produced four alternative elevation studies, reflecting the different tacks on which the two offices were already sailing. One pair of designs evinced a rather robust and Roman spirit, and offered options both with and without a dome (figs. 29–30).[35] In the other, a Palladian portico was attached to the center of the composition and the detailing was drier and thinner. It, too, was worked out in domed and undomed variants (figs. 31–32). The contrast between these two pairs may be taken as representative of the differences between the two firms. The first pair was evidently Zantzinger, Borie, and Medary's strong and somewhat daring composition. It did not, to be sure, offer much evidence of Zantzinger's French training except when compared to the pair of precise and rather lifeless Palladian drawings. Their more explicit use of precedent was typical of the Trumbauer workshop's conscientious historicism, and their use of perspective reflected his approach to architecture through picture-making.

The drawings suggest that the two offices had taken up the project that summer independently, although agreeing to adopt the little bird's-eye view that Cret had sketched in 1907 (see fig. 14) as a starting point for the massing and overall proportions of the building. They had also agreed to experiment with domes and to work from the same floor plan. Behind all of their elevation studies would lie at first only a double-loaded corridor of galleries, sky lit on the top floor and window lit below; the great, glass-roofed courtyards of 1895 were given up. Eventually the architects intended to expand the museum into a huge complex of roughly trapezoidal shape, but the details of this were vague. As Charles Borie recalled years later, "'The architects were a bit handicapped in their work as we had but little idea as to the use

to which the building would be put—after all the City owned damned little art!'"[36]

Not surprisingly, it was one of Trumbauer's prototype designs that was chosen for further development. Although not much older than Zantzinger, Borie, or Medary, he was vastly more experienced than they and may have already designed a museum for Widener. It was his domeless Palladian variant that continued to be studied. Its Corinthian portico remained untouched at the center, but the corner pavilions were progressively strengthened and the vast approach stairway was thoroughly reconsidered. A first revision gave each pavilion a pair of in-antis columns instead of pilasters on their front faces and created a kind of sunken plaza between two flights of steps (fig. 33). In September 1912 the Trum-

Fig. 33. Borie, Trumbauer, and Zantzinger, *Philadelphia Museum of Art*. Southeast elevation, spring 1912. Horace Trumbauer office, delineators. Hand-colored photograph of lost watercolor. City Archives of Philadelphia, 140.3, 81, PW 1210

Fig. 34. Borie, Trumbauer, and Zantzinger, *Philadelphia Museum of Art*. Southeast perspective, September 1912. Horace Trumbauer office, delineators. Watercolor and graphite on paper, 23¼ x 51½″ (59 x 130.8 cm). Philadelphia Museum of Art, Archives, 20.7

bauer office refined this further, attaching unpedimented porticoes to the pavilion fronts (while removing their side porticoes) and creating a single stairway of enormous width (fig. 34).[37] Price forwarded this last design together with his own report to his fellow commissioners, and they met to discuss the museum on March 12, 1913.[38] He told them that the total cost of the building and its approaches would be $3 million, and he asked for permission to obtain estimates for site preparation and to submit the design to the Art Jury for approval. They agreed, and the next day the newspapers were full of illustrations of the long-awaited museum.[39]

The Art Jury, to whom the design was now delivered, was another of John Reyburn's legacies to the artistic well-being of his city. It had been chartered in 1907 and

charged with the power to review the city's acquisitions of art. But Reyburn had had difficulty appointing a panel that would agree to serve together, and for several years he relied on the advice of his Comprehensive Plans Committee instead. He finally named the jurors on October 8, 1911, and their review powers were almost immediately expanded to include all buildings built with public funds and all privately financed buildings erected in or adjacent to parks. With this vast authority, they had almost complete control over the buildings of the parkway.[40]

It was to a committee of this body that the museum came for the first time on March 26, 1913. The conditions appeared highly favorable for the design, for the committee chairman was Joseph Widener, P.A.B. Widener's son, and another committee member was Price; their feelings

Fig. 35. Borie, Trumbauer, and Zantzinger, *Philadelphia Museum of Art*. Porticoed model from east, 1914. Photograph of lost model. Philadelphia Museum of Art, Archives, SF/PHO, PMA Proposed Models

about it were certain. But the charter of the Art Jury stipulated that there be one architect member, and Reyburn had appointed Paul Cret to that position. He too served on the committee to which the art museum was assigned, as he did on virtually every architectural committee of the Art Jury, and his role on questions of architecture had become decisive. It can only be imagined what he felt about the rather brittle project now proposed for the head of the boulevard that he had planned in 1907. But he certainly recognized it in that devotion to "styles" against which he had warned his students. It was probably he who suggested that the committee adjourn before taking any formal action, intending, no doubt, to have words with his friends Zantzinger and Borie.[41]

A Cliff-Hanger

No immediate conference was necessary. While the commission signed a contract with Robert Patton to prepare

the site on August 4, 1913, and work then began with the $200,000 appropriated from the old loan of 1897, Philadelphia's new reform mayor was unable to produce the funds needed to proceed further. Rudolph Blankenburg, true to his scrupulous reputation, had not put the museum in his first budget of 1912 because no design was in hand. Moreover, the careful control of construction budgets was an essential element of his campaign to overthrow the contractor-dominated Republican machine.

In 1913 a design was ready although not yet approved, but Blankenburg again hesitated. Anxious to release taxpayers from the costly burdens imposed by corrupt administrations like Reyburn's, he omitted the museum from his September budget while publicly hoping "'that some public-spirited citizen may come forward'"—an obvious reference to Widener's promise of six years earlier.[42] P.A.B. Widener was no longer rising to such bait, however, and so it was left to the newspapers, by their tumult of protest, to convince Blankenburg that some way must be found to pay for the museum.[43] His ingenious solution was to transfer $1.5 million from the defunct project for a convention hall in Fairmount Park, and at first the Republican Councils seemed to be ready to go along. But at the last minute John Connelly, the Finance Committee chairman and a leader of the machine, withdrew his support and the plan collapsed. His action was intended to embarrass the mayor, but the tactic backfired, clearly painting the organization with a tarry brush instead, for it happened that at the same time that the Councils quashed the art museum they were also rejecting the pleas of neighbors to close down the insalubrious, machine-protected pig yards of South Philadelphia. The *Record* adroitly pinned the Republicans with the slogan, "We Want Hogs, Not Art."[44]

The architects must have viewed this state of affairs with bewilderment, but the imposed delay cost them nothing, for while they were waiting the contractor at work on Fairmount discovered that the terrain would

not permit them to build what they had intended anyway. The Park Commission reported that what had seemed to be a gentle slope on the southeast face of the hill, facing the parkway, was actually "a nearly vertical cliff" and that it was therefore necessary for the architects to make "a careful restudy of their plans . . . ."[45] This offered the Zantzinger office, bolstered by Cret's apparent criticism, the opportunity to turn the design in another direction.

The new topography posed an exhilarating challenge, and during the latter part of 1914 the architects struggled with solutions, constructing an enormous set of models to place on a mock-up of the terrain. While they made some effort to adapt a version of the Palladian design to a position on the edge of a cliff, Trumbauer's influence over the work seemed to wane and his collaborators began to play a dominant role. It was they who produced a series of suave alternative designs, like the earlier plan intended to be realized in parts with the first piece to be a single block facing the parkway.[46] But now this block was to be perched over the edge of the newly discovered cliff, with two floors of exhibition space on the top of the hill and a "basement" at the level of the parkway (fig. 35). At this lower level visitors could enter a lobby whence elevators would whisk them up to the museum proper. The Zantzinger office worked this out in models, sketches, and finished drawings, at first preferring either an austere facade or one articulated only by paired pilasters (figs. 36–39).

The largest set of completed drawings, however, depict a slightly more festive, arcuated solution with an arcaded porch (figs. 40–41). This was apparently the architects' favorite version. Although the roots of its straight-linteled classicism were found in mid-eighteenth-century France, the lessons of that period were so well absorbed by Ecole men like Zantzinger that individual sources are not detectable.

Paul Cret probably did not see this new design before leaving for his annual holiday in France in the summer of 1914.[47] This time, however, he did not return to Philadelphia until 1919, having decided to join the French

Fig. 37. Borie, Trumbauer, and Zantzinger, *Philadelphia Museum of Art*. Sketch perspective from east, bird's-eye perspective from east, transverse section, and northeast elevation of colonnaded variant; 1914. Zantzinger, Borie, and Medary office, delineators. Graphite and colored crayon on tracing paper, 14⅜ x 15¾" (36.4 x 40 cm). Philadelphia Museum of Art, Archives, 30.4

Fig. 38. Borie, Trumbauer, and Zantzinger, *Philadelphia Museum of Art*. Sketch southeast elevation of colonnaded variant with obelisk in forecourt, 1914. Zantzinger, Borie, and Medary office, delineators. Graphite and colored crayon on tracing paper, 9½ x 18¼" (24.1 x 46.3 cm). Philadelphia Museum of Art, Archives, 30.15

Fig. 39. Borie, Trumbauer, and Zantzinger, *Philadelphia Museum of Art*. Entrance and typical gallery floor plans of astylar variant, September 24, 1914. Zantzinger, Borie, and Medary office, delineators. Graphite, wash, watercolor, and colored pencil on illustration board, 20 x 24¼" (50.8 x 61.6 cm). Inscribed: *SEPTEMBER 24 1914*. Philadelphia Museum of Art, Archives, 30.6

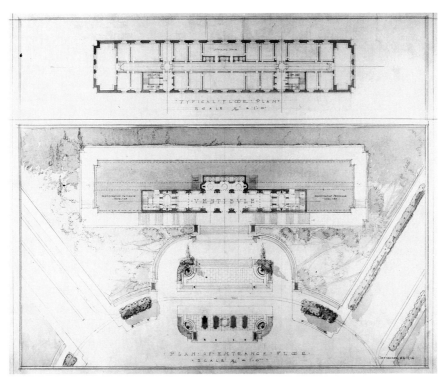

army when Germany declared war in early August. But before leaving, Cret had seen a good deal of Zantzinger and his partners, for in July they had just finished making revisions in the design of their first large collaborative project, the Indianapolis Public Library. They must have been thinking of him as they assembled the various models and prepared alternative elevation studies that fall.[48] He was, after all, the architect-member of the Art Jury, to whom the design would return for approval, and their work with him on the Indianapolis project—where his had certainly been the guiding hand—had shown them his methods. It is probably not coincidental that their museum designs of 1914 abandoned the complicated facade composition that had been worked out in 1911–12, with its central block, wings, and corner pavilions. The urbane single prism of the new first-phase design may have consciously emulated Cret's similarly disciplined library, although he would probably have criticized the rather mannered slenderness of their plan.

To be sure, Cret was often exasperated by what he saw in his American friends' work, and while in France he watched with trepidation as they revised the Indianapolis design to meet its budget. His feelings were certainly complicated by what he imagined to be the "*progermanisme*" of Zantzinger (who had gone to school in Germany) and Borie.[49] He did his best to offer advice from the trenches, even revising some drawings there, and although he told Zantzinger to "rest assured, I have no doubt about the final result," he fretted privately about the dessicating effects of his friend's "*raison raisonnante*."[50] Nevertheless, he must have been pleased to think of their design replacing Trumbauer's on Fairmount. When he collaborated with them again in 1921 in the competition for Kansas City's Liberty Memorial, they produced an elegant variation of the cliff's edge parti of 1914, complete with the embracing arms that enframed the forecourt on the lower level (see figs. 40–41).[51] But by then a very different museum was being built in Philadelphia.

The Compromise of Howell Lewis Shay

In 1914, although the design of the museum was still under revision, Mayor Blankenburg at last committed

Fig. 40. Borie, Trumbauer, and Zantzinger, *Philadelphia Museum of Art*. Southeast elevation of arcuated variant, 1914. Zantzinger, Borie, and Medary office, delineators. Graphite, ink, watercolor, and wash on illustration board; 10¼ x 23¾" (26 x 60.3 cm). Philadelphia Museum of Art, Archives, 30.7

Fig. 41. Borie, Trumbauer, and Zantzinger, *Philadelphia Museum of Art*. Close perspective of arcuated variant from east, 1914. Zantzinger, Borie, and Medary office, delineators. Graphite on illustration board, 21⅞ x 29⅞" (55.6 x 75.9 cm). Philadelphia Museum of Art, Archives, 30.13

himself to the project in his budget, and in November the voters approved a loan issue of $800,000. This confidence at first seemed to have been misplaced, for the building was still being adjusted to its site in the spring of 1915, some two years after the initial submission to the Art Jury. To make matters worse, the Zantzinger office had abandoned its carefully studied design for a building set on the edge of Fairmount, and they were now exploring a radically different solution. Then the Fairmount Park Commission issued an ultimatum, and Horace Trumbauer once more insisted on having his say in the project. From the resulting turmoil emerged a design recognizably like the one that was built.

What exactly compelled Zantzinger, Borie, and Medary to cast away the designs that they had worked out in the latter part of 1914 cannot be determined. However, they apparently grew dissatisfied with the spartan accommodations provided by their elegantly slender but impractical first-phase building. They may also have wanted to create a design that raised a more commanding central feature at the head of the parkway. They therefore let one of the brightest young men in their office, William Pope Barney (1890–1970), take up the problem, and it was he who turned the design in the direction of its final form.

Following his graduation from the University of Pennsylvania in 1913, Barney entered the office of Paul Cret, with whom he had studied. He remained there, working on the Indianapolis Library design, until after Cret enlisted; he then moved to the Zantzinger partnership, where he found the firm embroiled in the museum problem. Between March and May 1915, Barney worked out a fresh design on a radically different parti, one that celebrated the diversity of the museum's holdings (and the several independent collections that it might attract) by assembling a number of quasi-independent buildings around a court of honor. The central unit would place its great pedimented portico on the parkway axis, and the others might be erected as budgets allowed and needs developed, responding with suppleness to the still unsettled program of the proposed museum. He first envisioned the buildings as fully detached from each other (fig. 42), but later studies show the several blocks connected by passages, including graceful quadrants linking the front units to those on the sides (fig. 43).

Barney's drawings had the kind of panache produced by the best students trained in the manner of the Ecole, for they took a vague description of purpose and somehow translated it into a credible plan. It was his plan that was the ingenious invention. Graceful and unmannered, it stepped back from the cliff to make use of the entire Fairmount hilltop, although it still dropped elevators from the frontmost pavilions down to lobbies at the

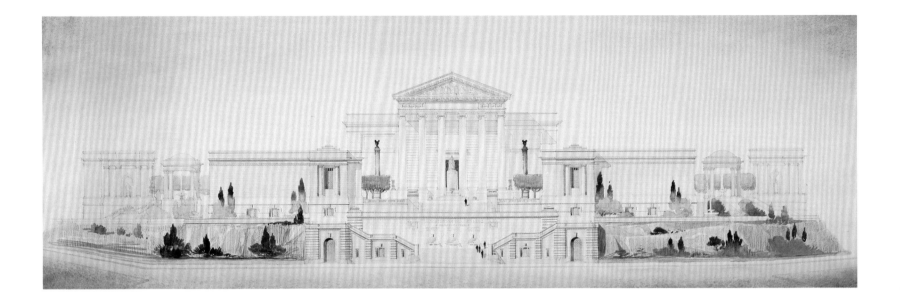

level of the parkway. The elevations, by contrast, seemed rather primitive, with scattered concentrations of historicist detail that could not reproduce the unity that had been so easily achieved in the plan. It was certainly the kind of design to make a serious architect ponder, and this is what Zantzinger, Borie, and Medary were doing when an ultimatum arrived from the Fairmount Park Commission, pointing out that two years had elapsed since the associated architects had produced a preliminary design and threatening to turn the work over to others.

A similar message was received by Horace Trumbauer's office, where Julian Abele, almost surely the highest-placed black architect in America, played a leading role among the diverse and talented staff that produced the variety of historicist designs desired by Trumbauer's clients. One of these designers was Howell Lewis Shay (1884–1975), who had graduated from Pennsylvania in the same year as Barney. He has left a report of the frenzy of activity that followed the receipt of the threatening letters, in which he convincingly claims credit for working

out a compromise design that took into account both the Barney plan that had bewitched Zantzinger and the Palladian design of which Trumbauer was so proud. Shay's story begins with the warning from the Park Commission:

"Mr. Trumbauer showed me the letter. It said they had just three weeks to get the plans done—or they would turn the contract over to other architects.

"'I want you to handle this, Shay,' he said, 'or are you afraid of it?'

"I wasn't afraid. I had heard the three of them [Trumbauer, Zantzinger, and Borie] arguing many times. I knew why they hadn't been able to agree on a final design. Mr. Trumbauer wanted one monumental building to be at the end of the Parkway, like the one with the flat facade he had worked out before. But Mr. Zantzinger and Mr. Borie wanted the Fairmount 'Acropolis' to be more like the Acropolis at Athens, with several 'temples' around at random.

"I had to be sure they wanted me to handle it, too. But Zantzinger and Borie had seen my work, and knew of my awards

Fig. 42. Borie, Trumbauer, and Zantzinger, *Philadelphia Museum of Art.* Southeast elevation, May 1, 1915. William Pope Barney (1890–1970), delineator. Graphite, ink, crayon, and watercolor on paper; 15 x 43¼″ (38.1 x 109.9 cm). Inscribed: *May 1 1915* WPB. Philadelphia Museum of Art, Archives, 40.3

Fig. 43. Borie, Trumbauer, and
Zantzinger, *Philadelphia Museum
of Art.* Bird's-eye perspective
from east, May 1915. William
Pope Barney, delineator.
Graphite on tracing paper,
11¾ x 17¾" (29.8 x 45.1 cm).
Philadelphia Museum of Art,
Archives, 40.7

*[medals from the Society of Beaux-Arts Architects in 1912 and
1913]. 'You go ahead, Shay,' they said.*

*"'All right,'" I said. 'Now, Mr. Zantzinger, you'd like
to have it like the Acropolis at Athens . . . well, let's start with
one big temple, right on the axis of this mile-long Parkway. I
think that the tallest temple in the world is the Temple of Zeus,
with columns 60 feet high—so let's make these columns 63 feet
high, tallest in the world, a fitting terminus for the long vista.*

*"'Let's put one more temple on this side,' and I sketched it
in, 'and another on this side, facing each other.' And Mr. Zantzinger and Mr. Borie were pleased, but Mr. Trumbauer had two
more buildings than he wanted.*

*"Then I reminded them, 'Now we have to think about cli-
mate. Greece has very little rain, and mild temperatures. You can
go between the temples on the Acropolis easily. But here we'd have
rain and snow and you'd have to put on your galoshes. So why
don't we connect these three temples with a series of galleries—
exhibition galleries to house some of the art, big enough so full-
scale rooms could be brought in—and connect these, forming a*

*forecourt? That would make a beautiful approach from city hall
down the Parkway.'"*[52]

The disputing architects agreed to Shay's solution, and
they set him up with a bottle of bourbon and a small office
of his own on Juniper Street. There, in ten days, he produced the design that was submitted to the Art Jury on
June 21, 1915 (figs. 44–45). Trumbauer later paid him a
bonus of $350.

For all the talk of compromise, Shay's design
adopted only Barney's idea of a court of honor; otherwise,
it was far more like the work of Trumbauer than that of
the Zantzinger office. Ponderously historicist, it strung together its three great porticoes by means of an ungainly E
plan whose long center bar had slipped backward. The
side arms, despite Shay's announced intentions, were
inconveniently narrow; there was only room for a wasteful system of single-loaded corridors. In addition, a great
proportion of the main block was occupied by a single-run
ceremonial stair of staggering length, but one that led the
visitor only to a few galleries at the very back of the building. Externally, this arrangement managed to generate a
composition of splendid geometric clarity, but this abstract beauty was purchased at the expense of intelligent
planning. Despite apparent organizational similarities,
Shay's work was the very reverse of Barney's design,
where appearance had been sacrificed to plan.

The appearance of the Shay design seems to have
been shaped by several immediate precedents. Most important was probably the Minneapolis Institute of Fine
Arts, which had opened on January 8, 1915, just a few
months before he set down the Philadelphia design. The
plan that the McKim, Mead, and White office made for
the Minneapolis building does not appear to have influenced him, at least at first, but its austere Grecian portico,
rising from amid plainly detailed side wings, seized a
place in his memory. He would have found even greater
Hellenism in the Albright Art Gallery of Buffalo (Edward
B. Green and William S. Wicks, architects, 1900–1905),

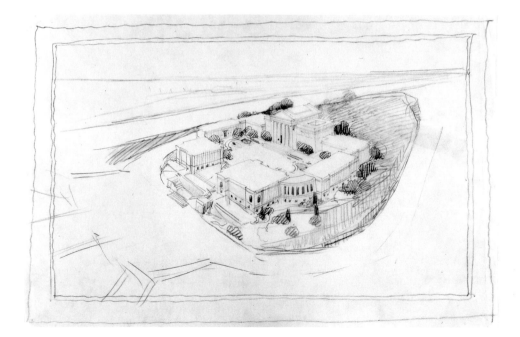

Fig. 44. Borie, Trumbauer, and Zantzinger, *Philadelphia Museum of Art*. Perspective from southeast, June 1915. Howell Lewis Shay (1884–1975), delineator. Photograph of lost drawing. Inscribed: *Rec'd by Art Jury June 21, 1915. Approved . . . Andrew Wright Crawford 6-29-15 Secretary Date of Action by Art Jury June 25, 1915*. Philadelphia Museum of Art, Archives, SF/PHO, BOX 1

where the Greek Ionic portico of the central block was echoed in a different key by replicas of the Erechtheum caryatid porch on each of the corner pavilions. The most striking overall resemblance lies between the Philadelphia museum and the Academy of Science of Athens, designed by the Danish architect Theophilus Hansen in 1859 but not completed until 1887 in what was by that time a very out-of-fashion Greek Revival style. With its three porticoes facing onto a forecourt, it mirrored in miniature the Fairmount design, although, of course, it cannot be certain that Shay knew of it. What is clear is that the young architect, like those of the cited buildings, was seduced by historicist detail and overall visual effect. In his later work, Shay turned these tastes to great advantage, creating some of the best of Philadelphia's skyscrapers of the 1920s with

a detailing that ranged over the gamut of historical vocabularies before turning to Art Deco. But Zantzinger, Borie, and Medary, and any other architects sensitive to the systematic plan-making of the Ecole, must have looked on his solution with a pang of regret.

The Art Jury committee showed no hesitation, however, in approving the general design "in principle" on June 24, 1915.[53] But of course Cret was in France, and to replace him the chairman had selected Medary, who could certainly make no public objections. Howell Lewis Shay was asked to go ahead with a further consideration of the problem, and just after Christmas Eli Kirk Price saw to it that a great display of the new museum design was set up in a temporary pavilion in City Hall courtyard. The centerpiece of this exhibition, created to dispel the accumu-

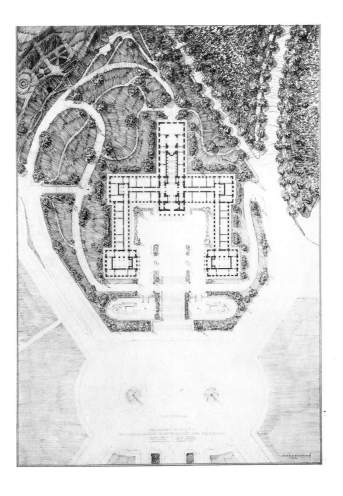

Fig. 45. Borie, Trumbauer, and Zantzinger, *Philadelphia Museum of Art*. First-floor plan, June 1915. Howell Lewis Shay, delineator. Photograph of lost drawing. Inscribed: *Rec'd by Art Jury June 21, 19[15.] Approved . . . Andrew Wright Crawford 6-29-15 Secretary Date of Action by Art Jury June 25, 1915*. Philadelphia Museum of Art, Archives, SF/PHO, Box 1

lated doubts of the people and their elected officials, was a large plaster model (fig. 46). Despite a cold rain, holiday crowds numbering 7,500 came to see the show on the first two days of public admission, and the newspapers published Shay's design with joyful thoroughness.[54] Some pointed with regret to the fact that P.A.B. Widener had died less than two months earlier.

The design represented by the displayed model differed subtly from that approved by the Art Jury (fig. 47). Although almost impossible to detect, the proportions of its plan had been judiciously altered, thickening the emaciated lateral wings although still not making them wide enough for central corridors. The main block, too, had been slightly shortened and widened, and an eight-column portico was required where six had sufficed before. A rendering now gave a glimpse of the stupendous central stair hall inside, with its endless perspectival recession beneath a partially glazed barrel vault (fig. 48). The side pavilions were more strongly emphasized with full-width six-column porticoes, and their rather crudely organized, two-story interior courts shown in the Art Jury design had been regularized and refined. (These courts now closely resembled those planned by McKim, Mead, and White for the corners of the Minneapolis museum.) The most visible alteration was the elimination of the first-floor windows that had looked out on the park-

Fig. 46. Borie, Trumbauer, and Zantzinger, *Philadelphia Museum of Art*. Model seen from southwest, fall 1915. Photograph of lost model. City Archives of Philadelphia, 140.3, 81, PW 1209

way from the ends of the wings. Their deletion under-scored the geometrical simplicity of his composition.

By mid-February, fifty thousand visitors had trooped past the model. Among them was Mayor Thomas Smith, the enthusiastic builder of the parkway, whom Price guided through the exhibition on January 12, 1916.[55] Optimism was in the air, and the new mayor, who had restored Boies Penrose's authority over the public affairs of the city, promised to ask the people for an additional $3 million for the museum—enough to cover those estimated expenses that would not be met by the $1 million available from the loans of 1897 and 1914. But Smith found it impossible to make a place for the museum in the budget he announced on February 29, and Price, unwilling to wait for another uncooperative mayor to pass from office, took up the offensive.[56] Fortunately, with the restoration of machine rule, the antipathy between the mayor and Councils had evaporated, and so on March 7 Price could sit down in conference with Smith, Joseph P. Gaffney (Finance Committee chairman), and "Hogs Not Art" Connelly himself, now the city solicitor. Price advanced a plan to transfer $1,202,000 to the museum from other Park Commission items in the loan bill, and Connelly placidly agreed.[57] In the end, only $1 million could be moved, but the machine had been brought on board.

Outside Experts

The Art Jury, too, inspected the model, and its committee met on January 22, 1916, to discuss what they had seen. Medary was still serving as Cret's substitute, however, and before proceeding on the museum it was decided to ask the American Institute of Architects to appoint some other architect to avoid an apparent conflict of interest.[58] In May, the AIA responded with the suggestion that it appoint three advisers because of the importance of the building.[59] These were John Russell Pope, whose entry in the Lincoln Memorial competition (1911–12) and design for the Scottish Rite Temple in Washington (1910–15) had marked him as McKim's natural successor as head of the

Fig. 47. Borie, Trumbauer, and Zantzinger, *Philadelphia Museum of Art*. Perspective from east, fall 1915. Photograph of lost drawing. Philadelphia Museum of Art, Archives, SF/PHO, Box 1

American classicists; Burt L. Fenner, who had become one of the guiding hands in the office of McKim, Mead, and White after the deaths of White and McKim and who had played a large role in the firm's work for the Metropolitan Museum of Art in New York (1904–26) and the Minneapolis Institute of Fine Arts; and Arnold Brunner, who had been Daniel Burnham's coadjutant for Cleveland's vast remaking as a "city beautiful." This was a most impressive panel, but not one by disposition inclined to make trouble for Shay's design, as Cret might have done. Although Pope had trained at the Ecole des Beaux-Arts, his most important schooling had come under McKim, and the others had had no difficulty putting aside the Ecole-based features of their MIT degrees. They were not, however, inclined to ignore the defects of the design, and they made specific recommendations. Indeed, the work of these three nationally prominent architects for the Art Jury reshaped its role along more activist lines. It was this new role that Cret took up when he returned from France, but by then the museum design had been fixed.

The Jury committee met for the first time with its AIA advisers on June 30, 1916, with chairman Joseph Widener, Zantzinger, Borie, and Trumbauer all present. Fenner was absent, but Pope and Brunner inspected the model and visited the site in the company of the architects and the committeemen. They must have been struck by the majestic view looking up the Schuylkill from Fairmount and puzzled at the blank elevation that Shay had placed beneath the broad pediment on that side of the building (see fig. 46). They may have doubted, too, whether visitors were likely to relish either the arduous

Fig. 48. Borie, Trumbauer, and Zantzinger, *Philadelphia Museum of Art*. Perspective of stair hall, fall 1915. From *Yearbook of the Twenty-Second Annual Architectural Exhibition Held by the Philadelphia Chapter of the American Institute of Architects and the T-Square Club* (Philadelphia, 1916). The Athenaeum of Philadelphia

climb up the monumental stairs that led from the parkway or the drive up the serpentine access road to the front entrance; visitors might in fact prefer to approach the building from the "back," where only a service door was shown (see fig. 45). Accordingly, they recommended revisions, and the committee resolved "that the architects be requested to continue their studies of the northwest façade of the Philadelphia Museum of Art, treating the river and park façades of the building as of equal importance with the Parkway façade, and to submit a revised design of the northwestern end of the building as a completed structure . . . ."[60]

The changes proceeded slowly, and with $2 million now appropriated for the building and with site preparation well advanced, restlessness about the apparent lack of progress began to be publicly expressed. On January 11, 1917, Mayor Smith explained with some annoyance that the design was still waiting for approval from the Art Jury and the Fairmount Park Commission, and said that he hoped to begin construction "'as soon as possible.'" On the same day Price ventured to predict that ground would be broken during the spring. "'However,'" he added, "'I feel that when the question in hand involves such a large expenditure of the people's money that it is best to proceed with great care.'"[61]

At last, on February 6, 1917, the three advisers assembled for a conference with Price and Andrew W. Crawford, the secretary of the Art Jury. They reviewed a set of revised drawings and expressed satisfaction with the portico that now stood at the center of the northwest facade (fig. 49). While they made a variety of small suggestions about the appropriate landscaping for a building that now faced two directions at once, their most important recommendation was for the further modification of the side wings. These were still very slender, and the four corner pavilions were inexplicably of unequal size. To correct this awkwardness, the advisers asked "that both side pavilions, of the northeast and the southwest façades, be made equal in projection . . . ."[62]

No mention was made in these deliberations of one of the most notable features of the revised plan—the further shortening of the main block. Recognizing its wasteful extravagance, the architects had pared another twenty feet from its rearward extension, and this had forced a drastic reconfiguration of the great stair. Still designed so that it would reach the second-floor level in a single, straight run, the stair now filled most of the available space (fig. 50). It was met at the top by a balcony that ran all around the hall atop Ionic columns, at last offering visitors a direct connection between the stair and the second-floor exhibition galleries.

The recommendations of the three advisers were taken up by the full Art Jury committee on February 13 and adopted, and on March 13, 1917, the Art Jury itself formally approved the design, stipulating only that the suggestions made by Pope, Brunner, and Fenner were to be carried out.[63] On March 11, Price carried this news to the Fairmount Park Commission, and they granted their approval as well.[64] The architects plunged ahead with renewed enthusiasm, over the summer producing a set of plans for use by those who would bid for the construction contract (fig. 51). Jacques Gréber, who had been hired by the Park Commission on March 3 to study the landscaping of the parkway, also turned his hand to making a series of handsome watercolors and crayon perspectives of the new museum (figs. 52–53).

These latest drawings showed that the final footprint of the building had been established, with substantially thickened side wings and with equally proportioned pavilions at the four corners. Inside the central block, the great stair had been redesigned, dividing it between a straight run at the bottom (that no longer demanded the entire space) and a divided upper flight that departed to

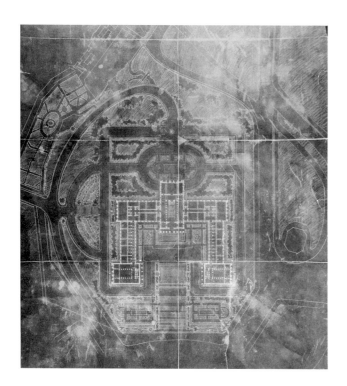

Fig. 49. Borie, Trumbauer, and Zantzinger, *Philadelphia Museum of Art*. Ground-floor plan, late 1916–early 1917. Detail photograph of damaged blueprint, 39¼ x 43½″ (99.7 x 110.5 cm) (original blueprint). City Archives of Philadelphia, 140.3, 81, V

Fig. 50. Borie, Trumbauer, and Zantzinger, *Philadelphia Museum of Art*. Perspective of stair hall, late 1916–early 1917. Blueprint, 16⅜ x 15¼″ (41.6 x 38.8 cm). City Archives of Philadelphia, 140.3, 81, Q

Fig. 51. Borie, Trumbauer, and Zantzinger, *Philadelphia Museum of Art*. First-floor plan, summer 1917. Photographic print, mounted on linen; 31¾ x 37¼″ (80.6 x 94.6 cm). Inscribed: *C. L. BORIE, JR. HORACE TRUMBAUER C. C. ZANTZINGER ASSOCIATE ARCHITECTS*. Philadelphia Museum of Art, Archives, 50.24

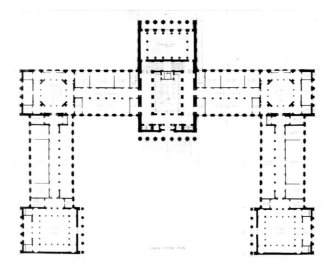

the left and right from a landing. The circumferential balcony was replaced by the more comfortable two-story elevation of the executed building, although some of the details had not yet been fixed. The exterior surfaces were enlivened by a great sculpted frieze across the cityward faces of the front pavilions (as introduced experimentally in the 1915 model and specifically approved by the three advisers) and by a rich system of Corinthian pilasters attached to the flanks of the central block (fig. 54). Even more precise and restrainedly classical in its overall massing than before, the building welcomed this almost baroque enrichment of texture.

Price showed this design to Langdon Warner, the director of the Pennsylvania Museum, in October 1917. This was one of the few formal consultations between the Fairmount Park Commission and their prospective tenant, for Price had just been elected a trustee of the museum and usually looked after its interests himself. Warner criticized some of the details of circulation, but he later wrote to Price, "I have not that soft place in my heart for architectural grandiloquence [*sic*] that I should have if I had been trained at the Beaux Arts. Please do not think me a captious critic."[65] His misunderstanding of the ideals of

the Ecole aside, he need not have worried about offending Price; Price knew that it was his design to choose.

Wartime and Postwar Battles

As the museum design took on its penultimate form, the world in which it would be built was transforming itself. America declared war on Germany on April 6, 1917, and construction materials gradually became unavailable. But even when normalcy returned, nine more years elapsed before the building was opened to the public, dogged through much of that time by the rapid seesawing of Progressive Era politics.

On the eve of the war, Mayor Smith had chafed angrily at the delay caused by the Art Jury when it referred the design to a panel of outsiders, but it was soon his own administration's financial difficulties that posed the greatest threat to the project. Because the state legislature had not raised the ceiling on the amount that the city was allowed to borrow, Smith found himself early in 1917 without the power to ask for another loan with which to build the museum. He announced this grim news on February 7, probably confident that the earlier appropriations of $2 million would see the slow-moving project into the next fiscal year.[66]

Such confidence was not felt by John G. Johnson, however. He had served as a judge of the design competition in 1895, and he had seen plan after plan pass into oblivion since then. The plaster model of the latest proposed museum had stood in the courtyard of City Hall for more than thirteen months, and, so far as he knew, the Art Jury was still quibbling with its advisers over details. Then came the news that Smith could not ask the people for further funding. Doubtful about the suitability of the site and the design from the beginning and now uncertain that it would even be realized, on February 12, 1917, Johnson penned a codicil to his will. Whereas he had previously promised his art and a great endowment to the city without setting any conditions, he now specified that his paintings were to remain in his house at 510 South Broad

Street, which he would give to the city as a museum. Moreover, he directed that "'the art objects shall not be removed for permanent exhibition to any other place, unless some extraordinary situation shall arise making it exceedingly judicious.'"[67]

At least Johnson thereby insured that his collection would not have to wait for a home, and in 1933, in the depth of the Depression, the city finally moved his paintings into the Fairmount museum as an economy measure. But that seemed an impossible scenario when Johnson died on April 14, 1917, just after America had entered the war. It was after receiving this blow that the art museum project retreated from public attention for the war's duration. The design work did go ahead until Zantzinger, having been appointed to the War Trade Board, departed in November for Sweden. Jacques Gréber shuttled back and forth between Paris and Philadelphia throughout the conflict, working on drawings for the Park Commission. But there was no public discussion of this modicum of progress.

When the war clouds parted, the gloom that hung over the art museum was also briefly dispelled. Restrictions on building materials were lifted even before the armistice of November 1918, and this prompted Mayor Smith to resume his campaign against what seemed to be the dilatoriness of the Fairmount Park Commission. On January 13, 1919, he met with Joseph Widener, Price, and others to impress upon them the importance of a speedy start for the work.[68] Widener had himself increased the stakes for the project by publicly promising his father's pictures to the city on December 5, 1918, provided only that a satisfactory gallery was built for them.[69] At the same time, Widener was promoting a plan to move the Johnson pictures to a museum of their own on the parkway, thereby preserving, he claimed, the spirit of Johnson's will, and in this mood of art euphoria bids were invited and received for the foundations on Fairmount. Price reported to the Park Commission on June 25 that the lowest bid had come from the Frank W. Mark Construc-

tion Company, but there was some controversy over his calculation of totals, and Price's reckoning was also challenged by a taxpayers' suit. In the end, the suit was dismissed and the contract awarded, without entirely disposing with the questions of financial propriety. Construction began, without ceremony, on July 28, 1919.[70]

Good news continued. In October, the city received George W. Elkins's bequest of his paintings and those of his father, William L. Elkins. His only condition was that there be an art gallery ready to receive them within five years of his death. To this Clarence Zantzinger confidently responded, "'Any building, within reason, can be finished in five years. . . . Barring unexpected conditions, such as strikes or a calamity like the late war, the structure should be completed much sooner than that.'"[71] He must have regretted those words many times in the eight years that lay ahead.

After this favorable season, 1920 began a period of setbacks. J. Hampton Moore had swept into the mayor's office in the previous November on the strength of a campaign directed against "contractor rule" in general and the Vares in particular. As it had under Blankenburg, however, honest government slowed construction work in the city, and Moore placed the parkway projects under partic-

Fig. 52. Borie, Trumbauer, and Zantzinger, *Philadelphia Museum of Art*. Perspective from east, 1917–18. Jacques Gréber, delineator. Ink and crayon on tracing paper, mounted on card; 26 x 34″ (66 x 86.4 cm). Inscribed: *J. GREBER*. Philadelphia Museum of Art, Archives, 50.1

Fig. 53. Borie, Trumbauer, and Zantzinger, *Philadelphia Museum of Art*. Longitudinal section, October 20, 1917. Jacques Gréber office, delineators. Watercolor and ink on paper, 32⁵/₁₆ x 82¼" (82.1 x 208.9 cm) (plexiglass package). Inscribed: *J. GRÉBER. S.A.D.G., PARIS, X-20th 1917*. Philadelphia Museum of Art, Archives, 50.3

ular scrutiny. There was no sensible reason for the government to build a large museum on Fairmount *and* a smaller gallery, as Joseph Widener had proposed for the Johnson paintings, and Moore said so in blunt language. Widener had been a friend of Mayor Smith, but he saw no chance of exerting his usual influence in the teeth of such reformist zealotry. On July 22 he quit the Art Jury, to which the Johnson collection had been entrusted, and he rescinded his offer to give his father's paintings to the city.[72] Eli Kirk Price vainly sought to effect a reconciliation, but he failed, as did the Pennsylvania Museum, which strove for twenty years to regain Widener's confidence. The collection went to the National Gallery in Washington in 1942.

Construction of the museum proceeded slowly, reportedly because of difficulty in obtaining large quantities of concrete. Another $1.5 million was voted in 1920, but work on the foundations and retaining walls stretched on through that year and 1921. The public grew suspicious of the secrecy with which the Fairmount Park Com-

mission was conducting the project, and in October 1921, the *Public Ledger*'s reporter found it impossible to get a statement on the building from Price, Art Jury chairman John F. Lewis, or Charles Borie. Horace Trumbauer only stirred the tempest when he told the investigator, "'Mr. Price . . . has instructed those under him not to say a word about the museum.'"[73] Price responded with a series of site tours for reporters and city officials, showing them that, out of sight, two foundation stories had been constructed.

These doldrums were partly offset by the news that John McFadden, who died on February 16, 1921, had emulated Elkins by leaving his paintings to the city on the condition that a suitable gallery be erected. He allowed what by then seemed a more reasonable seven years for completion, however. Then came the word that the foundations were at long last completed, allowing the commission to invite bids for the building's steel skeleton. That contract was awarded on January 5, 1922, to the American Bridge Company.

Fig. 54. Borie, Trumbauer, and Zantzinger, *Philadelphia Museum of Art*. Perspective from north, 1917–18. Gouache, crayon, and graphite on tracing paper, mounted on card; 25 x 51¾" (63.5 x 131.4 cm). Philadelphia Museum of Art, Archives, 50.7

But the steel, like the concrete, was slow in arriving on the site, and complaints resumed about this and about the lack of progress on the long gash of a trolley underpass that cut across the parkway just in front of the museum.[74] The mayor had grown furious at the Park Commission's independent fiefdom, where abuses were allowed to flourish without review, and he attacked at their meeting on November 8, 1922, demanding an accounting from the architects. Their report, made by Price and Borie at a special meeting on November 22, must have shocked everyone. Price explained that the work already completed or under contract would exhaust almost all of the appropriated funds but leave the city with only a steel skeleton. An additional $5,272,188.62 would be needed "to put the building under roof," and it was made clear that even this total expenditure of more than $8.5 million would leave the interior unfinished. Most in the audience remembered that before the war they had expected to complete the project for $3 million, and they were aghast. The only good news came from Borie, who

predicted that the museum could be ready within two years—in time to meet the Elkins deadline. But those who knew what the site looked like must have found this hard to believe (fig. 55).[75]

The newspapers naturally complained about the conduct of the Park Commission, which had acted "in disregard of the rights of the city to a voice in its proceedings," and the mayor now demanded a full report on all contracts awarded to date.[76] The attack amounted to an assault on the personal integrity of Eli Kirk Price, and this was not deflected by Price's often arrogant behavior. To one reporter he riposted, "'What does it matter what it costs? . . . What difference does it make? Who cares? All the people are interested in the Art Museum, not in what it cost. Look at it; the work speaks for itself.'" The same newspaperman received an equally unguarded statement from Borie:

"We don't know now what it will cost to finish the building entirely. We never made such an estimate. How could we? How

can anybody tell what it is going to cost? Why should we make such estimates? We are interested only in the designs and the plans, and that's all the public is interested in."[77]

On the morning of the January 1923 Park Commission meeting at which Price was to give an account of all the contracts, the *Evening Public Ledger* broke the story that the very first contract, for site clearing, had not gone to the lowest bidder. Although Robert Patton, the contractor selected by Price, did submit the lowest estimate for the removal of rock, the vast majority of the work consisted of the excavation of dirt, and for dirt removal Patton had been underbid by five competitors.[78] With this analysis in mind, Price's complete but superficial listing of the dates and amounts of contracts was received with skepticism, and the mayor insisted on the appointment of a

small review committee to explore the matter in greater detail. He chaired that committee himself, and while it reported no malfeasance, neither did it clear up the questions that hung over the Mark and Patton contracts. It did recommend that in the future contracts should only be signed if appropriated money was available, an estimate had been made, and an invitation for bids had been advertised. Contracts were always to go to the lowest bidder.[79] This was accepted, and the subsequent construction bids were handled by the Park Commission with a huge show of openness—enough to stop most of the critics.

The museum was still a horrendously slow and expensive project. Although the Moore administration appropriated $7.5 million over the next two years and although a contract for the superstructure masonry was at last awarded to George A. Fuller on March 5, 1924, meeting the terms of the Elkins bequest proved almost impossible. The paintings had to be temporarily exhibited in an unfinished section of the basement for a few days in October 1924, and only because of the generosity of the executors was this counted as satisfactory compliance with the will. As construction of the superstructure began, Price convinced the commission that they should build the two outermost pavilions first to obtain the greatest possible amount of space for the available money, and so in the summer of 1925 the building raised two detached roof lines at the end of the parkway (see fig. 1). It escaped no one's notice that Price's stratagem would also embarrass the city into providing funds for completion of the missing central portion of the building. It would take a good deal of embarrassing indeed, because in April 1924 the architects estimated that finishing the interior would cost another $8.5 million, bringing the total to $17 million.[80]

In 1925 the tone in which these often difficult proceedings were conducted was improved by several important changes in personnel. Mayor W. Freeland Kendrick had taken office in 1924, and with him and new City Council President Charles Hall came a return to the comfortable certainties of the Vare machine. In the fall of 1925

Fiske Kimball arrived in Philadelphia to head the Pennsylvania Museum, and Price, elected president of the museum a few months later, at last had a museum director to whom he thought it was worth talking. In a kind of celebration, the architects obtained a dramatic rendering of the new building from Hugh Ferriss (1889–1962), the foremost architectural illustrator of the day (fig. 56). He showed it standing high above a deeply shadowed parkway, where the multitudes had gathered as though in religious reverence before its bright facade.

City appropriations amounting to about $9 million rolled in over the next four years, and in December 1927 the Fairmount Park Commission said a fond farewell to Mayor Kendrick and Council President Hall as their terms of office expired. The mayor averred that "the little part that I was permitted to play in helping to finance the great Art Gallery in the Parkway gave me inspiration and pleasure . . . ." Hall was more specific:

When the Commission said that it would cost a certain amount to finish the exterior of this Art Museum, through the staunch support of his Honor, the Mayor, we made the appropriation. Some of my colleagues in Council, of course, did not approve of it. They have different interests and what appeals to one man particularly as a necessity does not appeal to another. I have been subject to some criticism for taking the advanced step that I have, and that criticism I am proud to receive.[81]

With this kind of reliable service from the machine, the building was ready to be shown to the press on January 3, 1928. On March 7, 13, and 26 the museum was opened to increasingly large numbers of invited guests, in the midst of which Kimball's *American Architecture* arrived from the publisher. On March 27 the doors opened to the public. Much of the interior decoration was still unfinished, and there were only ten period rooms and ten galleries filled with the best art that Kimball could scrounge from Memorial Hall or borrow from local collectors, but no one seemed to look at what was not there or to think

about the long and costly route that the project had taken. There was much to look at and admire, not the least of which was the building itself, whose design had taken a joyous and original direction as it encountered the 1920s.

Local Color

What everyone *could* see, and what they all commented on, was the color of the new building. Almost all of the masonry was a bright, natural yellow, and polychromatic terra-cotta ornament, its details based on the evidence of ancient Greek practice, brightened the inside and outside. Column capitals, cornices, coffered ceilings, and the acroteria and antefixes that adorned the roof were all splashed with intense primary colors, and work was going ahead on polychromatic sculpture for the museum's eight pediments. A great deal had evidently changed since the model of a white marble building had been displayed in City Hall in 1915.

The transformation had been wrought by Charles Borie, who became the project architect after Shay left Trumbauer's office in 1918. It was he who had to answer the difficult questions posed by the mayor and the press, but it was also he who created the museum's most beloved features. Borie evidently sympathized with the impulse that had attached so much sculptural enrichment to the austere blocks of the building in 1917, but he had wondered if there was not a better way to achieve the same effect. Like many American architects in the teens, he began to think about the greater use of color, and the groundswell of their interest launched the decorative exuberance of Art Deco in the 1920s.[82] The Philadelphia Museum of Art, despite its archaeological character, thus became the first "moderne" design in the city.

Borie turned for help in realizing his intentions to Leon V. Solon, an architectural writer who had made a special study of polychromy. He had read Solon's "Principles of Polychrome in Sculpture Based on Greek Practice," published in 1918,[83] and in 1921 he arranged to meet him. Although some of Borie's collaborators at first

Fig. 56. Borie, Trumbauer, and Zantzinger, *Philadelphia Museum of Art*. Perspective from southeast, 1925. Hugh Ferriss (1889–1962), delineator. Crayon on paper, 19½ x 34¾" (49.5 x 88.3 cm). Inscribed: *Hugh Ferriss del*. Philadelphia Museum of Art, Archives, 50.30

accused him of having "a frivolous attitude" toward the project, with Solon as an ally he was able to win them over.[84] They next had to convince Eli Kirk Price of the soundness of their plan, and they plied him with scholarship on the subject, including a long, new series of articles by Solon.[85] In this they were abetted by the prejudices established during Price's youthful study of the classics, and by the summer of 1922 a favorable decision had been made. That November Borie announced that the background for the polychromy would be five slightly different shades of tawny yellow, quarried from the Mankato and Kasota dolomite beds of Minnesota.[86]

Not only was it decided to replicate ancient polychromy, but Borie also consulted William H. Goodyear of the Brooklyn Museum, and together they determined how the complex optical "refinements" that Goodyear had studied in Greek architecture might be applied to a modern building. Creating the subtle curvatures that were necessary was a complex and costly process. Because the entire building had to swell upward, the masons who cut its half-million cubic feet of stone had to shape almost every block according to separate specifications. Some of

the effects were nonetheless very hard to detect: The columns of the great porticoes were inclined toward each other in such a way that lines extended upward from their axes would meet—but at a point two and one-half miles above the earth.[87]

To design and make models of the polychromatic ornament, the Park Commission turned to Paul Jennewein, who was already engaged with the sculptural decoration of the museum's retaining wall. Pleased with the preliminary results, which were tested on an eighth-scale model erected in the old carrousel building in Fairmount Park, the commissioners asked Jennewein and the better-known John Gregory to make small-scale studies for pedimental sculpture for the two side pavilions of the great courtyard.[88] Jennewein and Borie traveled together to Italy to study polychromy, and Jennewein stayed on for five months, working up his design for a pediment. Upon his return, Price admired his work, and on February 13, 1924, both he and Gregory were commissioned to prepare larger, one-third-size models of the terra-cotta figures.[89] In the end, only Jennewein's *Western Civilization* was realized at full-scale and placed in its pediment. It was unveiled in March 1933. Gregory's *Eastern Civilization* remained a model,[90] but both of the sculptors had established useful Philadelphia connections. Jennewein, who also designed the museum's bronze elevator doors, remained a close friend of Borie for the rest of the architect's life, and he went on to work with the Zantzinger office on the Department of Justice Building in Washington (1932–34). Gregory was chosen to carve the wonderful panels on the facade of Cret's Folger Library, also in Washington (1928–32).

Warmed by Borie's color, in the final years of its construction the great temple on Fairmount was at last also illuminated by a vision of its special place among the museums of the world. This was Fiske Kimball's contribution. Whereas the architects had heretofore struggled with almost no program to guide them, he now directed them to design the second exhibition floor to accommodate period rooms, which he intended to purchase and install as the appropriate settings for the art of their times. Among the first to be acquired was an early eighteenth-century room from the Treaty House at Upminster, England, donated by George Elkins's son for the hanging of his father's paintings (fig. 57). By the time the museum opened, ten such interiors were in place, arranged around a trio of cool neoclassical galleries on the axis of the north wing. Many more were added as work on the unfinished interior continued, with federal support, during the Depression. The complementary installation of study collections that Kimball intended on the first floor was never mounted, and his vision was thus left incomplete. But the

stately enfilades of the period rooms are an enduring reminder of his architect's eye.

And so it was that a project long beset by inertia and scandal and torn by debate between architects of different philosophies was held on course by Eli Kirk Price and delivered into the hands of those who could bring it to life. On opening day the Ionic columns of the great stair hall still lacked their terra-cotta capitals, and the unfinished roof of the temporary exhibition gallery at the head of the stair had to be disguised by a bright awning (fig. 58). But there was no hint of sarcasm in the words of the observer from New York's Metropolitan Museum who called the new building "A Philadelphian Acropolis."[91]

Fig. 57. Borie, Trumbauer, and Zantzinger, *Philadelphia Museum of Art*. Perspective of room from the Treaty House, Upminster, England; c. 1927. Crayon on tracing paper, mounted on illustration board; 22¼ x 23¾" (56.5 x 60.3 cm). Philadelphia Museum of Art, Archives, 60.2

Fig. 58. Borie, Trumbauer, and Zantzinger, *Philadelphia Museum of Art*. Perspective of stair hall, c. 1927. Crayon on tracing paper, mounted on card; 16 x 18⅞" (40.6 x 47.9 cm). Philadelphia Museum of Art, Archives, 60.1

*A Constellation
of Institutions*

At the same time that Eli Kirk Price was guiding the creation of an art museum on Fairmount, he and those who thought like him were also working to see that the museum was joined on the parkway by nearly a score of other institutions. Although the dimensions of this project waxed and waned over the years, it was always taken for granted that the city's cultural life would reassemble itself on the new avenue and around Logan Circle.

The report on the realignment of the parkway made by Paul Cret, Clarence Zantzinger, Charles Borie, and Horace Trumbauer in 1907 gave first expression to this vision of a cultural boulevard. Cret's sketch in the report portrayed the assemblage of art schools that Borie dreamed would "creat[e] about the foot of an acropolis devoted to the presentation of works of art the institutions in which artists should be locally trained" (see fig. 14).[1] Chief among those institutions were to be the Pennsylvania Academy of the Fine Arts and the Pennsylvania Museum's own school of art, depicted by Cret on either side of Fairmount Plaza. It was also announced in 1907 that the Franklin Institute and the Free Library, both badly overcrowded in their existing accommodations, would join the art schools in building on the parkway. They had selected sites at the other end, close to City Hall and Broad Street Station.

Little was done, however, while the route of the parkway was still under discussion. It was Mayor John Reyburn—the person responsible for seeing that the axis of the boulevard was shifted back to Fairmount in 1909—who joined with Eli Kirk Price in leading the campaign to move the city's institutions to the new thoroughfare. Price was strategically positioned on the boards of many of the very organizations that the mayor wished to move, and by 1911, with Reyburn's Comprehensive Plan as a backdrop, they could announce that a large number of additional sites had been assigned (see fig. 18). At the City Hall end of the parkway they showed the Franklin Institute occupying a domed building on the west side of a great public plaza. On the north side of the plaza stood new law courts.

The city had agreed to provide the American Philosophical Society with a triangular building lot on the north side of the parkway between Sixteenth and Seventeenth streets, and on Logan Square the existing Roman Catholic Cathedral and the Academy of Natural Sciences would be joined by the Free Library, now shifted to the site it occupies today. To the west, the location ultimately selected for the Rodin Museum at Twenty-Second Street was assigned to the Central Manual Training School, while Fairmount Plaza, at the foot of the acropolis, was flanked by the Pennsylvania Academy and the Pennsylvania Museum School, as Cret had shown. By the time Reyburn left office, serious discussion was under way with a host of other potential tenants, including Temple University, the Philadelphia College of Pharmacy, the architecture department of the University of Pennsylvania, the Post Office, the American Catholic Union, and the Medico-Chirurgical Hospital.

Of course, the densely built-up boulevard that Reyburn envisioned was not to be. Few of the identified institutions had even begun to raise the necessary funds when the war began, and then, in 1917–19, Jacques Gréber recast the parkway as a wedge of greenery in which only a few scattered buildings were indicated (see figs. 24, 26). The easternmost section was now to be almost entirely commercial, while Logan Circle received a much greater concentration of institutions: The Free Library on its north side was to be paired with a building that Gréber sometimes marked as the Commercial Museum, the Franklin Institute was to join the Academy of Natural Sciences on the south side, and the law courts were to occupy a vast structure on the west. Out along the western parkway, he first showed an Episcopal cathedral, modeled on the Sacre Coeur in Paris, on the present Rodin Museum site, but by early 1919 this had been replaced by a small gallery for the Johnson collection, and the proposed cathedral had been Gothicized and moved to a site south of the parkway, close to Fairmount Plaza. No other buildings stood among the trees until one reached the

plaza, where the Pennsylvania Academy and the museum school were to take up positions, now augmented by a small exhibition pavilion for the Art Club on the north side of the square.

Fulfilling even this more constrained construction program required decades of work, and the individual buildings, either planned and built or planned only, tell a complicated political and artistic story. The projects were hemmed in by byzantine lawsuits that reflected increasing vigilance over the public purse, and they were also tugged between the two schools of modern classicism. That so many were realized owes not a little to the perseverance of several strong-willed architects. Horace Trumbauer, Paul Cret, and John Windrim were each responsible for more than one of the designs for new parkway buildings, and they were joined by a handful of other architects who each contributed one building to the avenue.

Horace Trumbauer

Horace Trumbauer was a formidable figure in Philadelphia architecture throughout the period of the building of the parkway. His position as the favorite architect of P.A.B. Widener, William Elkins, Edward Stotesbury, and their descendants had earned him an entrée to the board of virtually every cultural organization in the city. Such connections had also helped to secure his appointments to study the parkway for the Fairmount Park Art Association in 1907 and to design the museum of art in 1911. They also brought him the commissions for the Free Library and for a gallery for the Johnson Collection.

The Free Library
P.A.B. Widener was a long-serving trustee of the Free Library, and he saw to it that Trumbauer was hired to design its new home. Shunted from one temporary lodging to another during the relatively short period since its founding in 1891, the library had initially hoped to build on the new plaza north of City Hall, and this was what the Library Committee of City Councils recommended in

Fig. 59. Horace Trumbauer, *Free Library*. Perspective from southeast, 1912. Photograph of lost watercolor. Free Library of Philadelphia, Print and Picture Department

April 1907. But then came the realignment of the parkway under Reyburn's Comprehensive Plan of 1911, in which the library was shown on the north side of Logan Square, one of a pair of buildings that both resembled Henri Labrouste's Bibliothèque Sainte-Geneviève, Paris (1838–50; see fig. 18). This site was formally assigned to them in April 1911, and Trumbauer was appointed shortly thereafter.[2] The strenuous story of the Free Library that followed introduced many of the artistic and legal themes that echoed through the other buildings of the parkway.

Site acquisition proceeded very rapidly, and within a year Trumbauer had prepared a design that plainly alluded to the similarities between the planned Logan Square, with its pair of south-facing monumental buildings, and the Place de la Concorde in Paris (fig. 59). Trumbauer's library remained an allusion rather than a copy, however, for he eschewed the luxurious extravagance of a freestanding arcade at ground level and a detached colonnade above with which Ange-Jacques Gabriel had invested the palatial townhouses in Paris (1755–63). Thus, while the design clearly placed him among the more archaeological classicists, it was sufficiently liberated from precedent to allow Paul Cret, acting in his role as

chairman of the Art Jury committee on this project, to approve it on April 26, 1912. The Free Library was only the sixteenth submission that they reviewed, and it was their first parkway case.[3]

The library planned to break ground in June 1912, starting work on the foundations with $1 million that Councils had appropriated for them from an old loan, but those plans were halted by the decision in the taxpayer's suit of *Wakelin* v. *The City of Philadelphia*. This landmark case, whose effects were also felt by the other parkway buildings, forbade the city from commencing projects unless it had the money on hand to complete them.[4] The suit was intended to curb the excesses of the contractor bosses, but, ironically, its effects fell first on reformer Rudolph Blankenburg. Such additional funds could not be generated during the years when his administration was locked in combat with the Councils, and so the library languished. The idle site had been cleared of its houses, and in 1915 it was used for revival meetings by evangelist Billy Sunday.

Only in 1916, when Thomas Smith restored machine rule to the mayor's office, did the project revive. In his first month in office a special ordinance was passed to allow the Free Library to enter separate contracts for each part of the building, and in June Smith signed an appropriation for $2.46 million from a just-voted loan. It was calculated that this amount, combined with the old loan, would be enough to build the entire building, rendering the new ordinance unnecessary.

In the four years since the last design had been put forward, the city had decided to widen the streets surrounding the library, and so Trumbauer was compelled to revise his design (fig. 60). This was submitted to the Art Jury on November 23. Julian Abele represented Trumbauer before the jury committee on that date, and the design appears to have been his work. While the building had been altered in plan to conform to the new site lines, the most striking changes were on the outside, where the architect had reduced the height of the entrance stairway and made the Corinthian colonnade freestanding. These alterations rendered the building a much more faithful copy of its Parisian prototype, and Cret, had he not been in France at war, might well have registered a protest. But Milton Medary was substituting for him on the Art Jury, and he was unable even to attend the meeting. On the next day he recorded his comments as a postscript to the meeting minutes, only predicting blandly that "the building will be a very distinguished one."[5] The design was approved.

Builders were invited to bid early in 1917, but when the contract was awarded on April 2 the matter was swamped by another species of legal complication: The next day John Flynn filed a taxpayer's suit against the city for failing to comply with the 1894 and 1895 ordinances requiring that all stone used for city projects be cut in the city rather than at the quarry. This costly stipulation was intended to protect local stonemasons, and the courts upheld Flynn's case. The library authorities accordingly went ahead with a groundbreaking ceremony on May 12, 1917, but they also advertised for new bids. No sooner was a new contract, in compliance with the old ordinances, signed, however, than another taxpayer's suit was filed, attacking from the other side. W. R. Taylor's action, initiated on August 2, challenged the constitutionality of the 1894 and 1895 laws, and this position was in turn upheld by the state supreme court on June 3, 1918. It was agreed that the terms of the latest general contract, with John Gill and Sons, could be rewritten to allow the stone to be cut at the quarries, but wartime restrictions prevented the full resumption of work, and when peace did come Gill found himself unable to do the job at the bid prices. On November 22, 1919, the contract was cancelled, with only some excavation work to show for nearly four years of effort. Similar taxpayer litigation, amounting to a war against Philadelphia's bosses, was to bedevil most of the parkway buildings.

With the inauguration of J. Hampton Moore in January 1920, contractors were under even greater scrutiny. But in the fall of that year, a loan for another $1 million for the library was voted by the people, and in December a new set of bids was opened, this time restricted to foundation work. Construction began again on February 14, 1921, and one year later the contract for the superstructure was awarded. Just as this final phase of the project began, Trumbauer submitted a final set of revised drawings to the Art Jury. Even more archaeological than the 1916 design, this one replicated even the niches, swagging, and (so far as different floor levels would allow) fenestration pattern of Gabriel's eighteenth-century buildings. Cret could not be present when this was discussed by committee on April 24, 1922, and they approved the design. Little else was possible, since it had been reviewed favorably in 1916, but a few days later Cret set down his views for the record:

The Place de la Concorde buildings [by Gabriel] being a master work, there is no doubt that the Philadelphia Library will be successful on the whole, as far as general proportions and detail are concerned. However, it will be a matter of regret to some that such an important building built by the city will not deserve more than the doubtful praise of being a copy of a good example.[6]

On January 24, 1923, in the rain, the formal cornerstone laying was staged, five and one-half years after the groundbreaking, and construction proceeded uneventfully under the rule of Mayor Kendrick. On January 20, 1927, the first books were moved into the library, and on June 2 the great building was opened. Its total cost had mounted to $6.3 million (figs. 61–62).

Johnson Collection Gallery
Like the library, the commission for the Johnson Collection gallery came to Trumbauer because of his Widener connections, and it too was immediately engulfed in Philadelphia politics. Unlike the library, however, the gallery was never built, and the confidences damaged in the process enormously magnified the loss.

Fig. 60. Horace Trumbauer, *Free Library*. Perspective from southwest, c. 1916. Watercolor and ink on paper, 25 x 53″ (63.5 x 134.6 cm). Free Library of Philadelphia

When John G. Johnson added the codicil to his will on February 12, 1917, specifying that his collection was to remain in his South Broad Street house, he had been convinced that the plans for the Fairmount museum would never be realized and doubted that he would like the museum even if it were built.[7] His death a few months later, on April 14, and the publication of his will presented a thorny problem to those who had dreamed of uniting all of the city's great private collections in the new museum. Not the least of these dreamers was Joseph Widener. The deaths of his father (P.A.B.) and brother (George) had left him in charge of the family collection, and in 1916 he had been appointed president of the Art Jury. After Johnson's death his name was also added to the Fairmount Park Commission, for which he oversaw the Wilstach Collection. In every respect he was now the leader of the city's art-owning gentry, and although his own hobby was horse racing, he took this position seriously. The Johnson codicil worried him; he was selected by the city to head a special committee in charge of looking after the Johnson pictures, and he wanted to show respect for the wishes of his old family lawyer, but he also hoped to assemble a great public collection for the city.

Throughout 1918 the press was abuzz with the Johnson story. Widener's committee ordered that the paintings be taken from his house for their safety, having judged it to be a firetrap, and the Orphans' Court prepared to hear a suit backed by Johnson's own trustees. The litigants argued that the poor condition of the house, coupled with the prospect of moving the paintings to the new art museum, constituted the kind of "extraordinary situation" that the codicil had said would allow the removal of the collection.[8]

While Widener supported the lawsuit, he also sought to show some understanding for Johnson's wish to keep his pictures apart from other collections. He probably also knew of the disenchantment that Johnson had felt toward large art museums during the last years of his life. A member of Mayor Blankenburg's cabinet remembered that the collector had said, "'I don't intend that my pictures shall ever be used as a bait for the construction of any —— —— marble palace. I shall provide that the city of Philadelphia may have them if it is willing that they shall be housed in a plain brick building. If not, they will go elsewhere.'"[9] John F. Lewis, president of the Pennsylvania Academy of the Fine Arts, had warned Eli Kirk Price in 1914 that Johnson believed that the Fairmount museum "would be an architect's monument rather than a suitable place in which to display pictures . . . ."[10] Accordingly, late in 1918 Widener asked Trumbauer to design a separate gallery, which would bring the Johnson paintings to the parkway but preserve their identity. He unveiled this news to a gathering of influential guests—including Price—at the Ritz-Carlton Hotel on December 5, and at the same time he announced that his father's paintings would be given to the city for the museum (if suitable) on Fairmount.[11] These two pieces of information were received with general rejoicing.

Trumbauer's design was simple, if not exactly the "plain brick building" of which Johnson had spoken (fig. 63). True to his usual methods, it was based very closely on precedent, in this case borrowing its central feature from the façade of the Pazzi Chapel in Florence (c. 1460). This contained the entrance vestibule, while one-story galleries extended outward from either side and encircled

Fig. 61. Horace Trumbauer, *Free Library*. Main reading room, c. 1930. Free Library of Philadelphia, Print and Picture Department

a courtyard at the back. Intended for the site on which Gréber had first sketched the Episcopal cathedral and ultimately occupied by the Rodin Museum, the little gallery won the full support of Mayor Thomas Smith. Smith, who called Widener "'my very good personal friend,'" struggled throughout 1919 to find the $500,000 needed to erect the gallery—by selling the Johnson house, if necessary—but without luck.[12] Without a securely funded alternative location, however, the courts refused to break Johnson's will.

Such were the conditions when Mayor J. Hampton Moore was inaugurated on January 5, 1920. Pledged to root out the corrupt contractors, he controlled the city budget with an iron hand. As mayor, Moore was automatically a member of the Art Jury, and at his first meeting he clashed violently with Widener over the latter's request for funds to restore the Johnson pictures.[13] By April he had concluded that there was ample room for the Johnson Collection in the new museum on Fairmount—where it could be hung in a wing of its own—and that there was no need to build Trumbauer's separate gallery.[14] On July 14 the mayor explained these views to the Fairmount Park Commission (Widener was absent), and on July 19 he formally announced that he would not "'scatter the pictures belonging to the city around in separate buildings to satisfy separate estates or individuals.'"[15] The *Public Ledger* spoke for many when it called this proposal "sensible," but Moore had not taken into account the wishes of Johnson—or Widener.[16] Moore and Widener met in what was called a "battle royal" at the Art Jury on July 21, and, finding no common ground, Widener abruptly resigned, saying only that he and the mayor "'did not understand each other at all.'" He retaliated by revoking his pledge to give his father's pictures to the city.[17] Price's efforts to effect a reconciliation were in vain, and so the city lost both a pretty building and its greatest private collection.

Paul Cret

Paul Cret's connections were unlike Trumbauer's but they were equally useful. Although his work on the 1907 study

of the parkway for the Fairmount Park Art Association did not lead, as it did for Trumbauer and Zantzinger, to an appointment on the design team for the art museum, Eli Kirk Price came to rely heavily on his advice.[18] After Cret returned from the war, their association, and the public knowledge of it, brought a series of parkway projects into his office.

Rodin Museum

Of the several buildings that he designed for parkway sites, only the Rodin Museum was realized. It was created for Jules Mastbaum, Philadelphia's great movie theater mogul, who had begun to buy bronzes from the Rodin studio and wished to build a gallery for them on the parkway. He consulted with Price, and in January 1926 he dispatched his agent, the portrait painter Albert Rosenthal, to ask Jacques Gréber to design such a building.[19] Price wrote to Gréber at the same time, saying that although the matter had not yet been discussed by the Fairmount Park Commission, he was sure that the site of the intended Johnson gallery could be reassigned to Mastbaum's project.[20]

Gréber accepted the commission and began to prepare an "avant projet," but although he had been trained as an architect, he recognized his limitations in the field and asked to be allowed to invite Cret to collaborate with him. He wrote to Cret with such an invitation on January 23, 1926, but his assertion that all of the drawings would be executed in Paris led Cret, who had been approached by Mastbaum himself a few months earlier, to believe that Gréber was only looking for someone to supervise the work on the site. Gréber had clearly stated that both the preliminary and final designs would be submitted for Cret's review, but Cret's recollection of Gréber's opportunistic wartime behavior made him suspicious, and he refused the offer. Disquieted by this rebuke, Gréber replied from Paris with a most conciliatory letter, enclosing copies of all of his correspondence with Mastbaum, Rosenthal, and Price, and begging Cret to "set for your-

Fig. 62. Horace Trumbauer, *Free Library*, 1911–27. Photograph of March 4, 1927. City Archives of Philadelphia, 116.01, 23902

self" the conditions of their collaboration. Doing all of the drafting in Paris, he explained, was intended only to save Cret's time. Cret then spoke directly with Mastbaum, and on March 22 he agreed to work on the project.[21]

In the meantime Gréber had gone ahead with the design, and on April 3 the Art Jury received three drawings from his office, dated in February and March, that showed a five-bay-wide building standing behind a garden. This arrangement minimized the impact of the already small building upon Gréber's great wedge of park. Following Mastbaum's instructions, the garden gate was to be a replica of the montage of architectural fragments from the Château d'Issy that Rodin had assembled at his Meudon studio. Cret was on the committee that approved the design on April 7, knowing that it meant very little, for the drawings did not even show the facade of the museum and Gréber was due in Philadelphia in late June for consultation.[22]

Gréber's brief visit to Philadelphia was followed by another meeting with Cret, joined by Mastbaum, in Paris during Cret's summer holiday abroad. Although Gréber had undergone an appendectomy on the eve of this second conference, the two architects were able to revise the Art Jury design. They made the plan simpler than Gréber had shown, with the several rooms pulled together within an almost unbroken rectangle, and they began to study its elevations. After parting, they exchanged sketches and comments. Gréber, sensitive to American tastes, defined their choice as being between modernity and archaeology, which was shorthand for the two schools of contemporary classicism:

One can suppress, if you think it possible, more or less of the antique elements in order to make of it an architecture approaching the simple lines of Tony Garnier or [Auguste] Perret, or, on the other hand, one can stay within the antique tradition, as much in the proportions as in the details of the elements, . . . and thus remain in the mode which I believe always gives pleasure in the United States.[23]

Cret expressed the same views in his reply: "What has been shown on these sketches retains somewhat a modern feeling, and, as I told you before, I am not absolutely sure that we ought to do that." His doubts were sparked by a warning from Rosenthal, who had told him that the design looked too "'funereal'" and had suggested something more like the Petit Trianon at Versailles.[24] Although trapped between their own inclinations to modernize and simplify and their American client's desire for a more festive building with a historical pedigree, they were able to work out a compromise that retained the contours of eighteenth-century classicism while rearranging its details (fig. 64). At the center of the facade, they created a setting for Rodin's *Gates of Hell* (1880–1917) between a pair of Roman Doric columns. This parti was developed with

Fig. 63. Horace Trumbauer, *Johnson Collection Gallery.* Perspective, 1919. Jacques Gréber, delineator. Photograph of lost crayon drawing. Inscribed: *J. Greber del. Paris 1919.* The Commissioners of Fairmount Park, Philadelphia

a full set of drawings in Gréber's Paris office in October 1926, and at the end of the month he brought them to Philadelphia.[25]

Cret and Gréber spent a month together this time, and Gréber came to marvel at his collaborator's talents. He wrote from the steamship that took him home on December 8, "Let me tell you again that I am taking away from these several days passed in work at your side one of the most pleasant memories of my career. To see you study and direct the fine tuning of your projects is a real education that I hope not to lose."[26] In the course of Gréber's November tutelage, the design was carefully

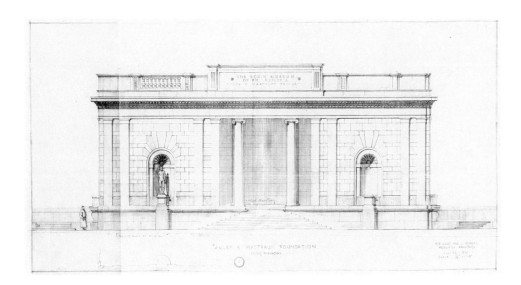

restudied. The triple-bay frontispiece was now replaced by a single compositional unit that was pulled back into the body of the building. Its columns were Ionic rather than Roman Doric. Having received Mastbaum's approval, Gréber's staff redrew this simpler scheme in December.[27] It was also represented in the set of finished presentation drawings that Cret's office produced seven months later (figs. 65–66).

The maturation of the design came, however, at what was otherwise a troubled time for the project, for Jules Mastbaum died on December 7, 1926, as Gréber sailed back to France. His executors were his widow and Morris Wolf, an attorney, and they called for an immediate cessation of labor and a fresh calculation of the cost of the museum building alone. An estimate of $350,000 was duly produced, but the stop-work order came too late, much of the stonework for the replica of the Meudon portal having already been cut in France. Eli Kirk Price now entered the scene, and, as Cret reported to Gréber in January 1927, he strove to convince Mastbaum's widow Etta at least to build the museum and donate the collection. She could not provide the operating endowment that her husband had promised, however, and Price undertook to get the city to replace this with a subvention of its own.[28]

In the early summer of 1927, Gréber again came to Philadelphia, and he and Cret met with Wolf to discuss the situation. They agreed to reduce the total cost of the project, including the garden and the portal, to $325,000, less than the December 1926 estimate for just the building.[29] They judged that this could be accomplished without radically changing the program, provided, as now seemed likely, that the city agreed to meet the operating expenses.

Gréber went back to France, and Cret took up his pencil again. By late August 1927, the needed economies had compelled him to "completely revise the studies."[30] Reduced in length from more than one hundred feet to little more than sixty, the museum now assumed the taut proportions of the executed design (fig. 67). Despite this

compression, the organization of the plan was almost un-changed. Cret warned Gréber that they would be "very, very squeezed," but he did admit that the artistic effect pleased him.[31] At the same time, Cret replaced the Ionic order with Greek Doric, which managed to be archae-ological while at the same time evincing the clean lines of modernity. He had also used Greek Doric at the Indian-apolis Public Library.

Cret showed the new design to Wolf in Philadel-phia, and Gréber showed it to Etta Mastbaum in Paris, and with their approval the work at last went ahead. In March 1928 Cret prepared a set of blueprints that were passed by the Art Jury on the sixteenth of that month.

Construction began within a month and proceeded rap-idly, despite the bankruptcy of the general contractor. The Rodin Museum was inaugurated on November 29, 1929, by which time a large marble copy of *The Kiss*, exe-cuted by Gréber's father, had been installed in the main gallery (fig. 68).

Despite its rocky beginnings, the Cret-Gréber col-laboration had worked smoothly, in large part because of the neatly divided lines of responsibility. As Gréber later explained, "If the general composition and the lay out of the garden are my work, the building itself as it appears now executed, ought to bear more the signature of Cret than mine."[32]

Fig. 66. Paul P. Cret and Jacques Gréber, *Rodin Museum*. Transverse section, July 25, 1927. Graphite and colored pencil on tracing paper, 17¼ x 36″ (43.8 x 91.4 cm). Inscribed: *P. P. CRET AND J. GREBER ASSOCI-ATE ARCHITECTS JULY 25, 1927*. Philadelphia Museum of Art, Archives, 100.3

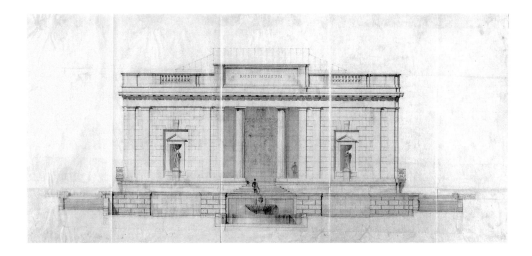

Fig. 67. Paul P. Cret and Jacques Gréber, *Rodin Museum*. Southwest elevation, August 1927. Graphite and colored pencil on tracing paper, 18½ x 41¾" (47 x 106 cm). The partners of H2L2 Architects/Planners, Philadelphia

Fig. 68. Paul P. Cret and Jacques Gréber, *Rodin Museum*, 1926–29. Photograph of March 1, 1929. City Archives of Philadelphia, 116.01, 26509

American Philosophical Society

Throughout the years of his collaborative project for the Rodin Museum, Cret was working alone on the design of new headquarters for the American Philosophical Society, which had outgrown its home on South Fifth Street next to Independence Hall. Members of the society met with Mayor John Reyburn on February 3, 1911, when he was lining up tenants for the parkway, and after hearing a

report that argued against replacing old Philosophical Hall *in situ*, a special meeting of the members on May 10 voted to move.[33] They agreed with the mayor to trade their land for a parcel on the north side of the parkway between Sixteenth and Seventeenth streets.

There the matter stood for fourteen years, punctuated only by the appointment of a committee to study the site question again in 1919. Eli Kirk Price, who served as treasurer of the society for fifteen years, was its most active member,[34] and it was he who finally persuaded the committee to revive consideration of the parkway location. This occurred at its meeting on March 5, 1925—only the third time the committee had convened since its creation. Price had clearly laid secure foundations for this maneuver, because the next day the society's executive council authorized the committee to proceed with a consideration of the problem, and on March 11 the committee reconfirmed the decision to move to the parkway and "expressed themselves informally as in favor of a colonial style of architecture for the new building." On Price's motion, he was dispatched to discuss this matter with Paul Cret.[35]

Among the needs of the society that Price outlined to his friend were two auditoriums (seating one hundred and three hundred, respectively), a library with a bookstack that could be expanded to hold half a million volumes, an exhibition gallery, a dining room, offices, conference rooms, and a residence to be used by the librarian or the secretary. Cret must have expressed some misgivings over the specified style of the building—intended to memorialize the society's eighteenth-century origins—but he agreed to prepare a design. Price sent him his contract on May 6, and Cret made a preliminary report three weeks later.[36]

Cret showed his drawings to the committee on December 16, 1925, and they enthusiastically asked him to make a presentation perspective (fig. 69). His design filled the triangular site with a Y-shaped building whose arms enfolded a porticoed main entrance, a conceit whose

quirky ingenuity was more reminiscent of the work of Edwin Lutyens, the great twentieth-century English classicist, than the Ecole des Beaux-Arts. The style was a mixture of British and American Georgian, rendered in brick with light-colored trim. Handsome as it was, the design was more a measure of Cret's respect for his American friends than an expression of his artistic will.

The architect must have been secretly relieved when the Philosophical Society found itself unable to move immediately to the construction of this building. The question was allowed to lapse while various funding schemes were considered, including possible cooperation with the plans being made by the Poor Richard Club, the fraternity of Philadelphia's advertising community, for a national memorial for Benjamin Franklin. Cret made use of this time, and late in 1927 he presented a design that accorded better with his own tastes (fig. 70). This showed a serene composition with simplified neoclassical detail-

ing, assembled on top of a more academic T-shaped plan. An enormous blank attic enclosed the bookstack. Price was apparently won over to this design, for when the society finally authorized a fund drive in 1929, the promotional literature was illustrated with a slightly reduced version that Cret estimated would cost just over $1 million (fig. 71).[37] Now with a frontispiece reduced to five bays, the latest design was shown executed in brick as a gesture to those who had wanted a "colonial" building.

Unfortunately, the fundraising campaign was formally announced on October 15, 1929, just nine days before the Wall Street crash, and at first it proceeded slowly. On July 1, 1931, as the Depression deepened, the building committee asked Cret to eliminate the residence from the program and to look once again at reusing the old building.[38] Cret's report on the latter question strongly reiterated the findings of the 1911 study; on October 26 the committee endorsed his recommendation for a new

Fig. 69. Paul P. Cret, *American Philosophical Society*. Perspective of neo-Georgian design from southwest, c. 1925–26. Watercolor, ink, graphite, gouache, and crayon on paper; 11½ x 28¾" (29.2 x 73 cm). Inscribed: *Paul P. Cret*. American Philosophical Society, Philadelphia

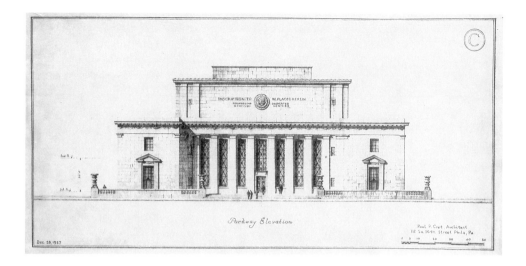

Fig. 70. Paul P. Cret, *American Philosophical Society*. Southwest elevation of seven-bay neoclassical design, December 28, 1927. Photographic print of lost drawing, 10¼ x 19¼" (26 x 48.9 cm). Inscribed: *DEC. 28, 1927 Paul P. Cret, Architect.* American Philosophical Society, Philadelphia

Fig. 71. Paul P. Cret, *American Philosophical Society*. Southwest perspective of five-bay neoclassical design, May 1929. Photograph of lost drawing. American Philosophical Society, Philadelphia

building on the parkway and sent it along to the executive council.[39] There it was decided to push ahead, doubtless emboldened by a bequest of $4 million from Dr. Richard Penrose.

On December 30, 1931, Cret returned to the committee with schematic drawings that managed to preserve the main outlines of his 1927–29 work. With their assent he spent January of the new year making elevation studies in which he tested nearly a dozen combinations of fenestration patterns and orders for the main colonnade, now restored to seven bays. He considered but rejected the use of both square piers and Greek Doric columns along with a variety of other possibilities (figs. 72–73). His preference fell in the end upon an Ionic colonnade, lightening with its graceful proportions the otherwise rather austere facade. On March 2 he won approval for this variant, and at the end of May he prepared presentation drawings of the exterior (fig. 74). Work on the interior followed, with each set of drawings being approved in turn by the building committee (fig. 75).[40]

It appeared that the final resolution was nearing. Arrangements were made in the fall of 1932 to invite contractors to bid on the construction, and on February 27, 1933, the mayor signed an ordinance to trade the parkway site for the society's present land. The Art Jury committee approved the design (with Cret abstaining) on March 16, 1933.[41] But the project suddenly found itself at risk, challenged by another of that species of taxpayers' suits with which the reformers struggled to tame the political machine. In this case, it was the proposed land swap that came under scrutiny, with protestors claiming that the city was exchanging a piece of parkway property worth $900,000 for an old building whose value was $50,000 or less.[42] Suit was brought against the deal in the Court of Common Pleas on April 25 by Ernest T. Wright, and litigation dragged on inconclusively into the fall. The society no longer had the benefit of Price's unflagging enthusiasm for the project, for he had died in January 1933, and they were dispirited by this turn of events. They were also

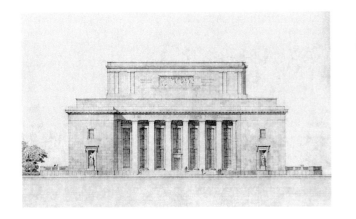

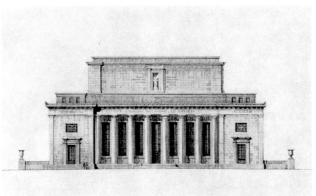

Fig. 72. Paul P. Cret, *American Philosophical Society*. Southwest study elevation with square piers (detail), January 29, 1932. Graphite on tracing paper, 19¼ x 34½″ (48.9 x 87.6 cm). Inscribed: *JAN 29. '32*. American Philosophical Society, Philadelphia

Fig. 73. Paul P. Cret, *American Philosophical Society*. Southwest study elevation with Doric columns (detail), January 1932. Graphite on tracing paper, 19¼ x 34½″ (48.9 x 87.6 cm). American Philosophical Society, Philadelphia

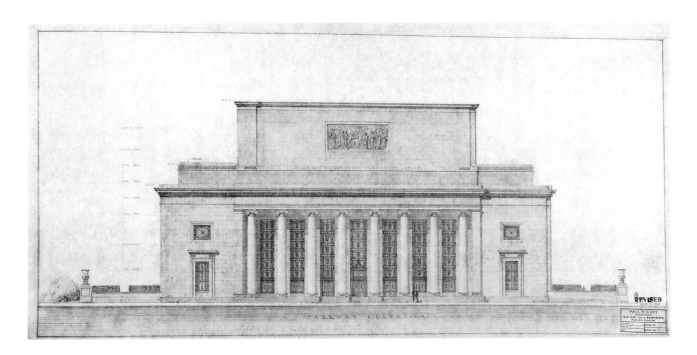

Fig. 74. Paul P. Cret, *American Philosophical Society*. Southwest elevation, May–June 1932. Graphite on tracing paper, 21 x 41½″ (53.3 x 105.4 cm). Inscribed: *REVISED JUNE 21. 1932 PAUL P. CRET ARCHITECT 5.31.32*. American Philosophical Society, Philadelphia

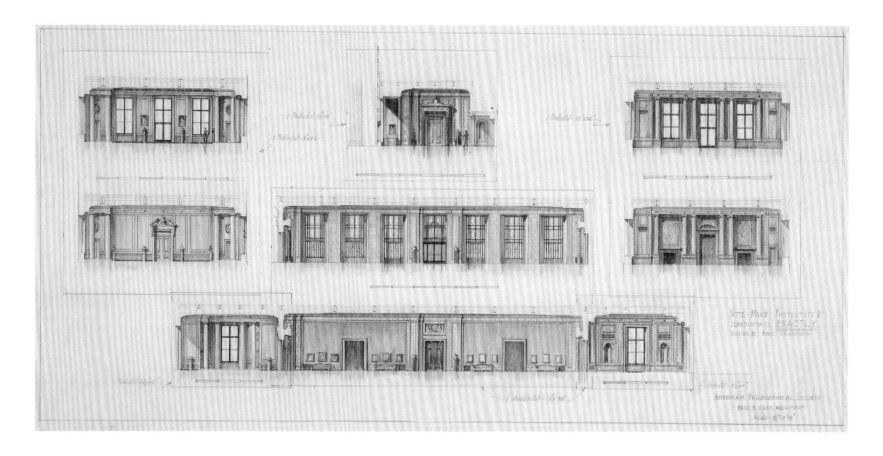

Fig. 75. Paul P. Cret, *American Philosophical Society*. Sections through lobby and meeting rooms, 1932. Graphite and colored pencil on tracing paper, 21 x 38½" (53.3 x 97.8 cm). Inscribed: *PAUL P. CRET, ARCHITECT*. American Philosophical Society, Philadelphia

increasingly pressed by members from outside Philadelphia who wished to retain the historic address, and thus the Building Fund Committee decided on November 13, 1933, to poll the preferences of all those who had given money.[43] As a result, Cret's design was retired, and he helped them plan the renovation of Philosophical Hall. The library was moved into an office building across the street in 1934, and it only acquired a building of its own in the 1950s when the society built a replica of William Thornton's Library Hall, the eighteenth-century home of the Library Company.

City Hall Tower

Also unbuilt and even more controversial was Cret's plan to demolish all but the tower of City Hall, thereby restoring the intended openness of the central square in William Penn's city plan while also preserving the terminus of the parkway. Cret was certainly not alone in his disrespect for John McArthur's vast Second Empire style building, whose scandal-ridden construction had dragged on from the 1870s into the first years of the twentieth century. Making it the focus of the parkway had brought even greater scrutiny to bear upon it, and in 1911, during the much-vaunted City Planning Conference sponsored by Mayor Reyburn, it was the object of much ridicule from visitors. The architect Ernest Flagg opined,

"Notwithstanding its immense cost, I do not think that public money could be spent in any other way so advantageously for the improvement of the city as in the removal of the Philadelphia City Hall, for, standing where it does, it is nothing less than a monument to bad taste . . . . [It is] nothing but a disfigurement to the city in blotting out as it does the square on which it stands and . . . destroying the vista of the streets which it obstructs."[44]

Cret must have had similar thoughts on January 26, 1924, when he sketched Penn Square as it would be if all but the tower of City Hall were razed. He showed his drawings to the Philadelphia Chapter of the American Institute of Architects on March 24, as illustrations to a lecture on the parkway, and the audacity of his design sparked considerable interest.[45] Among those most impressed was the philanthropist Edward W. Bok, former editor of Cyrus H. K. Curtis's *Ladies' Home Journal* and Curtis's son-in-law. Bok called together a group of civic-minded friends, including Eli Kirk Price, on October 23, 1925, and they incorporated themselves as the "Philadelphia Commission," which was "Devoted to the Beautification" of the city. They had two main objectives: reducing litter and tearing down City Hall.[46]

After unexplained delays, a committee devoted to the question of City Hall was created under the chairmanship of Milton Medary, who was later to design the Bok Carillon Tower in Mountain Lake, Florida, and they invited Paul Cret to show his drawings to them on October 4, 1926. Medary met with Cret several times for further discussion, and Cret agreed to develop his ideas in detail. He asked to be associated in this with his former pupil Harry Sternfeld (1888–1976), then a fellow instructor at the University of Pennsylvania.

Cret and Sternfeld made their report to the commission in May 1927, at which time they showed Stern-

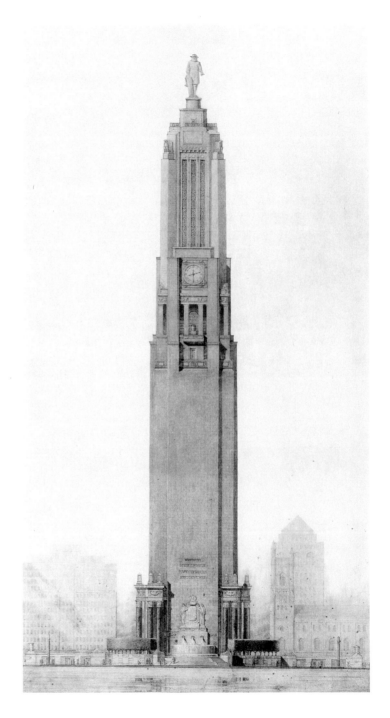

feld's finished drawings of their scheme (fig. 76).[47] After summarizing the functional inadequacies of City Hall, they went on to conclude that it "will never become good architecture, except for the Tower, which on account of its size rather than of its design, is unique among belfries; and we feel, likewise, that it is the Tower alone, with the figure of William Penn atop, that has become for the majority of Philadelphians, the landmark of their birthplace, and the object of civic pride . . . ." So it was that they only spared the tower, standing unencumbered in Penn Square, and unlike Cret's 1924 design, they now replaced its "ugly metal roof" with a masonry structure that would frame the clock faces and provide a pedestal for Alexander Milne Calder's statue of Penn. The entire design was treated in a uniformly cool neoclassical style, save at the base, where freestanding columns and a large fountain on the south face afforded some vitality. Beneath the tower would lie a new central station for the existing Market Street subway and the line planned for Broad Street, designed on a generous scale because it was no longer necessary to dodge the foundations of City Hall, and around the tower would flow automobile traffic in a simple circular pattern. The work of city government was to be relocated to a municipal building on the plaza that

had just been cleared north of Penn Square, where the Municipal Services Building (1962–65) stands today.

The commission admired this proposal, and they shared it with City Council President Charles Hall and Senator-elect William S. Vare. But some members apparently thought that Cret might have proposed something more radical—perhaps advocating an even more complete remodeling of the tower—and so on November 25, 1927, they asked him to make a new design of the proposed tower "without limitation of any kind." Work on this went ahead throughout 1928, and on May 20, 1929, a press luncheon was held at which a revised and illustrated report was made public.[48] In fact little distinguished this design from that of two years earlier, although there was now an even greater amount of unarticulated planar masonry and the colonnade around the base had been reduced to eight square piers.

When the Philadelphia Commission's plans were announced, they caused a brief flurry of interest in the press, but this died away quickly. Soon the project was foundering. First came the death of Milton Medary on August 6, 1929. Then, five months later, Bok died. Although Zantzinger succeeded Medary as chairman of the City Hall committee and W. Curtis Bok was elected to take up his father's position, the commission rarely again obtained a quorum. It last met on November 2, 1932.

2601 Parkway

Paul Cret was better served in his work for the developer Joseph J. Greenberg, for whom he designed an apartment building to be erected at 2601 Pennsylvania Avenue, due north of the art museum.[49] The project, which for marketing purposes was always called "2601 Parkway," occupied Cret's office for about nine years, during which time he began to experiment with the vocabulary of modernism. The first sketches of around 1931, however, were strictly historicist. A twin-towered, twenty-eight-story Gothic design, in some of the drawings detailed very much like Eliel Saarinen's second-place entry in the Chi-

cago Tribune competition of 1922, was worked out at the same time that a three-block classical variant was being tested (fig. 77). Then, after conducting massing studies in May 1932, in which the building was stripped of all detail, the office produced a series of "moderne" alternatives that compared the different effects of horizontal and vertical alternating banks of limestone and orange brick. Sketched in colored crayon in sharp perspective, some of these studies assumed an expressionist guise (fig. 78).

"Moderne" led Cret to modern, as in his contemporary work for the Chemistry Building at the University of Pennsylvania (1940) and the Camden Athletic Club (c. 1938), and by the late 1930s the design had grown sharply geometrical and been covered with ribbon windows (fig. 79). In some of this last work for Greenberg, Cret was associated with the architects Sydney E. Martin

Fig. 78. Paul P. Cret, *2601 Parkway*. Perspective of "moderne" design from south, c. 1932. Crayon and colored crayon on tracing paper, 7 x 15¼″ (17.8 x 38.7 cm). The partners of H2L2 Architects/ Planners, Philadelphia

Fig. 79. Paul P. Cret, *2601 Parkway*. Perspective of modern design from southwest, late 1930s. Graphite on tracing paper, 4½ x 7¼″ (11.4 x 18.4 cm). The partners of H2L2 Architects/Planners, Philadelphia

Fig. 80. Paul P. Cret succeeded by Aaron Colish (born 1910), *2601 Parkway*, 1931–40. Photograph of October 17, 1940. City Archives of Philadelphia, 1176, 37587, **B**

and Walter H. Thomas, and in the end he joined forces with his former student Aaron Colish (born 1910). Their design was approved by the Art Jury in 1939, marking the end of Cret's evolution toward modernism (fig. 80).

John T. Windrim

Joining Trumbauer and Cret in that coterie of architects who played large roles in designing the buildings of the parkway was John T. Windrim (1866–1934). Schooled in architecture by his father James H. Windrim, author of Mayor Stuart's parkway plan of 1891–92 (see fig. 10), the younger Windrim was a shrewd and well-connected member of the architectural fraternity. He was the company architect of both the Bell Telephone Company and the Philadelphia Electric Company, and he bequeathed these lucrative connections to W. R. Morton Keast (1888–1973), his long-time assistant and eventually his successor. The Windrim-Keast contribution to the parkway was enormous, although not all of their designs were realized.

Bell Telephone Building
John Windrim's association with the Bell Telephone Company led to the construction of the first major building on

the parkway, the firm's fifteen-story office tower at Seventeenth Street. First discussed at an early Art Jury meeting on October 24, 1912, the design reached its final form in January 1914 (fig. 81).[50] Windrim adopted what was by that date the conventional tripartite division of the exterior of a tall office building into base, shaft, and crown, and he clothed it with restrained eighteenth-century details that accorded well with the older architecture of the Quaker City. The Bell Telephone Building, completed in 1916, established the commercial character of the southeast end of the parkway (fig. 82). It was soon joined by other major works from the same designer.

The Franklin Institute
By the middle of the nineteenth century, the Franklin Institute, founded to continue Benjamin Franklin's scientific work, had outgrown the little Greek Revival building on Seventh Street that John Haviland had built in 1825. When the architect Joseph M. Wilson was president of the institute in the 1890s, he prepared several designs for a new rental office building that would also include expanded quarters. But the project did not move ahead until 1906, when it seemed that the long postponement of the art museum project was likely to deprive it of the Franklin Fund, the endowment set up in Benjamin Franklin's will for the city's cultural betterment. Reckoning that these moneys might rightly be transferred to its own building account, the institute began fundraising and obtained from the city a site on the southeast corner of the intended parkway and Sixteenth Street. On April 10, 1907, the Board of City Trusts did transfer the Franklin Fund to the institute—amounting to only slightly more than $130,000—and on the next day the newspapers published a sketch design for a handsome Wrenian building from the office of Cope and Stewardson, architects of most of the new buildings on the University of Pennsylvania campus (fig. 83).[51]

Both Walter Cope (1860–1902) and John Stewardson (1858–1896) had died by the time that the Franklin

Fig. 81. John T. Windrim, *Bell Telephone Building*. Parkway and Arch Street elevations, early 1914. Photograph of lost drawing. City Archives of Philadelphia, 140.3, 106

Fig. 82. John T. Windrim, *Bell Telephone Company*, 1912–16. Bell Telephone Company of Pennsylvania, Philadelphia

Institute commission came to their office, and so the work was probably overseen by James P. Jamieson, who served as chief designer for the firm between 1902 and 1912. The pedimented east facade was to look over a triangle of park that the city was expected to create, while the west front was pressed up against Sixteenth Street. Much of the interior was filled by a large auditorium, around which were arranged the library, offices, laboratories, and classrooms.

Cope and Stewardson's association with the project was short-lived. In January 1908, the Board of City Trusts, guardian of the Franklin Fund, communicated their desire that the commission be transferred to the office of James Windrim, whose extensive work on the large properties managed by the estate of Stephen Girard had won him favor among the trustees.[52] James Windrim's son John had for some years been overseeing the design work in the office, and it was to him that the Franklin Institute now turned for a design. He took up the problem with enthusiasm. In the meantime, the city had ceded all of the intended triangular park to the institute,

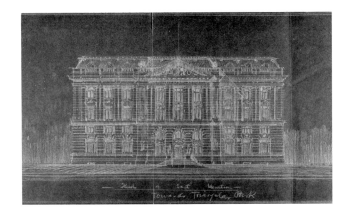

and so it was for a large, three-sided site, stretching almost to Fifteenth Street, that he sketched a design that was unveiled on February 14, 1908 (fig. 84). With around $400,000 already in hand for construction, Windrim created a vastly more imposing building, Roman in proportions and authority and topped by a grave saucer dome like that of the Pantheon in Rome.[53] Its model was clearly McKim's Low Library at Columbia University, and it was with that brand of Americanized classicism that the Windrim office worked most comfortably.

This second design was also quickly superseded when the parkway was realigned on June 8, 1909, following the recommendations of the Fairmount Park Art Association. The institute's site having been eliminated by this action, it planned a retreat westward to a large rectangular parcel at the southwest corner of the parkway and Sixteenth Street. For this site Windrim produced a variation of his previous design, now, however, cloaking his Roman forms in more of the ornamental filigree that passed among the unsophisticated as the mark of the Ecole des Beaux-Arts (fig. 85). While such "cartouche architecture" was not much respected by the Ecole men themselves, especially those who, like Paul Cret, had been trained under the soberer influence of Pascal and Guadet, its presence here may reflect the admiration with which Windrim had watched the work of the newly arrived Frenchman. The next year, as chairman of the building committee of the Valley Forge Park Commission, Windrim saw to it that Cret received the commission for the Washington Memorial Arch (1910–12).[54] And while Cret was in the French army he sent him a gift of 5,000 francs and the warm promise that "one-half of all I have is yours for the asking. . . ."[55]

Windrim's 1909 design was shown on the model built for the City Planning Conference of 1911, but the institute never acquired the expensive site (see fig. 18). Instead, two years later it purchased several rowhouses at the southeast corner of Nineteenth and Race streets, including substantial frontage on the south side of Logan Circle between the Academy of Natural Sciences and Wills Eye Hospital, and it sold off its now unusable property east of Sixteenth Street.[56] Windrim produced two rather restrained designs for this new site; the first, with an attached portico facing the circle, must have been created shortly after the Sixteenth Street location was abandoned. The second, dated January 9, 1922, shows a group of three plain buildings reaching down Nineteenth Street from the circle.[57] In both, the laboratory and museum functions of the institute were given increased space, but the building campaign never went further than these preliminary designs.

The turning point came in 1926. That fall Morton Gibbons-Neff, president of the Poor Richard Club, began a campaign to build a national Benjamin Franklin Memorial on the parkway. Cyrus Curtis agreed to chair a corporation created to promote this project, and he contributed $2 million to its treasury.[58] Throughout 1927, the new organization worked with Paul Cret on a design to stand next to the Free Library, but negotiations with the Franklin Institute soon began as well.[59] On June 21, 1928, the Benjamin Franklin Memorial corporation and the Franklin Institute formally agreed to join forces, creating a building that would serve the interests of both, and seven days later Mayor Harry Mackey told City Council that a vast site, encompassing all of the block that lay west of Logan Circle, should be transferred from an intended courthouse to the newly allied organizations. On May 28, 1929, he signed legislation that accomplished this goal.[60]

With more than $5 million now in hand, the Windrim office went ahead with a design for the new site and the joint clients. The construction of the institute's Bartol Research Laboratory at Swarthmore College (c. 1927–29) meant that the building would be given over almost entirely to library, museum, and memorial purposes. For this program a preliminary plan was published in the newspapers in December 1929, showing a porticoed and saucer-domed main block facing Logan Circle.[61]

This proposal seems to have been prepared without the assistance of W. R. Morton Keast, who had joined Windrim's office shortly after the very first Franklin Institute designs had been made by 1910 and served for nearly twenty years as his chief designer. Keast had studied architecture under Cret at the University of Pennsylvania, and he had gone to work for his teacher after graduation to help with the design of the Bureau of the American Republics. In 1910 he won the Cope Memorial Prize of the T-Square Club for a "Treatment of a Public Square on the Parkway" in a competition judged by Cret, and at

about the same time he joined Windrim, then already deeply involved in real parkway commissions. But in 1927–30, just when the Franklin Institute project was at last gaining momentum, Keast was on leave from Windrim and working for Grant and Edward Simon on the Fidelity Trust Building (1927) at Broad and Walnut streets in Philadelphia.

When he returned to the office in 1930, Keast swiftly redirected the design. Rejecting the rather weak pastiche that had been created during his absence, he worked up a grave and grandiose substitute that seemed to be more appropriate to the dignity of the Franklin Memorial part of the program. By the time that ground was bro-

Fig. 85. John T. Windrim, *The Franklin Institute*. East elevation, October–December 1909. Photograph of lost drawing. Inscribed: *John T. Windrim Architect*. The Franklin Institute Science Museum, Philadelphia

· FRANKLIN · INSTITUTE ·

JOHN · T · WINDRIM · ARCHITECT ·

Fig. 86. John T. Windrim, *The Franklin Institute*. Perspective from east, c. June 1930. From The Franklin Institute, *A Living Memorial* (Philadelphia, [1930]). The Franklin Institute Science Museum, Philadelphia

ken on June 18, the new scheme had been published in fundraising material, lifting a brooding, shallow dome atop an octagonal central block at the center of the Logan Circle facade (fig. 86).[62] The centerpiece was unperforated save for a prodigious doorway. The memorial statue of Franklin was to stand beneath the dome, while rather utilitarian-looking wings for the functions of the institute stretched away on either side. In the fall, Keast simplified this design further by making the central block a simple rectangle, and it was in that form that it was presented to the Art Jury on December 2, 1930 (fig. 87).[63]

The proposal seems to have surprised the members of the jury. On December 18, 1930, at a committee meeting attended by Eli Kirk Price and Cret, the rather bald design was thoroughly reviewed. Although no admirer of Trumbauer's Free Library, Cret must have reckoned that good taste required that its neighbors adopt some measure of the same eighteenth-century decorum. He would also have noted that the building's north facade, facing the parkway, was almost devoid of interest. His friendship with Windrim and Keast probably prevented him from taking any action himself, and so Price was dispatched to the directors of the Franklin Institute and the Benjamin Franklin Memorial "with a view to conveying to them informally the Art Jury's opinion that the building as designed indicates an inadequate appreciation of the requirements of such a commanding site on the Parkway for a monumental building and to suggest that the building should be redesigned."[64] Windrim himself came to discuss the design with the committee on February 3, 1931, and it was recorded that he "took away with him . . . three pencil elevations on tracing paper, stating that he would be glad to submit a revised design in accordance with the suggestions made."[65] The sketches were apparently Cret's, and Windrim's mood must have been dispirited.

With such firm guidance, the work went quickly, and new drawings were prepared for the Art Jury between March 2 and April 6, 1932. These showed a suave but rather conventional Palladian building that was designed to raise great porticoes on each of its four facades, thereby doing service to the parkway as well as Logan Circle. It also paid respect to the eighteenth-century tenor set by the Free Library (fig. 88). The Franklin Memorial was to stand in a large room inside the east portico, while a huge exhibition gallery called Curtis Hall occupied the main north-south axis. The Art Jury approved this design on April 14, and construction began that fall.

Lacking sufficient funds to build the entire museum in the midst of the Depression, the allied clients erected only the most visible facades that faced north and east. Behind them, most of the building was just one gallery deep, forming a great L. Only the Franklin Memorial room and one of the four projected stairways lay inside its two arms; Curtis Hall and the other two facades were left for a later campaign. The museum opened on January 1, 1934, just six months before the death of John Windrim. The memorial, with its statue by James Earle Fraser, was dedicated in 1938 (fig. 89).

Fig. 87. John T. Windrim, *The Franklin Institute*. Model seen from southeast, October 1930. Photograph of lost model. The Franklin Institute Science Museum, Philadelphia

Fig 88. John T. Windrim, *The Franklin Institute*. Perspective from northeast, March 23, 1931. Photographic print of lost drawing. Inscribed: *JOHN T. WINDRIM ARCHITECT 3.23.31*. City Archives of Philadelphia, 140.3, 2285, o

Fig. 89. John T. Windrim, *The Franklin Institute*, 1928–34. Photograph of April 30, 1934. City Archives of Philadelphia, 116.01, 34532

Convention Hall

In its chase from site to site on the parkway, Windrim's Franklin Institute was like two other projects on which his office worked during this period: a convention hall and a building for the municipal courts. Like the Free Library and the American Philosophical Society, the convention hall was dogged by taxpayers' suits.

It was Mayor John Reyburn who first involved the Windrim office in the convention hall project. Perhaps recalling his work on the parkway when he was director of public works under Mayor Stuart, in 1909 Reyburn appointed the elder Windrim, James, to his Comprehensive Plans Committee. This committee identified the best site for a convention hall as a place called Snyder's Woods in Fairmount Park, located above the east bank of the Schuylkill at the crossing of the Reading and Pennsylvania railroad tracks, and it was to John Windrim that the city turned for a design. He presented his work to the Park Commission on October 14, 1910 (fig. 90), and, after visiting the site, the commissioners voted their approval on November 11.[66]

John Windrim's design, which was widely publicized during the first half of 1911 as part of the Compre-

hensive Plan report and as an exhibit at the City Planning Conference, was close in spirit to his 1909 scheme for the Franklin Institute. This was the type of work he did before Keast took over as his office chief. Assembled out of strong geometrical solids that possessed a Roman pedigree, the building was floridly ornamented in a manner that was probably imagined to be French. The hall was to be the largest in the world, with seats for 18,500, including 3,500 on stage, and it was only one unit in a complex that also included two stadiums.[67] In materials the building was to be modern in every respect: A steel skeleton was to support a carcass of terra-cotta and gray brick, while the dome was to be of bronze and glass. Instead of stairways, which might cause panic among the huge crowds during emergencies, the design showed only a great system of interior ramps.

Mayor Reyburn, in his last year in office, was eager to begin construction so that the great German *Sängerfest*, scheduled to meet in Philadelphia in the summer of 1912, might at least assemble within the framework of the hall. The public approved a $1.5 million loan, and with that the city signed a first contract for foundations with Charles McCaul and Company in October. But the estimated final cost was $4.43 million, and Logan M. Bullitt, leader of an ad hoc taxpayers' committee, threatened a lawsuit if the city began work without having sufficient funds in hand. Rudolph Blankenburg chose not to press the matter, and the city instead built a temporary wooden structure on North Broad Street for the *Sängerfest*. It also served other such meetings for more than a decade. John Windrim had to sue the city in 1914 to obtain payment for his unrealized design, and Paul Cret was one of the chosen arbitrators in the dispute.[68] His sympathetic judgment may have helped to prompt Windrim's generous gift a year later.

When Mayor Thomas Smith returned machine rule to City Hall in 1916, the convention hall project was quickly revived, and Windrim was asked to design a building for a new site on the parkway at Twenty-Second

Street, where the Rodin Museum was eventually erected. Morton Keast was then on loan to Cass Gilbert of New York, and so Windrim got help from John F. Harbeson, Cret's assistant and future partner.[69] A new solution was developed, and finished drawings were produced in September 1916 for consideration by the Art Jury (fig. 91).[70] The design was an extraordinary one. An enormous octagon with porticoes on three sides and a cavernous interior with a clear span of 235 feet, the hall was designed to accommodate the same vast crowds as the building at Snyder's Woods. The general treatment was more conventionally Roman than Harbeson, one of the Ecole's most passionate American polemicists, would have liked, but his hand can probably be seen in details like the crisp paneling covering the facades between the porticoes.

Although it was estimated that the auditorium would cost $2.25 million, only $1.52 million was placed in the loan question on the November ballot, and this situation once again attracted the ire of reformist citizens. Henry Raff brought a taxpayer's suit against the project, and on January 15, 1917, the state supreme court ruled in his favor.[71] Blocked from advertising for bids, Mayor Smith first suggested that he would ask for a larger loan at the next election, but in March he asked Windrim to see what could be built for the available sum. The architect dutifully sketched a rectangular building with a single portico that would hold six thousand, but the design had few admirers.[72]

In June, the state legislature amended the Philadelphia city charter to permit incremental appropriations for such projects, but by then Jacques Gréber had been hired to refine the plans for the parkway, and he went about converting the boulevard into a park. In his first plans he had showed an Episcopal cathedral on the suggested site, but even that seemed to impinge too strongly on the parklike setting, and thus he chose to replace it with the proposed Johnson Gallery and move the cathedral to a position south of the Fairmount Plaza (see figs. 22, 24, 26). Although Eli Kirk Price was among those elected to the ves-

Fig. 90. John T. Windrim,
*Municipal Auditorium, Stadium,
and Coliseum at Snyder's Woods,
Fairmount Park*. Bird's-eye per-
spective from southwest, 1910.
Photograph of lost drawing.
Inscribed: *John T. Windrim
Architect*. City Archives of
Philadelphia, 117.01, 9616

Fig. 91. John T. Windrim,
Convention Hall. Perspective
from south, September 1916.
Photograph of lost drawing.
Inscribed: *JOHN T. WINDRIM,
ARCHITECT*. City Archives of
Philadelphia, 117.01, 15593

Fig. 92. John T. Windrim,
Municipal Court. First-floor plan
for site on west side of Logan
Square (detail), May 1920.
Blueprint, 43½ x 34¾″ (110.5 x
88.3 cm). Inscribed: *May 1920
JOHN T. WINDRIM ARCHITECT*.
City Archives of Philadelphia,
140.3, 1216, B

try in charge of planning the cathedral in 1919, and
although Bishop Rhinelander held services on the site
throughout that summer, support for the building dwin-
dled and the project was shifted to Roxborough. Even
there, only a chapel of the intended cathedral was erected
before the work was abandoned.[73]

Municipal Court

In the meantime, discussion of the convention hall had
revived after the war, and it became enmeshed with Windrim's work on another major building on Logan Circle,
the Municipal Court. Although there had been talk at the
time of Reyburn's Comprehensive Plan of moving the
courtrooms out of City Hall and into a building of their
own, the movement to erect a courthouse only obtained a
clear rationale in 1913, when a new Municipal Court was
established to handle domestic disputes and cases involv-
ing children. Housed at first in a warren of interconnected
rowhouses west of Logan Circle, the new courts were

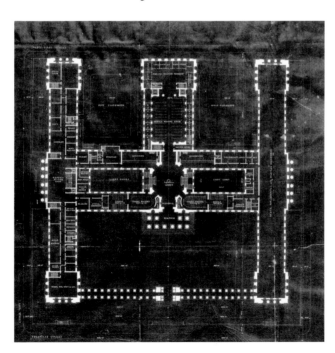

shown in Gréber's drawings of 1917–19 (fig. 26) as occupying a large, new building that filled that side of the circle completely. An ordinance passed in July 1919 officially
assigned this site to them, thus consolidating the properties that would ultimately be ceded to the Franklin Institute. At that date, however, the institute was still committed to a plot at Nineteenth and Race streets. John
Windrim was asked to produce a design for the courthouse, and in May 1920 his office made drawings for a
giant social service facility that would include a public
health hospital, a prison, and the headquarters for all the
agencies that dealt with children and families, as well as
the facilities needed by the courts themselves (fig. 92).[74]
The many-winged design faced Logan Circle with a
screen modeled on that with which the Admiralty faced
Whitehall in London. It may have been the memory of
this urbane solution that turned the Art Jury against Windrim's less adroit first submission for the Franklin Institute, when it was shifted to the same site.

While the design was being developed, Mayor J.
Hampton Moore was establishing himself firmly in power. As in the case of the art museum and the Johnson gallery, his scruples soon got in the way of this great building
project. He toured the intended site in April 1920 in the
company of Eli Kirk Price, and after some reflection he
announced publicly that the project would be too costly.[75]
The design work went ahead, however, and the Art Jury
committee granted preliminary approval on June 24. But
on July 21 the full jury accepted the mayor's request to
postpone any further consideration of the building. The
project had come to be called the "Palace of Justice," and
there was substantial support for Moore's decisiveness in
cutting it down to size.[76] His supporters might have been
fewer if they had known that it would be twenty-one
years before the new courts would be ready.

After this setback, the project went undiscussed
through the rest of Moore's term, but in the usual pattern,
when the machine placed W. Freeland Kendrick in office
in 1924, prospects for the courthouse again brightened. It

Fig. 93. Paul P. Cret, *Victory Hall*. Perspective from southwest, 1925. Photographic print of lost drawing, 8 x 20" (20.3 x 50.8 cm). Inscribed: *PAUL P. CRET, ARCHITECT.* University of Pennsylvania, Architectural Archives, Philadelphia. Gift of John F. Harbeson, 185.3

was at this point that the courts and the convention hall became entangled, for in 1926 the city architect, John Molitor, produced a scheme that lamely crammed both a giant civic arena and a modest building for the courts on the west side of Logan Circle. When this design was published, Cret exploded in protest, writing to the president of the Art Jury and calling it "by far the worst scheme suggested so far for [the convention hall] . . . or the Municipal Courts."[77] But Molitor wrote back to say that the project was already under critical review, and little more was done. It was this inaction that prompted Mayor Harry Mackey to transfer the intended site to the Franklin Institute in 1928.

With that decision, the convention hall and the courts were banished to other locations. The former was finally built on an eminently impractical site on Thirty-Fourth Street in West Philadelphia, for which Philip H. Johnson, the machine-connected architect of the Department of Public Health, produced the design in 1929. The Municipal Court fared better, although it waited longer. In 1930 Mayor Mackey and the judges agreed to place the building on the north side of Logan Circle, where it would twin the Free Library. Only a much smaller courthouse

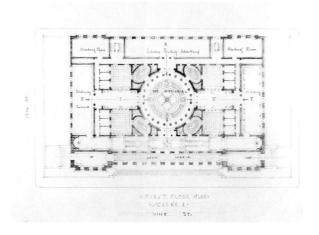

Fig. 94. Paul P. Cret, *Franklin Memorial*. First-floor plan ("Scheme A"), 1927. Graphite and colored pencil on tracing paper, 14 x 19¾" (35.6 x 50 cm) The partners of H2L2 Architects/Planners, Philadelphia

was possible on this site, but it enjoyed a commanding and convenient location, and it finally offered to complete the eastern half of Trumbauer's replica of the Place de la Concorde.

Dealing with the eastern building had been a long-vexed problem. In 1911 the Comprehensive Plan had shown a matched pair of structures on the north side of the circle, and when the design of the Free Library became

known, the facade of its neighbor was automatically fixed. Gréber indicated a commercial museum on that site in 1919, and for a while it was considered for the convention hall, after the Rodin Museum site had been given away. Following several years of public discussion, the Art Jury approved the location for that purpose on April 7, 1924,[78] with the expectation that the hall would be built as a war memorial, using money that had been collected in 1918 for Gréber's unrealized victory arch on South Broad Street. Several designs for such a "Victory Hall" were prepared in 1925, including one for a 12,000-seat arena by Paul Cret himself. In it, he necessarily submitted to the historicist formula that Trumbauer had set (fig. 93).[79] Cret was also the architect chosen by the Benjamin Franklin Memorial corporation in 1927, when they considered building a structure on their own. For them he produced a number of alternate studies that would fit behind his 1925 facade. Perhaps the most elegant of these placed a memorial rotunda at the center of the building, but he also designed several variants that combined the memorial function with a 3,500-seat concert hall (fig. 94). Cret's office produced a study that compared one of these with the Academy of Music at Broad and Locust streets, and it was perhaps this work that showed that a far more practical arrangement for the memorial would be an alliance with the Franklin Institute.[80]

It was to the site on Logan Circle next to the library that the Municipal Court came in 1930, with Windrim restored as its architect. Keast was responsible for the design, for which the drawings were completed in April 1931, and the Art Jury gave its approval on May 11 (fig. 95).[81] His exterior was even more archaeologically correct than Trumbauer's library had been, for, among other things, the floor levels of the courthouse matched those of the Paris example, enabling him to copy its pattern (fig. 96). But Cret could hardly complain now, having done the same thing himself in 1925 and 1927.

Approval of the design, however, did not guarantee anything during those days of Depression, and when

Fig. 95. John T. Windrim succeeded by W. R. Morton Keast, *Municipal Court*. Perspective of southwest corner, 1932. Photograph of lost drawing. Inscribed: *John T. Windrim, Architect 1932*. The Athenaeum of Philadelphia. Gift of Mrs. Grace G. Keast

Fig. 96. Logan Circle, with the Municipal Court under construction; October 21, 1939. Free Library of Philadelphia, Print and Picture Department, Dallin, vol. 22, no. 12650

J. Hampton Moore was elected to serve again after Mackey in 1932, the city was once more locked into a regime of utmost financial rigor. An honorable Republican, Moore steered the city on a course entirely opposite to that of Franklin Roosevelt's New Deal, cutting government expenditures just when public services were most desperately needed. It was not until September 17, 1938, that federal assistance finally permitted ground to be broken, and by the time the building was formally dedicated on January 22, 1941, Europe again found itself at war (see fig. 2).

The greatest glory of the Municipal Court (now called the Family Court) is the large program of decorative arts that was produced under the Public Works Administration (PWA), which included stained glass by the D'Ascenzo Studios of Philadelphia and paintings by nine artists (fig. 97). The latter, although installed in positions suitable for fresco, were painted on canvas in order to complete the building as rapidly as possible.[82] Everywhere the themes of family, childhood, and home were illustrated with a dignity that aspired to grandeur.

Pennsylvania Academy of the Fine Arts

After John Windrim's death in the dark days of the middle 1930s when nothing was being built, Morton Keast designed two more buildings for the parkway. Although both were for the Pennsylvania Academy of the Fine Arts, whose move to the new boulevard had been discussed for twenty-five years, neither was built. But then Keast had not been asked to design them, either.

Mayor Reyburn had done his best in 1911 to get the Academy to agree to transplant itself to Fairmount Plaza, but his lengthy discussions with its president, John F. Lewis, never produced an agreement.[83] Although in July 1916 the Academy formally asked the Fairmount Park Commission to assign it the northerly building site on the plaza, at the same time Lewis wrote to a friend to say that the rumor that they had "evolved a plan for a new building" was untrue.[84]

Fig. 97. John T. Windrim succeeded by W. R. Morton Keast, *Municipal Court*. Cartoon for stained-glass window *Justice Is the Queen of the Virtues* by D'Ascenzo Studios, c. 1939. Graphite and watercolor on paper, 24½ x 11½" (62.2 x 29.2 cm) (sight). The Athenaeum of Philadelphia. Gift of Mrs. Betty Bramnick

Fig. 98. W. R. Morton Keast, *Pennsylvania Academy of the Fine Arts*. Second-floor plan, February 14, 1935. Photograph of lost drawing. Inscribed: *Morton Keast, Architect. February 14, 1935*. Pennsylvania Academy of the Fine Arts, Archives, Philadelphia

Fig. 99. W. R. Morton Keast, *Pennsylvania Academy of the Fine Arts*. Southwest elevation, February 14, 1935. Photograph of lost drawing. Inscribed: *February 14, 1935. Morton Keast, Architect*. Pennsylvania Academy of the Fine Arts, Archives, Philadelphia

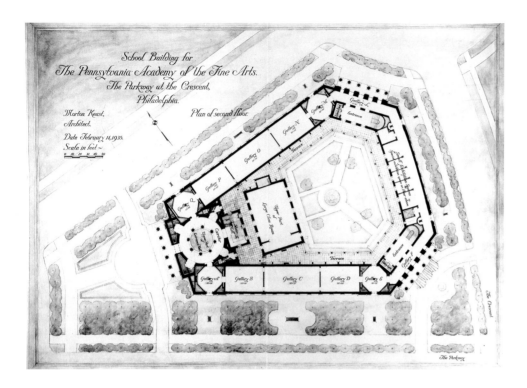

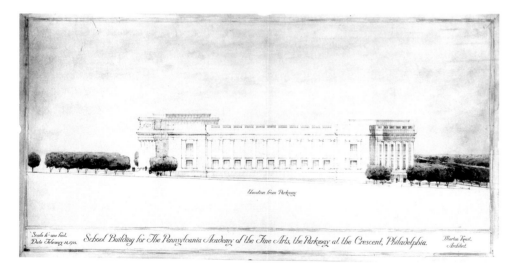

Then Eli Kirk Price was elected to the board of directors of the Academy on November 6, 1916, and he seems to have insisted on some action. In the following spring the directors agreed to hire a professional fundraiser to establish a "Building Endowment Fund."[85] Contributions trickled in for a while, but again in 1920 Price had to argue to Lewis that it was not "too soon to take up the matter of plans for the new building."[86] The Academy remained unconvinced of the advantages of moving to the parkway, however, and it is notable that the institution with which it was to be paired at Fairmount, the Pennsylvania Museum's school, also chose to remain where it was, at Broad and Pine streets. Despite the best efforts of its director, Leslie W. Miller, the fundraising campaign begun in 1920 never caught fire.[87]

So it must have been without much realistic hope of success that Keast addressed Academy president Alfred Steel on March 25, 1935, with the suggestion that Steel apply to the Federal Emergency Administration of Public Works for funds with which to erect Keast's design for a new building on the parkway (figs. 98–99).[88] Keast submitted small-scale drawings that showed a quiet, classical structure whose irregular hexagonal plan filled the triangular site. Despite the unusual plan, with its large interior courtyard, the internal organization was borrowed from the Academy building that Frank Furness had designed on Broad and Cherry streets, with ground-floor studios and second-floor exhibition galleries.

In addition to its new home, Keast later proposed that the Academy establish a "Fairmount Community Center" and seek additional federal support for the construction of a low-cost, 564-unit apartment building north of the new Academy on Pennsylvania Avenue between Twenty-Fourth and Twenty-Fifth streets (fig. 100). With three symmetrical towers detailed in a restrained form of modernism, the community center bears comparison with Cret's contemporary work at 2601 Parkway (see figs. 78–79). Despite the thoroughness of the Keast proposals, there is no record that the Academy seriously considered them. They were never formally discussed by the directors, and, indeed, their receipt seems to have gone unacknowledged.

Charles Z. Klauder: Philadelphia Council, Boy Scouts of America

Although Horace Trumbauer, Paul Cret, and John Windrim succeeded in obtaining the majority of parkway commissions, five important architects were responsible for five individual designs that merit discussion. Their work represents the range of talent that Philadelphia could tap in the twenties and thirties, ranging across the various schools of architectural thinking from historicism to modernism. Charles Z. Klauder (1872–1938) was a distinguished member of this group.

Klauder had been schooled in the traditional way, serving as an apprentice in the office of T. P. Chandler while taking classes at the school of the Pennsylvania Museum. In the 1890s he worked for most of the prominent architects of the city, including the Wilson Brothers, Cope and Stewardson, Frank Miles Day, and Horace Trumbauer, returning to Day's office in 1900 as chief draftsman. When Day died in 1918, Klauder continued the practice, eventually changing the name of the firm to his own. His reputation was established by Gothic buildings for college campuses, which he illustrated in pen and pencil sketches that reflected all of the strengths of the Anglo-American design tradition. It was such talent that he brought to the commission for the Philadelphia Council of the Boy Scouts of America.

Dr. Charles Hart, president of the Philadelphia Council, had begun to raise money for a building in 1920, and for this purpose he acquired a site at Twenty-Second and Winter streets that aligned with the north facade of the new building (whether it be a courthouse or the Franklin Institute) that was to be built on the west side of Logan Circle. The location offered an unobstructed view northward into Gréber's wedge of park. By 1928 Hart was able to ask Klauder for a design, and the drawings of

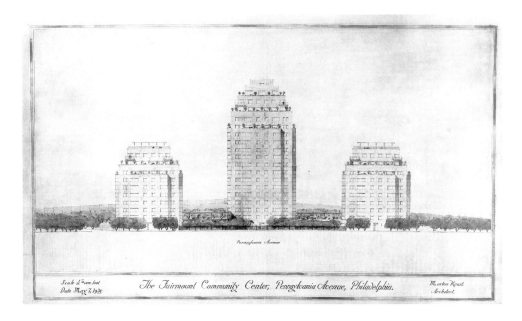

January 1929 show a compact building of Italian Renaissance pedigree, echoing the general mass and garden setting of the Rodin Museum that it faced across the parkway (fig. 101). Klauder's design was far more convincingly historicist, however, delighting in the rich textures of Florentine architecture of the sixteenth century. His pencil brought these to life with the same verve that he employed in his Gothic renderings.

Approved by the Art Jury on January 23, 1929, work on the little building proceeded rapidly.[89] Ground was broken that fall, and the building opened on October 23, 1930, after an expenditure of about $175,000. It was full of charming details.[90] At the center of the plan lay a miniature courtyard in the Italian fashion, but roofed in glass to serve as a reception hall. Beyond it lay a great lounge room, whose ceiling was wrought from aged cypress. The Renaissance exterior was marked to serve its modern American function by working Boy Scout badges into the ornamental program, and R. Tait McKenzie's 1914 statue of a heroic scout was erected in front of the

Fig. 100. W. R. Morton Keast, *Fairmount Community Center.* Southwest elevation, May 7, 1935. Hand-colored photograph of lost drawing. Inscribed: *May 7, 1935 Morton Keast, Architect.* Pennsylvania Academy of the Fine Arts, Archives, Philadelphia

Fig. 101. Charles Z. Klauder (1872–1938), *Philadelphia Council, Boy Scouts of America*. Perspective from northeast, January 1929. Photographic print of lost drawing, with graphite additions; 8¼ x 13⅞″ (21 x 35.2 cm). Inscribed: *C Z Klauder*. City Archives of Philadelphia, 140.3, 2137, B

building. Beside the front gate, the architect provided a ground-level water basin to refresh a boy's best friend.

Stewardson and Page: Insurance Company of North America

A different kind of historicism was practiced by the firm of Stewardson and Page in their contribution to the parkway, the building at the southwest corner of its intersection with Sixteenth Street. Their client was the Insurance Company of North America.

The partnership of Emlyn L. Stewardson (1863–1936) and George B. Page (1870–1948) had been created in 1912 to succeed the firm of Walter Cope and John Stewardson, which had continued until then under that name although both of the principals had died. John Stewardson's younger brother, who had taken charge of the business side of the office in the past, was now given public credit for his work, and Page left independent practice to oversee design. Like Klauder, Page had been

trained in the old apprenticeship system, but he had also spent eight months in a Paris atelier after winning a traveling scholarship in 1894.

The architects' commission came from the oldest shareholder-owned insurance company in the nation, founded in Philadelphia in 1792 and since 1916 led by the energetic Benjamin Rush, whose vision of the company had an architectural dimension. As soon as the First World War had ended in 1918, Rush created a building committee and began to plan a new office tower. Although the firm at that time had fewer than five hundred employees, he foresaw doubling or trebling that number within the next decades, and so his plans were large. Influenced by his friendship with Eli Kirk Price and also judging that proximity to Broad Street Station and the Market Street subway would be a boon to his workers, Rush began his search for a site at the City Hall end of the parkway.[91]

By early 1921, Rush's eyes had focused on the plot at the southwest corner of the parkway and Sixteenth Street that the Franklin Institute had briefly considered after its first parkway site had been eliminated by the realignment of 1909. Substantial difficulties lay in the way of moving his venerable company to this location, however, not the least of which was the resistance of his own directors, who respected the tradition that kept Philadelphia's financial institutions east of Broad and south of Market. But Rush was insistent, and he prepared a compelling docket of information for the board of directors and the Building Committee in which he argued that the new location would both be convenient and possess "value as an advertisement"—a matter of some note for a firm that had just begun its first national advertising campaign, and he went on to paint a picture of the new building that was designed to mollify the conservatives. He wrote: "While the building should be thoroughly modern, and up-to-date, the architect should be advised to try and preserve a colonial atmosphere, so as to take advantage of the past history of the Company, which your Officers have found to be of considerable value in the securing of business."[92] The board of directors yielded to this pressure, with the majority voting to accept Rush's site proposal on February 9, 1922. But two members resigned in protest rather than commit the company to the untested parkway.[93]

As soon as this decision was known, Rush began to receive inquiries from interested architects, but he proceeded deliberately. At the meeting of the building committee on June 22 it was decided to limit the selection of architects to Philadelphians, for reasons of convenience, and to team the architect with an efficiency expert.[94] The latter was a notion dear to Rush's heart, for he was a firm believer in the industrial management techniques fostered by Frederick Taylor. It was also his judgment that governed the choice of the architect, narrowing the field to just two: Edgar V. Seeler, whose office building for the rival Penn Mutual Insurance Company (1916) at Sixth and Walnut streets he admired, and Stewardson and Page, because George Page was a friend and because Rush was familiar with their substantial institutional work. Following the committee meeting, he wrote to both firms, enclosing the minutes of the discussion and asking if they were willing to collaborate with an efficiency engineer. Stewardson and Page replied immediately that there was nothing "unacceptable" in such an arrangement, but Seeler took longer to answer and was more critical. "Much depends on harmonious action between the architect and his engineers," he wrote, "and you will probably find that in this particular class of work an architect can render his best service with the instruments which he has already adapted to his own methods."[95] On August 8, 1922, Rush wrote to Stewardson and Page offering them the commission.[96] Stone and Webster, Inc., of New York were hired to work with them as efficiency and construction engineers.

At the time of these appointments, the company was still engaged in a protracted negotiation with William Steele and Sons, a building contractor who owned the Sixteenth Street end of the intended site. It was only in

Fig. 102. Stewardson and Page, *Insurance Company of North America.* Perspective from northeast, early 1923. From *Building for the Insurance Company of North America, Philadelphia. Stewardson and Page Architects* (Philadelphia, [c. 1923]). CIGNA Archives, Philadelphia, 13/8

Fig. 103. Stewardson and Page, *Insurance Company of North America,* 1922–25. Photograph of 1929. CIGNA Archives, Philadelphia, 1581

September that the architects were told to proceed, but on December 15 they could already submit a preliminary design and report.[97] The building was shown very nearly as it was built, a shaft of red brick rising from two stories of granite and ending in four stories of Indiana limestone (fig. 102). In detailing, Page had adopted the specified eighteenth-century vocabulary, entering into it with the same spirit that he showed in the firm's historicist work for universities. As the architects explained,

In adapting the Colonial style of Architecture to this type of building (a problem with which the Architects of that period were never confronted) it has been attempted to design the Building as it might have been designed in those days, had the opportunity been presented. The detail is all of the Georgian period and particularly of that phase of it as practiced by the Adam Brothers.

Gracefulness of proportion without over elaboration, in harmony with the purpose and dignity of your Company, and at the same time, with enough elaboration to justify its prominent position as the "Gateway to the Parkway" has been the thought that has suggested the design herewith presented.[98]

This was enough to satisfy the building committee, which approved the design on January 8, 1923. But some of the company's real estate advisers were aghast that the architects had not crammed all of the possible rentable office space into the building by adopting a U plan with a long, narrow light well. This proposal had to be discussed in detail, but Rush had his way and the more handsome (and less efficient) dumbbell plan was retained.

Artistic criticism could also be heard, notably that of John F. Lewis, a director of the company and president of the Pennsylvania Academy of the Fine Arts. He complained to Rush that the plan was "exceedingly ugly," concentrating his attack on the details of the main entrance: "The capitols [*sic*] for the front portico seem to me unsuitable, and will be lodgement for dirt and pigeons, and the mortuary urns might be allowable for a Life Insurance Company, but I think they are ugly upon any kind of an office building." The president was able to reassure Lewis that the urns, at least, had already been replaced by eagles mounted on globes.[99]

Most reviewed the building much more favorably. It was given preliminary clearance by the Art Jury in May, and they granted final approval after the full specifications were submitted on October 24, 1923.[100] Construction began immediately, and on November 15, 1925, the Insurance Company of North America moved into its new headquarters. Their expenditure had been $7.75 million. Next year the design won Stewardson and Page the annual medal of the Philadelphia Chapter of the American Institute of Architects (fig. 103).

The interior of the building was unusually lavish for an office structure. Upon entering from Sixteenth Street, a visitor traversed an entrance hall clad in Kasota stone in which public displays of historical materials were often maintained. Beyond that lay the wondrous room in which the company transacted business with its local clients.[101] In form very like a banking hall, with Kasota stone walls and polished verde antique counters, its breadth of sixty-nine feet required a system of huge trusses to carry the fifteen floors that rose above it. When they came to portray this space, the architects found themselves torn between their client's dual desires for a modern building and one that reflected the history of the company, and so they ordered two renderings. In one, the historical detail was lovingly depicted with a rather old-fashioned Queen Anne drawing technique (fig. 104). The other emphasized the verticality of the room and used highlighting and shadow to suppress detail and produce an almost "moderne" effect (fig. 105). Such nuanced interpretations meant a good deal in a time of architectural transition.

Zantzinger, Borie, and Medary: Fidelity Mutual Life Insurance Company

The directors of the other great insurance company to build on the parkway embraced the modern more whole-heartedly than did the Insurance Company of North America, although that may not have been the original intention of the Fidelity Mutual Life Insurance Company in 1925 when it hired Zantzinger, Borie, and Medary, Horace Trumbauer's collaborators in the design of the Greek temple on Fairmount. Since the site was an awkward trapezoid in the 2500 block of Pennsylvania Avenue, lying just below the art museum, it might have been assumed that the new insurance building would be in a cognate style. But in the adopted design, almost all of the historicist trappings were dropped away. It seemed that the firm was anxious to show what it could accomplish without Trumbauer's interference.

The Fidelity Mutual commission was assigned to Milton Medary, as Paul Cret recalled.[102] The preliminary design, dated March 31, 1925, was for a C-shaped build-

Fig. 104. Stewardson and Page, *Insurance Company of North America*. Perspective of central hall, November 1923. William E. White (dates unknown), delineator. Graphite on paper, 14⅞ x 22¹⁄₁₆″ (37.8 x 56 cm). Inscribed: *W.E.W. del Nov 1923*. CIGNA Archives, Philadelphia, 20/1.24

Fig. 105. Stewardson and Page, *Insurance Company of North America*. Perspective of central hall, 1923. Graphite on paper, 25⅜ x 20¾″ (64.4 x 52.7 cm). CIGNA Archives, Philadelphia, 20/1.39

Fig. 106. Zantzinger, Borie, and Medary, *Fidelity Mutual Life Insurance Company*. Southwest elevation, March 31, 1925. Watercolor and graphite on paper, mounted on card; 12¾ x 20½″ (32.4 x 52.1 cm). Inscribed: *ZANTZINGER BORIE & MEDARY ARCHITECTS MARCH 31 1925*. The Athenaeum of Philadelphia. Gift of Dr. Vaughan P. Simmons

ing that opened its arms wide toward the street (fig. 106). By necessity, the open space in the center of the **C** was filled by a two-story structure, and a central tower rose above the composition. The detail was classical but of the plainest kind, and the building looked rather weak and ineffective. It was apparently this design that was submitted to the Art Jury on November 16, 1925, and it provoked a long discussion, after which Cret was dispatched to talk to the architect. At this point Medary suggested expanding the design by vaulting over little Olive Street, which bordered the site on the north. This idea seems to have been approved by Cret, who always liked to see a building respond to special needs, and so the entire design was remade, taking the motif generated by the great arch over Olive Street on the west and repeating it as the main entrance on the east (fig. 107). Around the two large pavilions that were thus created, Medary composed three

wings that reversed the **C**-plan of his first design, turning its mouth away from the street. A sketch showing this revision was approved by the Art Jury committee on November 28, and complete drawings were passed by the committee on March 3, 1926.[103]

The peculiar building that was created in this process had been shaken by necessity out of the grip of history. But in devising its ornamental system, Medary could draw many lessons from Borie's experiments with Greek decoration at the art museum. He had only to adopt the principles without retaining the precise forms, and he even hired Leon Solon, Borie's polychromy adviser, as a consultant. The decorative scheme was huge for a relatively small, three-story design, celebrating the richness that had begun to seduce the architects atop Fairmount. Solon exaggerated only a little when he claimed that "structural interest has been deliberately subordinated in the desire to create decorative opportunity."[104] Neither talent nor money was in short supply when construction began, and the architects were able to commission Lee Lawrie, the most eminent architectural sculptor of the twenties, to realize the allegorical program. He carved stony personifications of Amicitia, Prudentia, Fidelitas, and Frugalitas to flank the big arches, and his smaller figures filled the bronze door screens and populated the acroteria with allegories of admirable behavior (fig. 108). Inside, the detailing was of a species of simplified Tudor, its medieval associations providing an appropriate context for the lavish display of handicraft.

The building was ready by the end of 1927, and Fiske Kimball looked upon it as a sign of Zantzinger, Borie, and Medary's growing powers. While the art museum managed to show "that the purest classic may still have vitality," the Fidelity Mutual Building went further. There,

without the slightest effect of the bizarre which would betray an exotic element, the simple forms have freed themselves from the chilling hand of precedent. The irregular site has been handled brilliantly to produce an unusual balanced composition. The two immense arched portals contrast with long ranges of simple piers. Rich sculpture and color and gilding enhance the effect.[105]

Irwin T. Catharine: School Administration Building

Modernity was also the objective of Irwin T. Catharine (1884–1944), who called his design for the School Administration Building a "modern classic."[106] A graduate of the architecture program at the Drexel Institute, Catharine had joined the architectural staff of the School Board at the beginning of his career, and when his father, Joseph W. Catharine, became vice-president of the board his fortune climbed. By 1920 he was the chief designer of the department, and between 1931 and his retirement in 1937 he served as superintendent of buildings.

Catharine established his architectural signature with a series of large neo-Tudor schools, the most striking

Fig. 107. Zantzinger, Borie, and Medary, *Fidelity Mutual Life Insurance Company*. Perspective from southwest, 1926. Birch Burdette Long (1878–1927), delineator. Lithograph on paper, mounted on card; 23½ x 40″ (59.7 x 101.6 cm). Inscribed: BBL (monogram). The Athenaeum of Philadelphia. Gift of Dr. Vaughan P. Simmons

Fig. 108. Zantzinger, Borie, and Medary, *Fidelity Mutual Life Insurance Company*, 1925–27. From *Architectural Record*, vol. 63, no. 1 (January 1928)

Fig. 109. Irwin T. Catharine (1884–1944), *School Administration Building*. Sketch perspective from northeast, June 1928. Photographic print of lost crayon drawing, 24½ x 18″ (62.2 x 45.7 cm). City Archives of Philadelphia, 140.3, 2111, B

Fig. 110. Irwin T. Catharine, *School Administration Building*. Perspective from northeast; 1928, with later changes of detail. Chester B. Price (1884/85–1962), delineator. Crayon on paper, 32 x 43″ (81.3 x 109.2 cm). Inscribed: *Chester B. Price 1928*. The School District of Philadelphia

of which may be Overbrook High School (1924), but by the late twenties he was regularly experimenting with modernism. The opportunity to build a great office building for the school system challenged him to explore further in this direction, and in June 1928 he sketched a soaring tower nineteen stories tall with a 99-foot pyramid modeled on the Mausoleum at Halicarnassus on top. This was to be built between the sites of the Franklin Institute and the Boy Scouts Building (fig. 109). Boldly expressionist in feeling, the design was a flight of imagination, and when he submitted it to the Art Jury on October 8, Catharine must have known that it could not be built without obtaining a waiver of the 160-foot height restriction for that part of the parkway. His awareness of this is evident in the fact that when he and his father arrived for the jury's committee meeting on October 10, 1928, he brought along a new drawing with a shorter tower.[107]

The two designs were examined at length, but Cret was absent and the committee postponed any decision. When they assembled again two weeks later, Cret helped them to see that neither design would meet the zoning regulations. Joseph Catharine promised that they would comply, and his son bent himself to the task and drew the elevation of a yet shorter design on October 30.[108] This was approved with the stipulation that full working drawings would have to be submitted for review, and before the end of the year Catharine ordered a perspective of the building from Chester B. Price (1884/85–1962), a professional renderer based in New York (fig. 110). It showed a building in which a three-story podium of conventional Renaissance detail wrapped itself around a courtyard. Above it rose a nine-story tower whose attenuated detail was almost Gothic in its verticality and modern in spirit. Rather awkwardly stitched together, the design reflected the mild artistic schizophrenia with which Catharine took up the project, seeking at the same time to preserve some of the vitality of his June design while acceding to the wishes of the Art Jury. Cret, whose support for zoning was very strong, did not cheer him on

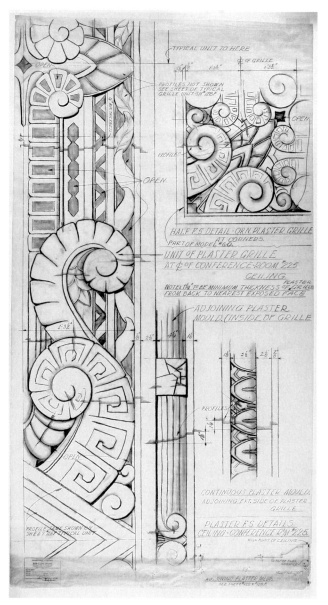

Fig. 111. Irwin T. Catharine, *School Administration Building.* Study of lower corner, February 1930. Graphite on tracing paper, 12 x 13″ (30.5 x 33 cm). City Archives of Philadelphia, 140.3, 2111

Fig. 112. Irwin T. Catharine, *School Administration Building,* 1928–32. Photograph of August 14, 1931. City Archives of Philadelphia, 116.01, 31621

Fig. 113. Irwin T. Catharine, *School Administration Building.* Full-scale details of auditorium ceiling plasterwork, May 13, 1931. T. L. Sime (dates unknown), delineator. Crayon and colored crayon on tracing paper, 77½ x 42″ (196.8 x 106.7 cm). Inscribed: *T. Sime Irwin T. Catharine 5/13/31.* The School District of Philadelphia

Fig. 114. Irwin T. Catharine, *School Administration Building*. Stained-glass panel of Fairmount (never installed as intended in the second-floor exhibition room) by Columbia Art Glass Company, after a design by Herman Schuh (in Catharine's office), c. 1931. 90 x 46¾″ (228.6 x 118.7 cm). The School District of Philadelphia

in this difficult work as he had done for Medary in his Fidelity Mutual design three years earlier.

The design languished for more than a year, and it was not until February 5, 1930, that Catharine submitted sixteen blueprints for final review. After discussing them carefully on February 11, the Art Jury committee dispatched Cret and Walter Thomas, the Ecole-trained city architect, to ask Catharine to revise certain features. The three architects met on February 14, and Catharine and Cret conferred again a few days later, producing agreement on all of the questions. Catharine sent in two sketches to show the most important of the changes, removing the pyramidal pinnacle and subduing the Art Deco character of the upper floor of the podium, and with these accepted he had another set of blueprints prepared (fig. 111). Final approval was granted on February 28, 1930, and work began later that year. On January 16, 1931, the ceremonial cornerstone was laid, and the building was formally opened on February 20, 1932 (fig. 112).

The difficult gestation period of the design left its imprint on some of the awkwardly disjunctive components of the twelve-story building, but a budget of $4 million, including $1 million for custom furniture, was able to disguise a good deal of this. On the outside, Jules Meliodon oversaw an extensive sculptural program that placed tympana over the principal courtyard entrances and encircled the top of the tower with portraits of major historical figures. Inside, Catharine's robust imagination enabled him to create a variety of environments. The main lobby was a serene "moderne" refuge of gray and black polished marble. As the architect explained, "It will be a striking contrast of quiet peace in there after the visitor passes in from the bright outside sunshine and the swift-shuttling automobiles of the Parkway."[109] The School Board Room, on the ground floor east of the courtyard, and the other administrative offices and meeting rooms on that floor were decorated in the Adam style, with delicate plaster ceilings and paneled walls. On the third floor was an auditorium for 350 whose plasterwork was molded in the paisley and abstracted floral motifs of Art Deco (fig. 113). (This was executed by Giuseppe Donato, the sculptor on the Art Jury.) Half of the tenth floor was given over to a Spanish-style cafeteria, with brightly tiled floor and dado and simple, heavy oak furniture. Diners could carry their food out to a terrace that surrounded the room. In the topmost two floors, where the tower narrowed to less than a third of its size at the base, Catharine installed the architecture department. His own office enjoyed a view up the parkway toward the art museum, like that created in the stained-glass windows of the exhibition room, and above his library fireplace was mounted the 1928 perspective of the School Administration Building itself (fig. 114).

Voorhees, Gmelin, and Walker: Concert Hall

The only parkway project to be designed by a non-Philadelphian was the concert hall promoted by publisher Cyrus Curtis, his son-in-law Edward W. Bok, and his grandson W. Curtis Bok. In the late 1920s, Curtis and his son-in-law, both ardent supporters of the musical life of the city, began to plan a replacement of the aging Academy of Music, to be built on the parkway. Soon after they took up the cause, Curtis spent more than $2 million to acquire Wills Eye Hospital on the south side of Logan Circle, and in January 1930 he added to this the adjacent property that the Franklin Institute had held while it was planning to build at Nineteenth and Race streets. In the meantime, Edward Bok, the prime mover behind the Philadelphia Commission and its plan to demolish City Hall, contacted C. Howard Crane, a theater architect from Detroit. Crane produced a preliminary design, but before they could go further, Bok died, leaving his widow to fulfill the promise of $850,000 that he had made toward the project.[110]

In July 1930, six months after Edward Bok's death, his son W. Curtis Bok incorporated "The Philadelphia Arts Association," dedicated to raising the additional money needed to build the new concert hall.[111] Among the directors were his mother and grandfather and Eli Kirk Price. They met for the first time on October 13, 1930, and among their early business was the creation of a small Committee on Architects, chaired by Bok with Price and prominent lawyer Samuel R. Rosenbaum as its other members. After an exhaustive interview process during December that included more than a score of New York and Philadelphia architects, Bok wrote a most perceptive report on the state of contemporary architecture and the requirements of their building. At a time when it was possible to commission anything from a replica of a Greek temple "to the refrigerator-like dwellings of Neutra or LeCorbusier," he concluded that the only way to secure a design that would remain satisfactory for a century or more was to avoid "a building of any set type." With this in mind, the committee had questioned each of the interviewees, and in the end they selected Ralph T. Walker, "a vigorous downright personality . . . ."[112]

Walker (1889–1973), the design partner in the New York firm of Voorhees, Gmelin, and Walker, was a renowned designer of Art Deco skyscrapers. He was probably best known for the craggy Bell Telephone Building that he had built in 1923–26 at Barclay and Vesey streets in lower Manhattan. Awarded the commission for the Philadelphia concert hall on January 22, 1931, he quickly accepted with words that were designed to accord with Bok's inclinations:

I feel very strongly that architecture is not a mere playing with structure and machine. While use is of prime importance, that which has always made for beauty transcends all these factors, and when they are no longer vital the beauty remains. It is in that spirit, which I find expressed in your philosophy of the building, that I gladly accept the commission offered, feeling that both of us having an earnest desire will achieve a true result.[113]

Philadelphia architect William Pope Barney, who had also been interviewed for the job, congratulated Bok on his choice, saying that Walker was "one of the *real* men of the modern school," and most were pleased with the selec-

Fig. 115. Voorhees, Gmelin, and Walker, *Concert Hall for the Philadelphia Arts Association*. Perspective at night from northeast, 1932. Chester B. Price, delineator. Photograph of lost drawing. Inscribed: *Voorhees Gmelin & Walker 1932 Chester B. Price 1932*. The Athenaeum of Philadelphia. Gift of the Bok Tower Gardens

a study tour of European opera houses. He submitted a report on his trip and forged ahead that fall with working out the interior organization of the building. After revising the design to reduce its cost below a level that had triggered Bok's "groans of agony," a series of presentation perspectives were prepared to show the likely alternatives.[115] These were ready by mid-February 1932 (fig. 115).

As Irwin Catharine had done, for many of the needed renderings Walker turned to Chester Price, who later joined his office.[116] Price's drawings emphasized the simple masses of the design, in which a single, mighty fly tower rose between the two larger halls, and a set of interlocking semicircular forms walked the building around the corner from Logan Circle and onto the eastern portion of the parkway. Convincingly modern without resembling a machine, Walker's design would have given the new avenue a contemporary air while bringing needed nighttime activity to its very center. But when Curtis Bok wrote to approve the final drawings later that year, he was gloomy about the prospects of the concert hall. "Practically," he explained, "any future work on the project involves the raising of money and I am afraid it will be a long time before we can put on the necessary drive."[117] The deaths of Cyrus Curtis and Eli Kirk Price in 1933 halted all organizing efforts, and even Walker's commission went unpaid. The concert hall project, Bok wrote, "is absolutely dead and will be until times improve materially." To explain this extraordinary failing Bok could only ask for sympathy. He lamented, "Because of the recent passage of all dividends on Curtis Publishing stock, my family is rapidly heading toward the ranks of the unemployed."[118] In the end, only a possible sale of the site to the federal government held out any prospect of rescuing the project from bankruptcy, but that deal collapsed. Save for the construction of the Municipal Court, paid for out of the national treasury, the great era of the building of the parkway was over.

tion. But Leopold Stokowski, the conductor of the Philadelphia Orchestra, expressed surprise that Frank Lloyd Wright had not been considered, although he admitted that "I have heard splendid things of Ralph T. Walker."[114]

Applying himself to the work at hand, by late spring Walker had produced a series of alternative plans for a building that would include two major auditoriums (of 4,000 and 1,500 seats) and a recital hall for five hundred. He brought these to Philadelphia on June 5, 1931, and discussed them with the Committee on Architects, and, having narrowed the choices, he set off in August for

Epilogue

In 1937, in preparation for the dedication of the statue of Benjamin Franklin that was to stand beneath the dome of the Franklin Institute, City Council voted to name the parkway after Philadelphia's most celebrated adopted son. By that date, the Benjamin Franklin Parkway seemed to be complete, although the Municipal Court had not yet joined the Free Library on the north side of Logan Circle. Attention shifted to other parts of the city after World War II, and while there was some erosion of the character of the parkway, it prevailed, becoming a part of the collective image that Philadelphians have of their city (fig. 116).

In the postwar years, the creativity and daring that Philadelphians had devoted to city planning were reassigned to the transformation of most of the central district of their city and its connection by means of new expressways to the growing suburbs. The City Planning Commission, under the forceful leadership of its executive director Edmund Bacon, was responsible for these vast plans, and because of its scale and the location, the new work had important repercussions for the parkway, although the parkway was not the center of attention. For instance, when the Schuylkill Expressway was joined to Vine Street in Center City by means of a sunken roadway, planned in 1947, it opened gigantic holes in the landscape of Logan Circle. These seemed to cut the ground from under the feet of the School Administration Building, the Boy Scouts Building, the Free Library, and the Municipal Court. West of City Hall, the demolition of Broad Street Station and the building of Penn Center in the 1950s reconfigured the parkway's southeast terminus. A fountain and a new tourist information office were erected, blocking the parkway in its last stretch before City Hall, between Fifteenth and Sixteenth streets, and the new Municipal Services Building (Vincent G. Kling and Associates, 1962–65) was built east of there on the great urban forum called Reyburn Plaza, north of City Hall. Thus did the city sacrifice the unimpeded parkway vista and the generously proportioned public square that had cost so much effort and money fifty years before.

Fig. 116. The Benjamin Franklin Parkway, 1989

The lining of the parkway with buildings proceeded slowly, especially northwest of Logan Circle, where Gréber's vision of a wedge of green parkland was preserved. The first major postwar construction was the Youth Study Center (1949–52), a prison for juveniles, erected on the north side of the 2000 block. Designed by Carroll, Grisdale, and Van Alen in a style that did not reject modernism in the search for dignity, the center was the first building with direct parkway frontage to forgo the trappings of the classical orders.

Other construction on this part of the parkway was residential in purpose. Parkway House (Gabriel Roth and Elizabeth Fleischer, 1950–53) was built in the 2200 block of Pennsylvania Avenue. With an active plan attuned to its triangular site and a restrained modernist vocabulary executed in brick, it continued the pattern established by Cret and Colish's 2601 Parkway (see fig. 80). On the other side of the parkway, the four apartment slabs of Park Towne Place (John Hans Graham and Associates, 1959) evinced the changes that American architecture had experienced in the intervening years. Their simple forms, placed with calculated nonchalance in the landscape, bespoke the tardy arrival of the International Style on the parkway and its degeneration into the language of real estate development.

Southeast of Logan Circle, postwar construction filled in most of the remaining gaps. Here the mix of building uses was more pronounced than in the park-like setting on the other side of the circle, and the buildings crowded the roadway more closely. While most of the new work was undistinguished, the United Fund Building (Mitchell/Giurgola, 1968–71) is an excellent example of the so-called Philadelphia School of contextual architecture. Respectful of its urban and historic setting, this philosophy found its center in Louis Kahn's design studio at the University of Pennsylvania, where Romaldo Giurgola had also begun teaching in 1958.

Contextualism had turned into postmodern historicism by the time Kohn Pedersen and Fox built the Four Seasons Hotel in 1982–83. It occupied the site on Logan Circle once acquired for Ralph Walker's concert hall (see fig. 115), but unlike the outspoken "moderne" of that design, the hotel echoed the general form of the colonnades with which the Free Library and Municipal Court greeted it from across the circle. The same architects built the One Logan Square office tower behind the Four Seasons as an exercise in abstract minimalist sculpture, but that design only serves to emphasize by contrast the historical forms and general visual environment that they discovered and protected in the parkway. At last, the perimeter of Logan Circle was nearing completion, although the gap at the northeast corner still demanded attention.

Protection and renewal have continued. In 1989 the diseased oak trees that lined the central roadway were removed and replaced. This project, funded by the Pew Charitable Trusts and an anonymous donor, returned the parkway to its appearance in the 1920s, when the trees were small and the new buildings loomed large above and beside it. Another generation has thus been permitted to enjoy the sense of accomplishment with which Philadelphians first greeted the new parkway.

Notes

Height precedes width in all dimensions. Translations are by the author unless noted. Location, including the place of publication of newspapers, is Philadelphia unless stated.

Figure numbers refer to illustrations in this book. Catalogue numbers refer to entries in the Checklist of the Exhibition. The inscriptions in both the figure captions and the checklist include only the information needed for the attribution or dating of the works; all writing on the objects was not transcribed. Life dates appear only with the first mention of an individual in either the captions or the checklist.

Abbreviations

AAUP	*University of Pennsylvania, Architectural Archives, Philadelphia*	
AIA	*American Institute of Architects, Washington, D.C.*	
APS	*American Philosophical Society, Philadelphia*	
Athenaeum	*The Athenaeum of Philadelphia*	
CPUP	*University of Pennsylvania, Cret Papers, Special Collections, Van Pelt Library, Philadelphia*	
FI	*The Franklin Institute Science Museum, Philadelphia*	
FPAA	*Fairmount Park Art Association, Philadelphia*	
FPC	*Fairmount Park Commission, Philadelphia*	
H2L2	*The partners of H2L2 Architects/Planners, Philadelphia*	
HSP	*The Historical Society of Pennsylvania, Philadelphia*	
PAAA	*The Athenaeum of Philadelphia, Philadelphia Arts Association Papers*	
PAFA	*Pennsylvania Academy of the Fine Arts, Philadelphia*	
PCA	*City Archives of Philadelphia*	
PMA	*Philadelphia Museum of Art (before 1938, Pennsylvania Museum)*	
PMAA	*Philadelphia Museum of Art, Archives*	

Chapter One

1. The Brooklyn Museum, *The American Renaissance, 1876–1917* (October 13–December 30, 1979), pp. 11–25.

2. For example, Paul Cret (see fig. 7) wrote and lectured often on the subject "Modern Architecture," and he spoke knowingly of "'we moderns'" to Fiske Kimball (see fig. 6). Cret to Kimball, December 19, 1927, CPUP, box 17.

3. Jacques Gréber, *L'Architecture aux Etats-Unis: Preuve de la force d'expansion du génie français* (Paris, 1920), vol. 1, p. 14.

4. See Ernest Flagg, "Influence of the French School on Architecture in the United States," *Architectural Record*, vol. 4, no. 2 (October–December 1894), pp. 218–22; H. Van Buren Magonigle, "Architecture," in Francis G. Wickware, ed., *The American Yearbook: A Record of Events and Progress, 1911* (New York, 1912), pp. 758–63. For recent discussion of the two camps see Elizabeth G. Grossman, "Paul Philippe Cret: Rationalism and Imagery in American Architecture" (Ph.D. diss., Brown University, 1980), pp. 7–8, 37–62; and Mardges Bacon, *Ernest Flagg: Beaux-Arts Architect and Urban Reformer* (New York, 1986), pp. 49–62.

5. See, for example, Talbot Faulkner Hamlin, *The American Spirit in Architecture*, The Pageant of America, vol. 13 (New Haven, 1926), pp. 165–78; Thomas E. Tallmadge, *The Story of Architecture in America* (New York, 1927), pp. 234–89; Fiske Kimball, *American Architecture* (Indianapolis, 1928), pp. 147–87.

6. Thomas E. Tallmadge, *The Story of Architecture in America* (New York, 1927), p. 195.

7. Flagg, "Influence of the French School," p. 223.

8. Thomas Hastings, "Architecture and Modern Life," *Harper's New Monthly Magazine*, vol. 94, no. 561 (February 1897), p. 406. Hastings wrote frequently and repetitively on these themes; see also "The Relations of Life to Style in Architecture," *Harper's New Monthly Magazine*, vol. 88, no. 528 (May 1894), pp. 957–62; "The Influence of the Ecole des Beaux-Arts upon American Architecture," *Architectural Record*, Beaux-Arts Number (January 1901), pp. 66–90; "The Evolution of Style in Modern Architecture," *North American Review*, vol. 191, no. 651 (February 1910), pp. 195–205; and "Principles of Architectural Composition" and "Modern Architecture," in Ralph Adams Cram, Thomas Hastings, and Claude Bragdon, *Six Lectures on Architecture: The Scammon Lectures for 1915* (Chicago, 1917), pp. 67–97, 98–120, respectively.

9. Hastings, "Modern Architecture," p. 105.

10. Hastings, "Principles of Architectural Composition," p. 88.

11. Hastings, "Evolution of Style," p. 195.

12. George Roberts and Mary Roberts, *Triumph on Fairmount: Fiske Kimball and the Philadelphia Museum of Art* (Philadelphia, 1959), pp. 26–28, 41–49. Lauren Bricker is completing a doctoral dissertation on Kimball at the University of California, Santa Barbara. I am most grateful for her assistance.

13. Fiske Kimball and George Harold Edgell, *A History of Architecture* (New York, 1918), pp. 560–65.

14. Fiske Kimball, "What Is Modern Architecture?" *The Nation*, vol. 119, no. 3082 (July 30, 1924), p. 128.

15. Ibid., p. 129.

16. Fiske Kimball, "Louis Sullivan—An Old Master," *Architectural Record*, vol. 57, no. 4 (April 1925), p. 304.

17. Ibid.

18. Kimball, *American Architecture*, p. 160.

19. Ibid., p. 168.

20. Ibid., p. 181.

21. Ibid., pp. 192–200.

22. Ibid., p. 217.

23. Roger Fry, "The French Post-Impressionists," in Fry, *Vision and Design*, 2nd ed. (London, 1925), pp. 237–43. The essay first appeared in the catalogue of the second Post-Impressionist exhibition at the Grafton Galleries in 1912 and was reprinted in the first edition of *Vision and Design* in 1920.

24. Kimball, "What Is Modern Architecture?" p. 129.

25. See Grossman, "Paul Philippe Cret"; Theo B. White, ed., *Paul Philippe Cret: Architect and Teacher* (Philadelphia, 1973). The T-Square Club was an association of younger Philadelphia architects that sponsored an atelier, founded in 1903, in which draftsmen could advance their training. The atelier was part of the national system organized by the Society of Beaux-Arts Architects.

26. Cret to Kimball, May 6, 1925, CPUP, box 17.

27. Cret to Kimball, December 19, 1927, CPUP, box 17.

28. Cret to Kimball, March 15, 1928, CPUP, box 17.

29. Kimball to Cret, March 16, 1928, CPUP, box 17.

30. Paul Cret, "The Ecole des Beaux Arts: What Its Architectural Training Means," *Architectural Record*, vol. 23, no. 5 (May 1908), p. 369.

31. Ibid.; Paul Cret, "Truth and Tradition," *Architectural Record*, vol. 25, no. 2 (February 1909), pp. 107–9; Paul Cret, "Training of the Designer," *Old Penn: Weekly Review of the University of Pennsylvania*, vol. 8, no. 18 (February 12, 1910), pp. 283–87.

32. Cret, "Training of the Designer," p. 285.

33. Julien Guadet, *Eléments et théorie de l'architecture*, 3rd rev. ed. (Paris, 1909), vol. 1, pp. 96–98.

34. Ibid., pp. 114, 115, fig. 29.

35. Ibid., p. 102.

36. Ibid., p. 135.

37. Quoted from Taine in Paul Cret, "The Classic *versus* the Modernist," *Yearbook of the Society of Beaux-Arts Architects . . .* (1934), p. 113.

38. Cret to Francis B. Swales, October 6, 1928, CPUP, box 17.

39. Paul Cret, "Modern Architecture" (TS), lecture presented to the T-Square Club, Philadelphia, October 25, 1923, CPUP, box 16.

40. Paul Cret, "Modern Architecture," in *The Significance of the Fine Arts*, ed. AIA, Committee on Education (Boston, 1923), pp. 208–9.

41. Paul Cret, "Modernists and Conservatives" (MS), lecture presented to the T-Square Club, Philadelphia, November 19, 1927, CPUP, box 16.

42. Ibid.

43. Paul Cret, "The Architect as Collaborator with the Engineer," *Architectural Forum*, vol. 49, no. 1 (July 1928), pp. 97–104.

44. Paul Cret, "Ten Years of Modernism," *Federal Architect*, vol. 4, no. 1 (July 1933), p. 8.

45. Cret, "Modern Architecture," p. 190n.

46. This notion was developed by Theodor Lipps. It had already been applied to classical architecture by Heinrich Wölfflin in *Renaissance und Barock* (1888).

47. Geoffrey Scott, *The Architecture of Humanism: A Study in the History of Taste*, 2nd ed. (New York, 1969), p. 159.

48. Ibid., p. 157.

49. Le Corbusier, *Towards a New Architecture*, trans. Frederick Etchells (London, 1927), p. 31.

50. Ibid., pp. 195–96.

51. Cret, "Modern Architecture," p. 206. See also the lecture cited in n. 39 above.

Chapter Two

1. Charles Mulford Robinson, *Modern Civic Art, or the City Made Beautiful* (New York, 1903), p. 3.

2. Lincoln Steffens, "Philadelphia: Corrupt and Contented," *McClure's Magazine*, vol. 21, no. 3 (July 1903), pp. 249–63.

3. Two important recent studies that include consideration of the "city beautiful" movement are M. Christine Boyer, *Dreaming the Rational City: The Myth of American City Planning* (Cambridge, Mass., 1983); and Giorgio Ciucci, Francesco Dal Co, Mario Manieri-Elia, and Manfredo Tafuri, *The American City: From the Civil War to the New Deal*, trans. Barbara Luigia La Penta (Cambridge, Mass., 1979).

4. Fiske Kimball, *American Architecture* (Indianapolis, 1928), p. 168. Written in the summer of 1927.

5. Daniel H. Burnham, John M. Carrère, and Arnold W. Brunner, *The Group Plan of the Public Buildings of the City of Cleveland: Report Made to the Honorable Tom L. Johnson, Mayor, and to the Honorable Board of Public Service* (New York, 1903).

6. U.S. Senate, Committee on the District of Columbia, *The Improvement of the Park System of the District of Columbia*, pt. 1, *Report of the Senate Committee on the District of Columbia*, pt. 2, *Report of the Park Commission*, ed. Charles Moore, 57th Cong., 1st sess., 1902, S. Rept. 166.

7. For Philadelphia politics of this era see Russell F. Weigley, ed., *Philadelphia: A 300-Year History* (New York, 1982); Donald W. Disbrow, "The Progressive Movement in Philadelphia, 1910–1916" (Ph.D. diss., University of Rochester, 1956); Donald W. Disbrow, "Reform in Philadelphia Under Mayor Blankenburg, 1912–1916," *Pennsylvania History*, vol. 27, no. 4 (October 1960), pp. 379–96; Lloyd M. Abernathy, "Insurgency in Philadelphia, 1905," *Pennsylvania Magazine of History and Biography*, vol. 87, no. 1 (January 1963), pp. 3–20; Philip S. Benjamin, "Gentlemen Reformers in the Quaker City, 1870–1912," *Political Science Quarterly*, vol. 85, no. 1 (March 1970), pp. 61–79; and George Morgan, *The City of Firsts: Being a Complete History of the City of Philadelphia from Its Founding, in 1682, to the Present Time* (Philadelphia, 1926), pp. 277–96.

8. William S. Vare, *My Forty Years in Politics* (Philadelphia, 1933), p. 19.

9. The story of the parkway is surveyed in several places, including Andrew Wright Crawford, George S. Webster, and William Perrine, "An Outline of the History of the Fairmount Parkway," in FPAA, *Fairmount Park Art Association: An Account of Its Origin and Activities from Its Foundation in 1871. Issued on the Occasion of Its Fiftieth Anniversary, 1921* (Philadelphia, 1922), pp. 244–52; W. S. Stanton, "Report: Outline History of the Fairmount Parkway, 1871–1935" (TS), March 1935, PCA, 145.12; and Cyrus Dezfuli-Arjomandi, "Benjamin Franklin Parkway in Philadelphia: A Study of the Forces Behind Its Creation and Evolution" (Ph.D. diss., University of Pennsylvania, 1985).

10. *Broad Street, Penn Square, and the Park* (Philadelphia, 1871), p. 10.

11. The history of the parkway from 1891 to 1894 is recounted in "The Boulevard Well Considered," *Inquirer*, July 2, 1894, p. 2.

12. Between 1796 and 1919, Philadelphia was governed by a bicameral legislature consisting of a Common Council and a Select Council. Until 1839 the Councils elected the mayor, and until 1887 they controlled most city departments. The reformer identified the Councils with Philadelphia's perennial corruption, and they gradually succeeded in reducing their power and creating a strong-mayor system through charter reform. In 1919 the bicameral legislature was abolished in favor of a single City Council.

13. "Pull Together for the Boulevard," *Inquirer*, April 11, 1894, p. 4; "Follow the Lead of the Mayor," *Inquirer*, April 13, 1894, p. 4; "Another Old Fogy Wail," *Inquirer*, April 26, 1894, p. 4; "A Few Objections Answered," *Inquirer*, June 3, 1894, p. 4.

14. "A Boulevard Will Beautify the City," *Inquirer*, April 15, 1894, p. 5.

15. "Stuart Will Veto the Boulevard Bill," *Inquirer*, July 13, 1894, p. 1; "The Boulevard Veto," *Inquirer*, July 13, 1894, p. 4; "The Mayor's Veto of the Boulevard," *Inquirer*, April 5, 1894, p. 8.

16. "The 'Concourse' Scheme," *Inquirer*, April 5, 1895, p. 4; "The Huey Concourse," *Inquirer*, May 10, 1895, p. 3; "That 'Concourse,'" *Inquirer*, May 16, 1895, p. 4. The Huey proposal is illustrated in Herbert C. Wise, "The Boulevard Project in Philadelphia," *House and Garden*, vol. 2, no. 7 (July 1902), repro. p. 319; and Albert Kelsey, ed. and comp., *The Proposed Parkway for Philadelphia: A Direct Thoroughfare from the Public Buildings to the Green Street Entrance of Fairmount Park* (Philadelphia, 1902), p. 15.

17. Albert Kelsey, "A Rational Beauty for American Cities," *Fairmount Park Art Association Twenty-Eighth Annual Report . . .* , no. 34 (1900), p. 68.

18. Kelsey, ed. and comp., *The Proposed Parkway*, pp. 17, 22.

19. Ibid., p. 22. Illustrated in Wise, "The Boulevard Project," repro. p. 320.

20. Kelsey, ed. and comp., *The Proposed Parkway*, pp. 9, 22.

21. Ibid.

22. James M. Beck, "Introductory Plea," in ibid., p. 7.

23. See n. 17 above and FPAA, *An Account of Its Origin*, pp. 255–56.

24. City Parks Association, *Special Report on the City Plan* (Philadelphia, April 15, 1902), p. 10. The report was signed by Crawford and J. Rodman Paul.

25. Andrew Wright Crawford, "Proposed Improvements in Philadelphia's City Plan," *Fifteenth Annual Report of the City Parks Association of Philadelphia*, pt. 1 (1908), pp. 3–8.

26. "Philadelphia Between New York and Washington," *Twenty-Fourth Annual Report of the City Parks Association of Philadelphia* (1912), p. 29.

27. Crawford to Miller, January 14, 1904, and January 20, 1904, HSP, FPAA Papers, box 55, folder 20.

28. Andrew Wright Crawford and Frank Miles Day, *The Existing and Proposed Outer Park Systems of American Cities: Report of the Philadelphia Allied Organizations* (Harrisburg, [1905]).

29. This meeting is discussed in more detail in Chapter Three.

30. See Miller to Cret, Trumbauer, and Zantzinger, April 30, 1907, HSP, FPAA Papers, box 31, letterbook for November 1906–March 1909, p. 135.

31. Kelsey to Cret, June 22, 1907, CPUP, box 13a.

32. Kelsey to Cret, February 3, 1908, and January 8, 1909, CPUP, box 13a.

33. "Study for the Improvement of the Schuylkill River Embankments and Adjacent Parks and Avenues," May 1905, AAUP, Cret 21.3.

34. Paul Cret to Marguerite Cret, December 2, 1915, CPUP, box 7b.

35. Ibid. Medary in fact was the design architect for the firm's Fidelity Mutual Life Insurance Building (for a discussion, see Chapter Four), a building that Cret admired.

36. Paul Cret to Marguerite Cret, July 24, 1917, CPUP, box 7b.

37. Cret to Leslie W. Miller, May 2, 1907, HSP, FPAA Papers, box 55, folder 21; Trumbauer to Miller, May 2, 1907, ibid.; Zantzinger to Miller, May 20, 1907, ibid.

38. Miller to Zantzinger, May 22, 1907, HSP, FPAA Papers, box 31, letterbook for November 1906–March 1909, p. 152.

39. Zantzinger to Burt Fenner, July 7, 1915, AIA Archives, Borie RG 803, box 219, folder 28.

40. Zantzinger to Miller, July 5, 1907 (enclosing the report dated July 3, 1907), HSP, FPAA Papers, box 55, folder 21.

41. C. C. Zantzinger (for the commission), *Fairmount Park Art Association: Report of the Commission Employed by the Association to Study the Entrance of the Philadelphia Parkway into Fairmount Park, as Presented at the Thirty-Sixth Annual Meeting of the Art Association, December 12th, 1907 . . .* (Philadelphia, 1908), p. 15.

42. Zantzinger to Cret, July 22, 1907, CPUP, box 13b.

43. This and subsequent detail is taken from the final report of the commission cited in n. 41. It is also published in *Fairmount Park Art Association Thirty-Sixth Annual Report . . .* , no. 42 (1908), pp. 35–49.

44. Trumbauer, Zantzinger, and Cret to Miller, October 15, 1907, HSP, FPAA Papers, box 55, folder 21; "To Beautify Parkway End,"

Record, November 12, 1907, p. 6.

45. "Mayor Reyburn's Address . . . ," *Fairmount Park Art Association Thirty-Sixth Annual Report . . .* , no. 42 (1908), p. 50.

46. For the quote see Sarah Dickson Lowrie, "Price Papers" (TS), 1936, pt. 2, p. 54, PMA Library. See also John H. Converse, "Thirty-Seventh Annual Report of the Fairmount Park Art Association," *Fairmount Park Art Association Thirty-Seventh Annual Report . . .* , no. 44 (1909), pp. 18–19; "Move for 'City Beautiful,' " *Press*, November 24, 1908, p. 3.

47. Daniel H. Burnham and Edward H. Bennett, *Plan of Chicago Prepared Under the Direction of the Commercial Club . . .* , ed. Charles Moore (Chicago, 1909).

48. The best published accounts of the committee are "Comprehensive Plans Number," *Philadelphia*, vol. 4 (March 1911); and *Annual Report of the Director of the Department of Public Works and the Chief of the Bureau of Surveys for the Year Ending December 31, 1911* (Philadelphia, 1912).

49. "Mayor Is Chairman of City Plan Committee," *Public Ledger*, February 28, 1911, p. 9.

50. "The Third Annual City Planning Conference," *American Architect*, vol. 99 (June 7, 1911), pp. 205–10; William E. Groben, "The Replanning of Philadelphia," *American Architect*, vol. 100, no. 1855 (July 12, 1911), pp. 9–11; "Conference on City Plans Opens Today," *Public Ledger*, May 15, 1911, p. 2; "Mayor Opens City Plans Conference," *Public Ledger*, May 16, 1911, p. 2; "City Planners Find Flaws in Housing," *Public Ledger*, May 17, 1911, p. 2; "City Planning Conference Ends," *Public Ledger*, May 18, 1911, p. 3.

51. "City Planning Exhibition," *Public Ledger*, May 16, 1911, p. 10.

52. "City Plans Committee," *Public Ledger*, July 8, 1911, p. 10.

53. Disbrow, "The Progressive Movement in Philadelphia," pp. 79–92; Kenneth E. Trombley, *The Life and Times of a Happy Liberal: A Biography of Morris Llewellyn Cooke* (New York, 1954), pp. 15–30.

54. FPC Minutes, vol. 12, pp. 462–65, December 13, 1916, PCA, 149.1.

55. "Mimic Fight Staged in Parkway Ruins," *Public Ledger*, May 3, 1917, p. 4.

56. "New Parkway Plans Ready in Two Weeks," *Public Ledger*, September 30, 1917, p. 22.

57. Jean-Claude Delorme, "Jacques Gréber, urbaniste français," *Metropolis*, vol. 3, no. 32 (1978), pp. 49–54; Pierre Lavedan, "Jacques Gréber, 1882–1962," *La vie urbaine*, n.s., no. 1 (January–March 1963), pp. 1–14.

58. FPAA, *The Fairmount Parkway: A Pictorial Record of Development from Its First Incorporation in the City Plan in 1904 to the Completion of the Main Drive from City Hall to Fairmount Park in 1919* (Philadelphia, 1919).

59. The details of the Gréber contracts were reported on January 10, 1923; see FPC Minutes, vol. 14, pp. 247–48, PCA, 149.1.

60. "City's Court of Honor, of Classic Outlines and Gorgeous Hues, to Greet Nation's Heroes," *Public Ledger*, December 8, 1918, p. 4.

61. A contract for $2,245 was awarded on March 3, 1922. Cat. nos. 33 and 34 were apparently produced under this contract.

62. Quoted in *Department of the Art Jury, Eighth Annual Report* (1918), p. 8.

63. Ibid.

64. Kelsey to Cret, January 31, 1918, CPUP, box 13b.

65. Paul Cret to Marguerite Cret, April 17, 1918, CPUP, box 7b.

66. Kelsey to Cret, [December 1918], CPUP, box 15.

67. Price to Cret, February 14, 1919, CPUP, box 13b.

Chapter Three

1. R. Sturgis Ingersoll, "The Creation of Fairmount," *Philadelphia Museum of Art Bulletin*, vol. 61, nos. 287–88 (Fall 1965–Winter 1966), pp. 22–29; George Roberts and Mary Roberts, *Triumph on Fairmount: Fiske Kimball and the Philadelphia Museum of Art* (Philadelphia, 1959).

2. John Maass, *The Glorious Enterprise: The Centennial Exhibition of 1876 and H. J. Schwarzmann, Architect-in-Chief* (Watkins Glen, N.Y., 1973), pp. 44–59.

3. "Stroll Among Art Centres: Nearly 400,000 Visitors to Memorial Hall Last Year," *Philadelphia Times*, January 6, 1895, p. 7.

4. "Plans for New Wings at Memorial Hall Condemned as Short-Sighted by Connoisseurs," *Evening Bulletin*, April 6, 1900, p. 8.

5. FPC Minutes, vol. 9, pp. 257–58, March 10, 1894, PCA, 149.1.

6. Ibid., vol. 9, pp. 266–67, April 14, 1894.

7. W94-1-2; purchased as *L'Amende honorable*.

8. W94-1-6; sold, Parke-Bernet Galleries, Inc., New York, *Nineteenth-Century American Paintings and European Genre Subjects . . .* (February 26–27, 1947), p. 30, lot 56.

9. FPC Minutes, vol. 9, pp. 283–84, June 4, 1894, PCA, 149.1.

10. Ibid., vol. 9, pp. 366–67, March 9, 1895, p. 370, April 13, 1895, pp. 387–89, May 11, 1895; FPC, Committee on Memorial Hall Minutes, pp. 7–8, March 9, 1895, pp. 12–14, May 11, 1895, PCA, 149.22.

11. FPC, Committee on Memorial Hall Minutes, pp. 15–17, June 27, 1895, PCA, 149.22.

12. FPC Minutes, vol. 9, pp. 432–33, October 11, 1895, PCA, 149.1; FPC, Committee on Memorial Hall Minutes, pp. 18–19, October 8, 1895, pp. 20–21, October 11, 1895, PCA, 149.22.

13. Christopher Thomas is completing a Yale doctoral dissertation on Bacon. He very kindly shared his insights and information about Bacon and the work then underway in the office of McKim, Mead, and White.

14. FPC Minutes, vol. 9, pp. 439–60, December 3, 1895, PCA, 149.1.

15. Ibid.

16. "Architects Angry Over the Awards," *Inquirer*, December 8, 1895, p. 17.

17. FPC Minutes, vol. 9, p. 464, December 13, 1895, PCA, 149.1.

18. "A Public Exhibit of Rejected Plans," *Inquirer*, December 11, 1895, p. 4.

19. FPC, Committee on Memorial Hall Minutes, pp. 23–24, December 13, 1895; pp. 31–35, May 22, 1896, PCA, 149.22.

20. Ibid., p. 31.

21. "City Trust to Withdraw Offer of Park Museum," *Inquirer*, March 14, 1907, pp. 1, 7.

22. As published in "Park Approaches," *Sixteenth Annual Report of the City Parks Association of Philadelphia* (1904), pp. 9–10. A fold-out map of the plan was also included.

23. "Address of Hon. John Weaver, Mayor of Philadelphia," *Fairmount Park Art Association Thirty-Third Annual Report . . .*, no. 39 (1905), p. 28.

24. "Study for the Improvement of the Schuylkill River Embankments and Adjacent Parks and Avenues," AAUP, Cret 21.3.

25. FPC, Committee on Memorial Hall Minutes, pp. 75–76, October 27, 1906, PCA, 149.22.

26. "Address of the Hon. Samuel Gustine Thompson," *Fairmount Park Art Association Thirty-Fifth Annual Report . . .*, no. 41 (1907), p. 48.

27. "Widener Offers to Crown Parkway with Magnificent $2,000,000 Art Gallery," *Press*, April 7, 1907, pp. 1, 2. See also "$10,000,000 Picture Gallery for City," *Public Ledger*, April 7, 1907, p. 1; "Offers $10,000,000 for an Art Gallery," *New York Times*, April 7, 1907; "Artists Rejoice at Widener Offer of Temple of Art," *Press*, April 8, 1907, p. 1.

28. Cret to Trumbauer, April 6, 1905, CPUP, box 13a; Trumbauer to Cret, April 8, 1905, ibid.

29. "Grecian Art Temple Planned by Widener for End of Parkway," *North American*, April 7, 1907, p. 1.

30. See Chapter Two, n. 48, above.

31. "Thirty-Ninth Annual Meeting of the Fairmount Park Art Association," *Fairmount Park Art Association Thirty-Ninth Annual Report . . .*, no. 47 (1911), pp. 29–30.

32. "Art Gallery Work to Start at Once," *Public Ledger*, March 5, 1911, p. 2. See also "Mayor to Start Work Promptly on Art Museum," *Inquirer*, March 5, 1911, p. 1.

33. FPC Minutes, vol. 12, p. 117, April 13, 1911; pp. 126–27, May 12, 1911, PCA, 149.1.

34. FPC, Committee on the Art Museum Minutes, pp. 343–44, June 29, 1911; pp. 345–46, October 19, 1911, PCA, 149.18.

35. Further drawings of the domed variant include PMAA, 20.1, 20.2, and 20.3.

36. Quoted in R. Sturgis Ingersoll, "The Creation of Fairmount," *Philadelphia Museum of Art Bulletin*, vol. 61, nos. 287–88 (Fall 1965–Winter 1966), p. 25.

37. Dated and attributed to the Trumbauer office on the basis of a photograph of a drawing that is dated September 25, 1912, and initialed by Charles F. Rabenold of Trumbauer's staff, Art Jury Submissions, file 81, PW 1218, PCA, 140.3.

38. Eli Kirk Price, "Memorandum of Report on Philadelphia Museum of Art, Fairmount Park" (TS), November 19, 1912, PMAA, BT: Eli Kirk Price; FPC Minutes, vol. 12, pp. 251–53, March 12, 1913, PCA, 149.1.

39. "Art Museum Plans Adopted by Commission," *Public Ledger*, March 13, 1913, pp. 1, 2, 11; "Plan for Great Art Museum in Park Approved," *Inquirer*, March 13, 1913, p. 1; "City Art Gallery Plans Approved," *Press*, March 13, 1913, pp. 1, 7.

40. "Choice of Art Jury Is Well Received," *Public Ledger*, October 9, 1911, p. 2.

41. "Meeting of the Committee," March 26, 1913, Art Jury Submissions, file 81, PCA, 140.3.

42. "Expects Citizens to Aid in Building Art Museum," *Public Ledger*, September 25, 1913, p. 1.

43. The campaign was led by the machine-controlled *Inquirer*; see "An Appeal for the Art Museum," *Inquirer*, September 25, 1913, p. 8.

44. "Hogs, Not Art, Wanted," *Record*, October 4, 1913, p. 8.

45. "Art Museum," *Report of the Commissioners of Fairmount Park for the Year 1914* (1915), p. 9.

46. In addition to the stylistic indicators noted below, the attribution to the office of Zantzinger, Borie, and Medary is corroborated by circumstantial evidence. It was Borie who gave the set of photographs of the study models to the PMAA, and one of the sketches is marked "Borie" (see cat. no. 66).

47. Borie reports that work on the new design was going ahead in November 1914; see Borie to Cret, November 6, 1914, CPUP, box 14.

48. Elizabeth G. Grossman, "Paul Philippe Cret: Rationalism and Imagery in American Architecture" (Ph.D. diss., Brown University, 1980), pp. 54, 67 n. 17.

49. Paul Cret to Marguerite Cret, May 24 and August 3, 1915, CPUP, box 7a.

50. Cret to Zantzinger, February 21, 1915, CPUP, box 14; Paul Cret to Marguerite Cret, November 30, 1915, CPUP, box 7a.

51. See Elizabeth G. Grossman, "Two Postwar Competitions: The Nebraska State Capitol and the Kansas City Liberty Memorial," *Journal of the Society of Architectural Historians*, vol. 45, no. 3 (September 1986), pp. 263–67.

52. Quoted in Doris Patterson, "The Invisible Man Behind the Art Museum" (TS), [1973], Athenaeum, Shay Papers.

53. "Meeting of the Committee," June 24, 1915, Art Jury Submissions, file 81, PCA, 140.3.

54. "Structure Which Will Crown Parkway Shown in Miniature: Model Forecasts Actual Grandeur of Art Museum," *Inquirer*, December 29, 1915, pp. 1, 8; "Model of the Art Museum on View," *Public Ledger*, December 29, 1915, p. 9.

55. "50,000 See Museum Model," *Evening Telegraph*, February 18, 1916, p. 13.

56. "Art Museum Item Omitted in Draft of New Loan Bill," *Inquirer*, March 1, 1916, pp. 1, 6.

57. "Loan Will Include $1,202,000 Item for Art Museum," *Inquirer*, March 8, 1916, pp. 1, 15.

58. "Meeting of the Committee," January 22, 1916, Art Jury Submissions, file 81, PCA, 140.3; Secretary of the Art Jury Committee to the President of the Philadelphia Chapter of the AIA, May 3, 1916, ibid.

59. "Meeting of the Committee," May 4, 1916, Art Jury Submissions, file 81, PCA, 140.3.

60. Ibid.; "Meeting of the Committee," June 30, 1916, ibid.

61. "Art Museum Delay Explained by Mayor," *Public Ledger*, January 12, 1917, p. 9.

62. "Memorandum of Conference," February 6, 1917, Art Jury Submissions, file 81, PCA, 140.3

63. "Meeting of the Committee," February 13, 1917, Art Jury Submissions, file 81, PCA, 140.3; "Memorandum in Regard to Submission No. 81," March 13, 1917, ibid.

64. FPC Minutes, vol. 12, p. 484, March 11, 1917, PCA, 149.1.

65. Warner to Price, October 19, 1917, PMAA, war.

66. "Mayor Takes Stand Against New Loans," *Public Ledger*, February 8, 1917, p. 4.

67. "Johnson Home and Art to City," *Public Ledger*, April 19, 1917, p. 4. Efforts to overturn the will were immediately launched, with important repercussions for the art museum and the rest of the parkway. See Chapter Four for extended discussion of this episode.

68. "City Will Resume Improvement Work," *Public Ledger*, January 14, 1919, p. 4.

69. "Widener Tells Plan for Great Court of Honor," *Public Ledger*, December 6, 1918, pp. 1, 10.

70. FPC Minutes, vol. 14, p. 78, June 25, 1919, pp. 92–93, July 24, 1919, pp. 95–96, October 8, 1919, PCA, 149.1; "Eleven Proposals for Museum," *Public Ledger*, June 5, 1919, p. 13; "Fairmount Museum Contract Held Up," *Public Ledger*, June 26, 1919, p. 13; "Injunction Denied on Parkway Job," *Public Ledger*, July 22, 1919, p. 5.

71. "Elkins' Art May Be in City Gallery Within Five Years," *Public Ledger*, November 1, 1919, p. 1.

72. "Widener Quits Art Jury; City Loses Pictures," *Public Ledger*, July 23, 1920, pp. 1, 4. This story is told in greater detail in Chapter Four.

73. Quoted in Charles Willis Thompson, "Park Commission and Art Jury Toploftically Refuse News of the Art Museum," *Public Ledger*, October 10, 1921, p. 2.

74. "Art Museum Delays," *Evening Bulletin*, November 10, 1922, p. 6. The gash remained but was lined, covered, and used as an underpass.

75. FPC Minutes, vol. 14, pp. 231–32, November 8, 1922, pp. 233–35, November 22, 1922, PCA, 149.1; "Art Museum Cost Put at $8,500,000; Finished in Two Years," *Public Ledger*, November 23, 1922, pp. 1, 5.

76. "The Costly Art Museum," *Public Ledger*, November 24, 1922, p. 10.

77. "Taxpayers Quiz $8,500,000 Cost for Art Museum," *Evening Public Ledger*, January 8, 1923, pp. 1, 13.

78. "Lowest Bidders for Art Museum Building Ignored," *Evening Public Ledger*, January 9, 1923, pp. 1, 6.

79. FPC Minutes, vol. 14, pp. 244–49, January 10, 1923; pp. 277–78, June 13, 1923, PCA, 149.1.

80. Ibid., pp. 316–18, April 17, 1924.

81. Ibid., pp. 473–75, December 14, 1927.

82. One early instance of this concern was J. H. Dulles Allen, "A Plea for Color in Architecture," *Journal of the American Institute of Architects*, vol. 2, no. 4 (April 1914), pp. 178–82.

83. Leon V. Solon, "Principles of Polychrome in Sculpture Based on Greek Practice," *Architectural Record*, vol. 43, no. 6 (June 1918), pp. 526–33.

84. This account draws heavily on Leon V. Solon, "The Philadelphia Museum of Art, Fairmount Park, Philadelphia: A Revival of Polychrome Architecture and Sculpture," *Architectural Record*, vol. 60, no. 2 (August 1926), pp. 97–111.

85. Leon V. Solon, "Principles of Architectural Polychromy," pts. 1–7, *Architectural Record*, vol. 51 (January–June 1922), pp. 1–7, 93–100, 189–96, 285–91, 377–86, 465–75.

86. "Art Museum Cost Put at $8,500,000; Finished in Two Years," *Public Ledger*, November 23, 1922, pp. 1, 5; Harold D. Eberlein, "The Philadelphia Museum of Art," *Architectural Forum*, vol. 49, no. 1 (July 1928), p. 3; Richard F. Bach, "A Philadelphian Acropolis: The New Building of the Pennsylvania Museum," *Bulletin of the Metropolitan Museum of Art*, vol. 23, no. 6 (June 1928), p. 162.

87. Bach, "Philadelphian Acropolis," p. 163.

88. Shirley Reiff Howarth, *C. Paul Jennewein, Sculptor* (Tampa, 1980), pp. 22–23, 25–26; Steven Eric Bronson, "John Gregory: The Philadelphia Museum of Art Pediment" (M.A. thesis, University of Delaware, 1977).

89. FPC Minutes, vol. 14, pp. 304–5, February 13, 1924, PCA, 149.1.

90. Now installed over the entrance of the Children's Shop in the museum.

91. Bach, "Philadelphian Acropolis," p. 160.

Chapter Four

1. Zantzinger to Burt Fenner, July 7, 1915, AIA Archives, Borie RG 803, box 219, folder 28.

2. "Purchase Site for Library," *Public Ledger*, June 17, 1911, p. 2.

3. Cret to the Art Jury, [April 26, 1912], Art Jury Submissions, file 16, PCA, 140.3.

4. These and other details are drawn from the *Free Library of Philadelphia Annual Reports*.

5. Committee Meeting Minutes, November 23, 1916, Art Jury Submissions, file 16, PCA, 140.3.

6. Committee Meeting Minutes, April 24, 1922, Art Jury Submissions, file 1434, PCA, 140.3; cat. no. 99.

7. For details of this story see Chapter Three.

8. "Court Will Determine Johnson Art Location," *Public Ledger*, December 3, 1918, p. 9.

9. George W. Norris, "Mr. Johnson's Opinion of Art Museums" (letter to the editor), *Public Ledger*, December 9, 1918, p. 8.

10. Lewis to Price, October 21, 1914, PAFA Archives, General Correspondence Files.

11. "Widener Tells Plan for Great Court of Honor," *Public Ledger*, December 6, 1918, pp. 1, 10.

12. "Mayor Upholds City's Art Jury on Paintings," *Public Ledger*, December 5, 1918, p. 3.

13. "City Has No Funds for Johnson Art," *Public Ledger*, February 28, 1920, p. 9.

14. "Mayor Inspects Sites on Parkway," *Public Ledger*, April 20, 1920, p. 13.

15. "Dual Art Gallery Idea Abandoned," *Public Ledger*, July 20, 1920, p. 1.

16. "A Single City Art Gallery," *Public Ledger*, July 21, 1920, p. 8.

17. "Widener Quits Art Jury; City Loses Pictures," *Public Ledger*, July 23, 1920, pp. 1, 4.

18. Sarah Dickson Lowrie, "Price Papers" (TS), 1936, pt. 2, p. 91, PMA Library.

19. Mastbaum to Rosenthal, January 6, 1926, CPUP, box 16.

20. Price to Gréber, January 6, 1926, CPUP, box 16.

21. Gréber to Cret, January 23, 1926, CPUP, box 16; Gréber to Mastbaum, February 5, 1926, ibid.; Cret to Gréber, February 16, 1926, ibid.; Gréber to Cret, March 3, 1926, ibid.; Cret to Gréber, March 22, 1926, ibid.

22. See Drawings A–C and Committee Meeting Minutes, April 7, 1926, Art Jury Submissions, file 1892, PCA, 140.3.

23. Gréber to Cret, August 14, 1926, CPUP, box 16.

24. Cret to Gréber, September 13, 1926, CPUP, box 16.

25. There are seventeen prints dated October 1926 in H2L2, box 384.

26. Gréber to Cret, December 8, 1926, CPUP, box 16.

27. Two November drawings survive: a southwest elevation dated November 29, 1926 (cat. no. 109), and a southeast elevation dated November 19, 1926 (cat. no. 108). A set of seventeen blueprints dated December 1926 is in H2L2, box 384.

28. Cret to Gréber, January 26, 1927, CPUP, box 16.

29. Gréber and Cret to Morris Wolf, July 6, 1927, CPUP, box 16.

30. Cret to Gréber, August 22, 1927, CPUP, box 16.

31. Cret to Gréber, September 17, 1927, CPUP, box 16.

32. Gréber to Lawrence Hills (editor of the *New York Herald* in Paris), April 4, 1930, CPUP, box 16. For an eloquent appreciation of the building as erected, see David Van Zanten, "Le Système des Beaux-Arts," *Architectural Design*, vol. 48, nos. 11–12 (1978), pp. 66–79.

33. "Report of the Special Committee on Site for a New Hall," May 2, 1911, APS Archives, IX,2.

34. Committee on Site for a New Hall and Committee on Ways and Means Minutebook, p. 77, January 16 and 24, 1919, APS Archives, IX,2.

35. Ibid., pp. 80–82, March 2 and 11, 1925.

36. Price to Cret, May 6, 1925, APS Archives, IX,2; Cret to Price, May 27, 1925, ibid.

37. APS, National Committee for the Building and Endowment Fund, *When Aristotle Comes Again* (Philadelphia, 1929); Cret to Price, May 11, 1929, APS Archives, IX,2.

38. Committee on Site for a New Hall and Committee on Ways and Means Minutebook, pp. 112–14, July 1, 1931, APS Archives, IX,2.

39. Paul Cret, "Report on Present Building of the American Philosophical Society," October 19, 1931, APS Archives, IX,2; Committee on Site for a New Hall and Committee on Ways and Means Minutebook, pp. 114–16, October 26, 1931, ibid.

40. Committee on Site for a New Hall and Committee on Ways and Means Minutebook, pp. 116–17, December 30, 1931; p. 118, March 2, 1932; pp. 119–20, May 25, 1932; pp. 121–22, June 7, 1932; p. 122, June 21, 1932; p. 123, October 4, 1932, APS Archives, IX,2.

41. Committee Meeting Minutes, March 16, 1933, Art Jury Submissions, file 2530, PCA, 140.3.

42. "Council Approves Parkway Site for Philosophical Society Home," *Public Ledger*, February 24, 1933, pp. 1, 14.

43. Building Fund Committee Minutes, n.p., APS Archives, IX,2.

44. "Mayor Opens City Plans Conference," *Public Ledger*, May 16, 1911, p. 2.

45. For the drawings see AAUP, Cret 187.1, 187.2. See also Cret's notes for a lecture to the Philadelphia Chapter of the AIA (TS), March 24, 1924, CPUP, box 16.

46. This and all subsequent information on meetings is taken from the Philadelphia Commission Minutebook, Athenaeum, Philadelphia Commission Papers.

47. Paul Cret and Harry Sternfeld, "Report on Improvement of City Hall Square—Philadelphia, Pennsylvania" (TS), [May 1927], CPUP, box 16.

48. Paul Cret and Harry Sternfeld, "Plans for the Improvement of City Hall Square, Philadelphia. Projected by the Philadelphia Commission" (TS), 1928–29, Athenaeum, Philadelphia Commission Papers. The report was illustrated with photographs of drawings, the originals for two of which are also in the Athenaeum collection. One, the "Plan of City Hall Square and Approaches," is dated December 31, 1928.

49. Information on this project is scanty. See Art Jury Submissions, file 3476, PCA, 140.3. Sixty-four drawings are preserved at H2L2.

50. Art Jury Submissions, file 106, PCA, 140.3.

51. The west facade is illustrated in "Hall of Science Is Now Planned for the Parkway," *Inquirer*, April 11, 1907, pp. 1, 2; "Franklin Institute to Adorn Parkway," *North American*, April 11, 1907; and "Franklin Institute Goes on Parkway," *Press*, April 11, 1907 (the latter two articles are in a scrapbook in FI Archives, Building Records, Projected New Buildings, 1859–1913).

52. George E. Kirkpatrick (superintendent of Minor City Trusts) to Walton Clark (president of the Franklin Institute), January 7, 1908, FI Archives, Franklin Fund Committee Correspondence, Building Records, 1906–31.

53. Persifor Frazer, "The Franklin Institute: Its Services and Deserts," *Journal of the Franklin Institute*, vol. 165, no. 4 (April 1908), pp. 245–96. Based on a lecture given on February 14, 1908.

54. Elizabeth G. Grossman, "Paul Philippe Cret: Rationalism and Imagery in American Architecture" (Ph.D. diss., Brown University, 1980), p. 65 n. 11.

55. Windrim to Cret, November 11, 1915, CPUP, box 14; see also Paul Cret to Marguerite Cret, November 27, 1915, CPUP, box 7a.

56. Minutes of Special Meeting, September 27, 1913, FI Archives, Building Records, Projected New Buildings, 1906–31.

57. Ibid.

58. Jack Lutz, *The Poor Richard Club: Its Birth, Growth and Activities; and Its Influence on Advertising, the City, State and Nation* (Philadelphia, 1953), p. 88.

59. The Cret project is discussed below.

60. "The Franklin Memorial, Franklin Institute and the Municipal Courts Building," *Thirty-Ninth Annual Report of the City Parks Association of Philadelphia* (1927–28), pp. 24–31; "Historical Extracts," *Franklin Institute Yearbook* (1928–29), p. 42.

61. "Monumental Museum of Science and Industry to Be Erected in Philadelphia in Memory of Ben Franklin," *Public Ledger*, December 15, 1929, Rotogravure Pictorial section, p. 4.

62. "Enough Evidence of Franklin's Greatness to Convince Any Skeptic About the Wisdom of Giving to This $5,000,000 Memorial," *Inquirer*, June 5, 1930, p. 13. This was a full-page advertisement, with a drawing of the proposed building, sponsored by the Benjamin Franklin Memorial, Inc.

63. Art Jury Submissions, file 2285, PCA, 140.3.

64. Committee Meeting Minutes, December 18, 1930, ibid.

65. Ibid., February 3, 1931.

66. FPC Minutes, vol. 12, pp. 89–90, October 14, 1910; pp. 92–93, November 11, 1910, PCA, 149.1.

67. "To Start Convention Hall," *Public Ledger*, July 19, 1911, p. 2; "Convention Hall Contract Awarded," *Public Ledger*, October 22, 1911, p. 8.

68. See the file "1914–1920 re Phila. Convention Hall (and Art Gallery)," CPUP, box 13b.

69. Harbeson to C. Emlen Urban, March 1, 1916, CPUP, box 14.

70. Art Jury Submissions, file 585, PCA, 140.3.

71. "Checks Convention Hall Construction," *Public Ledger*, January 16, 1917, p. 9.

72. "Convention Hall Favored by Mayor Smith," *Public Ledger*, March 12, 1917, p. 16.

73. "Site for Cathedral Blessed by Bishop," *Public Ledger*, June 4, 1917, p. 11; "Bishop Makes Call for New Cathedral," *Public Ledger*, March 26, 1919, p. 9. The Episcopal Diocese is unable to locate archival material related to this project.

74. Art Jury Submissions, file 1216, PCA, 140.3.

75. "Mayor Inspects Sites on Parkway," *Public Ledger*, April 20, 1920, p. 13; "The Overcrowded City Hall," *Public Ledger*, July 10, 1920, p. 8.

76. "A New Courthouse, Not a 'Palace,' " *Public Ledger*, July 23, 1920, p. 8.

77. Cret to John F. Lewis, July 12, 1926, Art Jury Submissions, file 2158, PCA, 140.3. See also "Mayor Announces Plans for Building of Convention Hall," *Inquirer*, July 11, 1926, pp. 1, 6; "Fine Features Shown in Plans for Great Hall," *Public Ledger and North American*, July 11, 1926, Editorials and Special Cables section, p. 1.

78. Committee Meeting Minutes, April 7, 1924, Art Jury Submissions, file 1698, PCA, 140.3.

79. Two drawings by Herman Miller for a design for this purpose also exist, dated March 19 and June 12, 1925, Athenaeum, MIL*013.1, MIL*013.2.

80. "Data—The Franklin Memorial—Scheme 3," n.d. (TS), H2L2, box 137; "Data Academy of Music Philadelphia" (TS), December 30, 1927, ibid.

81. Committee Meeting Minutes, May 11, 1931, Art Jury Submissions, file 2336, PCA, 140.3.

82. "Artists Win Municipal Court Mural Race," *Record*, October 13, 1940, Metropolitan section, p. 16.

83. "Mayor Urges Municipal Art Gallery on Park Site," *Public Ledger*, March 17, 1911, p. 2.

84. John F. Lewis to John E. D. Trask, July 6, 1916, PAFA Archives, John F. Lewis Correspondence.

85. Board of Directors Minutes, May 7, June 4, October 1, and November 5, 1917, PAFA Archives.

86. Price to Lewis, May 17, 1920, PAFA Archives.

87. "Art Building Plans Told," *Public Ledger*, February 13, 1920, p. 9.

88. Morton Keast to Alfred G. B. Steel (bound report), March 25, 1935, PAFA Archives, General Correspondence.

89. Committee Meeting Minutes, January 23, 1929, Art Jury Submissions, file 2137, PCA, 140.3.

90. "Scout Edifice, First in World, to Arise Here," *Record*, February 10, 1929, p. D (clipping, Art Jury Submissions, file 2137, PCA, 140.3); "New Scout Home Is Ready for Use," *Public Ledger*, October 22, 1930, p. 2.

91. Rush to Bayard Henry, December 3, 1918, CIGNA Archives, INA Coll. 13/5.1.

92. Rush to the Board of Directors, [early 1922], CIGNA Archives, INA Coll. 13/2.

93. Marquis James, *Biography of a Business, 1792–1942: Insurance Company of North America* (Indianapolis, 1942), p. 280.

94. Building Committee Minutes, June 22, 1922, CIGNA Archives, INA Coll. 13/2.

95. Stewardson and Page to Rush, June 24, 1922, and Seeler to Rush, June 27, 1922; both in TS report by Rush, [c. August 1922], CIGNA Archives, INA Coll. 13/2.

96. Rush to Stewardson and Page, August 8, 1922, CIGNA Archives, INA Coll. 13/5.1.

97. Stewardson and Page, "Preliminary Plans for a Building for the Insurance Company of North America, Philadelphia: The Architects' Report to the Building Committee," December 15, 1922, CIGNA Archives, INA Coll. 13/5.8.

98. Ibid.

99. Lewis to Rush, April 27, 1923, CIGNA Archives, INA Coll. 13/5.1; Rush to Lewis, April 30, 1923, ibid.

100. The appropriate documents are in Art Jury Submissions, file 1559, which is missing from PCA, 140.3.

101. This space was filled in 1952 by the construction of three mezzanine floors.

102. Cret to Fiske Kimball, March 15, 1928, CPUP, box 17.

103. Medary to Cret, November 25, 1925, Art Jury Submissions, file 1844, PCA, 140.3. See also the Secretary of the Art Jury to the Commissioners of Fairmount Park, November 28, 1925, ibid.; Secretary of the Art Jury to Zantzinger, Borie, and Medary, March 3, 1926, ibid.

104. Leon V. Solon and Harry Arthur Hopf, "The Fidelity Mutual Life Insurance Company Building, Philadelphia," *Architectural Record*, vol. 63, no. 1 (January 1928), p. 3.

105. Fiske Kimball, *American Architecture* (Indianapolis, 1928), p. 210.

106. Art Jury Submissions, file 2111, PCA, 140.3; "The New Administration Building for the School District of Philadelphia," *T-Square Club Journal*, vol. 1 (October 1931), pp. 22–23, 31.

107. Art Jury Submissions, file 2111, drawing 2111(I), PCA, 140.3.

108. Ibid., drawing 2111(J).

109. Quoted in Louis R. Winter, Jr., "Parkway Vista Gains New Dignity from Board of Education Building," *Public Ledger*, October 25, 1931, News section, pt. 2, pp. 1, 4.

110. "$6,000,000 Temple of Art to Rise at Logan Circle," *Inquirer*, June 20, 1930, pp. 1, 7.

111. This and all subsequent detail is taken from the records of the Philadelphia Arts Association at the Athenaeum.

112. "Report to the Committee of Architects to the Board of Directors of the Philadelphia Arts Association" (TS), [c. January 13, 1931], PAAA.

113. Walker to W. Curtis Bok, January 23, 1931, PAAA.

114. Barney to W. Curtis Bok, January 27, 1931, PAAA; Stokowski to W. Curtis Bok, February 12, 1931, ibid.

115. W. Curtis Bok to Eli Kirk Price, January 13, 1932, PAAA.

116. "Chester B. Price, Architect, Dies: Specialist in Illustration of Designs Was a Teacher," *New York Times*, July 4, 1962, p. 21.

117. W. Curtis Bok to Walker, June 29, 1932, PAAA.

118. Ibid., March 18, 1933.

Checklist of the Exhibition

1. John Penington & Son, publishers
Proposed Boulevards
Plan
From *Broad Street, Penn Square, and the Park* (Philadelphia, 1871)
Collection of Mrs. Joseph Carson, Philadelphia
Fig. 8

2. Charles K. Landis (1835–1900)
Map of the Grand Avenue to the Park
Plan and two perspectives
April 29, 1884
Lithograph with letterpress text
18¹/₁₆ x 21¼″ (45.9 x 54 cm)
Inscribed: *C. K. LANDIS, SEA ISLE CITY, N. J. April, 1884*
Collection of Mrs. Joseph Carson, Philadelphia
Fig. 9

3. James H. Windrim (1840–1919)
Park Boulevard from City Hall to Fairmount Park
Bird's-eye perspective from southeast
February 24, 1892
J. Hutchinson, delineator
Photograph of lost drawing
Inscribed: *Recommended February 24, 1892, —by—JAS. H. WINDRIM, Director of Public Works J. Hutchinson 1892.*
Free Library of Philadelphia, Print and Picture Department
Fig. 10

4. Albert Kelsey (1870–1950)
Parkway Plan as Prepared for the Art Federation
Plan
1900–1902
Inscribed: *Albert Kelsey, Chairman*
From Albert Kelsey, ed. and comp., *The Proposed Parkway for Philadelphia . . .* (Philadelphia,

1902), p. 17
University of Pennsylvania, Fine Arts Library, Philadelphia

5. Albert Kelsey
Parkway Plan as Prepared for the Art Federation
Bird's-eye perspective from southeast
1900–1902
From Albert Kelsey, ed. and comp., *The Proposed Parkway for Philadelphia . . .* (Philadelphia, 1902), p. 16
University of Pennsylvania, Fine Arts Library, Philadelphia
Fig. 11

6. Albert Kelsey
Parkway Plan as Prepared for the Parkway Association
Plan
1902
Inscribed: *JUNE 12TH. 1902*
From Albert Kelsey, ed. and comp., *The Proposed Parkway for Philadelphia . . .* (Philadelphia, 1902), p. 6
University of Pennsylvania, Fine Arts Library, Philadelphia
Fig. 12

7. Paul P. Cret (1876–1945), Horace Trumbauer (1868–1938), and Zantzinger and Borie
Parkway Plan as Prepared for the Fairmount Park Art Association
Bird's-eye perspective from east
1907
Paul P. Cret, delineator
Lithograph
34 x 31¾″ (86.4 x 80.6 cm)
Inscribed: *P.P.C. HORACE TRUMBAUER C. C. ZANTZINGER PAUL P. CRET*
Philadelphia Museum of Art, Archives, 90.1
Fig. 14

8. John T. Windrim (1866–1934)
Municipal Auditorium, Stadium, and Coliseum at Snyder's Woods, Fairmount Park
Bird's-eye perspective from southwest
1910
Photograph of lost drawing
Inscribed: *John T. Windrim Architect*
City Archives of Philadelphia, 117.01, 9616
Fig. 90

9. Department of Public Works, City of Philadelphia
City Hall Plaza
Perspective from west
From *Philadelphia Public Ledger*, March 19, 1911
The Franklin Institute Science Museum, Philadelphia

10. Department of Public Works, City of Philadelphia
The Parkway as Shown on the Comprehensive Plan
Model from southeast and plan of Fairmount Plaza
May 1911
Photograph of lost originals
City Archives of Philadelphia, 117.01, 4750
Fig. 18

11. Department of Public Works, City of Philadelphia
The Parkway as Shown on the Comprehensive Plan
Model from northwest
May 1911
Photograph of lost model
City Archives of Philadelphia, 117.01, 4749

12. Department of Public Works, City of Philadelphia
Fairmount Plaza and the Art Museum
Perspective from south

1911
William E. Groben (1883–1961), delineator
Photograph of lost watercolor
Inscribed: *William E. Groben, Architect—Department of Public Works. 1911.*
City Archives of Philadelphia, 117.01, 4762
Fig. 19

13. Department of Public Works, City of Philadelphia
Fairmount Plaza
Bird's-eye perspective from east
1911
William E. Groben, delineator
Photograph of lost watercolor
Inscribed: *William E. Groben Architect. Department of Public Works*
City Archives of Philadelphia, 117.01

14. Department of Public Works, City of Philadelphia
Art Museum in Fairmount Plaza
Southeast elevation
1911
William E. Groben, delineator
Photograph of lost watercolor
Inscribed: *William E. Groben Architect of the Department of Public Works*
City Archives of Philadelphia, 117.01, 4757

15. William L. Johnston (1811–1849)
North Side of Logan Square
Perspective from southeast
c. 1847
Lithograph
11½ x 16″ (29.2 x 40.6 cm)
Inscribed: *Drawn by Wm. Johnston, Archt. P.S. Duval Lith. Phila. On Stone by Jas. Queen.*
The Historical Society of Pennsylvania, Philadelphia, Bb87 L824a

16. Logan Square in the snow, looking north
December 16, 1915
Photograph
The Franklin Institute Science Museum, Philadelphia
Fig. 20

17. *Bement, Miles & Co., Twenty-First and Callowhill Streets*
Bird's-eye perspective from north
1892
Engraving
6¼ x 9¾″ (15.9 x 24.8 cm)
Inscribed: KEYS & WOODBURY WORCESTER
The Historical Society of Pennsylvania, Philadelphia. Campbell Collection, vol. 90, p. 135
Fig. 16

18. The first demolition for the parkway, with John R. Hathaway of the Department of Public Works removing the first brick from the chimney of 422 North Twenty-Second Street
February 22, 1907
Photograph
City Archives of Philadelphia, 116.01, 2453

19. 422 North Twenty-Second Street after partial demolition
February 22, 1907
Photograph
City Archives of Philadelphia, 116.01, 2449
Fig. 13

20. The future route of the parkway seen from City Hall tower, with the short stretch of the "temporary parkway" visible at top center
May 24, 1909
Photograph

City Archives of Philadelphia, 116, 3384
Fig. 15

21. Department of Public Works, City of Philadelphia
Pergolas for the Temporary Parkway
Plan and elevations
1909
William E. Groben, delineator
Photograph of lost watercolor
Inscribed: *Wm E. Groben*
City Archives of Philadelphia, 117.01, 684

22. Construction of pergolas on the temporary parkway
September 25, 1909
Photograph
City Archives of Philadelphia, 116.01, 3587
Fig. 17

23. The parkway looking toward City Hall, with one block east of Logan Square undemolished
March 30, 1917
Photograph
City Archives of Philadelphia, 116.01, 13575

24. The parkway from City Hall tower, with the Medico-Chirurgical Hospital still standing in the future roadway
March 18, 1918
Photograph
City Archives of Philadelphia, 116, 14806
Fig. 21

25. The parkway from the southeast, with the end pavilions of the art museum roofed but only the foundations of the central block in place. The INA Building, Bell Telephone Building, and Free Library are the only complete (or nearly complete) new structures.

August 22, 1925
Photograph
CIGNA Archives, Philadelphia, 20/1.19
Fig. 1

26. The parkway, with the soon-to-open art museum framed by the Soldiers and Sailors Monument
February 17, 1928
Photograph
City Archives of Philadelphia, 116.01, 25260
Fig. 25

27. Jacques Gréber (1882–1962)
The New Pennsylvania Railroad Station and Episcopal Cathedral
Elevations and sections
October 25, 1917
Gréber office, delineators
Brown line and watercolor
26¾ x 107¾″ (68 x 273.7 cm)
Inscribed: *J. GRÉBER, S.A.D.G. PARIS, X 25th 1917*
Philadelphia Museum of Art, Archives, 90.7
Fig. 22

28. Jacques Gréber
The Art Museum and the Pennsylvania Academy of the Fine Arts
Elevations and section
Fall 1917
Gréber office, delineators
Watercolor, gouache, metallic paint, and ink on paper
38¼ x 155″ (97.2 x 393.7 cm)
Inscribed: *Jacques Gréber TRUMBAUER, ZANTZINGER ET BORIE, ARCHITECTES*
Philadelphia Museum of Art, Archives, 90.8
Fig. 23

29. Jacques Gréber
Fairmount and the Art Museum
Plan
Fall 1917
Gréber office, delineators

Watercolor, gouache, and ink on paper
68¾ x 138¼″ (174.6 x 351.2 cm)
Inscribed: *Jacques Gréber*
Philadelphia Museum of Art, Archives, 50.4

30. Jacques Gréber
The Parkway, Looking from Logan Square Toward the Art Museum
Perspective
1918
Crayon on paper, mounted on card
19⅜ x 26¾″ (49.2 x 67.9 cm)
Inscribed: *Philadelphia 1918 J. Greber, del.*
The Commissioners of Fairmount Park, Philadelphia
Fig. 24

31. Jacques Gréber
The Parkway from Fairmount to Logan Square
Plan
c. February 1919
Gréber office, delineators
Watercolor and ink on two sheets of paper
55⅜ x 219⅜″ (140.6 x 557.2 cm) (overall)
Philadelphia Museum of Art, Archives, 90.9a,b
Fig. 26

32. Jacques Gréber
Fairmount Plaza
Bird's-eye perspective from east
1919
Photograph of lost crayon drawing
Free Library of Philadelphia, Print and Picture Department

33. Jacques Gréber
Parkway Landscaping at Logan Circle
Plan
1922
Gréber office, delineators
Watercolor, gouache, ink, and

graphite on paper
63 x 93½" (160 x 237.5 cm)
Philadelphia Museum of Art,
Archives, 90.12

34. Jacques Gréber
*Parkway Landscaping Southeast of
the Pennsylvania Academy Site*
Plan
1922
Gréber office, delineators
Watercolor, gouache, and ink on
paper
58 x 91" (147.3 x 231.1 cm)
Philadelphia Museum of Art,
Archives, 90.13

35. Hermann J. Schwarzmann
(1846–1891)
Memorial Hall
Exterior from the southeast,
showing the enclosure of the
arcades to create more exhibi-
tion space
c. 1930
Photograph
Philadelphia Museum of Art,
Archives, SF/PHO, "Memorial
Hall"

36. Hermann J. Schwarzmann
Memorial Hall
The large east gallery, used to
display tapestries and pottery;
the Wilstach Collection occu-
pied the identical west gallery
From *The Fortieth Annual Report
of the Trustees of the Pennsylvania
Museum and School of Industrial
Art* (Philadelphia, 1916)
Fig. 27

37. Hermann J. Schwarzmann
Memorial Hall
Plan and perspective from
southeast
1876
Photolithograph, annotated in
ink with room sizes
24½ x 32¼" (62.2 x 81.9 cm)
Inscribed: *Photo Lith. by J. Bien.*

N.Y.
Philadelphia Museum of Art,
Archives, 10.1

38. Henry Bacon (1866–1924)
and James Brite (dates
unknown)
Philadelphia Museum of Art
Perspective from southeast
1895, redrawn 1900
Photograph of lost drawing
Inscribed: *Feb 7th 1900*
Wesleyan University Archives,
Middletown, Connecticut
Fig. 28

39. Henry Bacon and
James Brite
Philadelphia Museum of Art
Ground-floor plan
1895
Photograph of lost drawing
Inscribed: *Submitted by Key Stone*
Wesleyan University Archives,
Middletown, Connecticut

40. Borie, Trumbauer, and
Zantzinger
Philadelphia Museum of Art
Southeast elevation with dome
December 1911
Zantzinger, Borie, and Medary
office, delineators
Photograph of lost watercolor
Philadelphia Museum of Art,
Archives, SF/PHO, Box 1
Fig. 29

41. Borie, Trumbauer, and
Zantzinger
Philadelphia Museum of Art
Southeast elevation without
dome
December 1911
Zantzinger, Borie, and Medary
office, delineators
Photograph of lost watercolor
Philadelphia Museum of Art,
Archives, SF/PHO, Box 1
Fig. 30

42. Borie, Trumbauer, and
Zantzinger
Philadelphia Museum of Art
Perspective from east with
dome
December 26, 1911
Horace Trumbauer office,
delineators
Blue-line print
11¾ x 26¼" (29.8 x 66.7 cm)
Inscribed: *DEC. 26. 1911 C. L.
BORIE HORACE TRUMBAUER
C. C. ZANTZINGER ASSOCIATE
ARCHITECTS.*
Philadelphia Museum of Art,
Archives, 20.5
Fig. 31

43. Borie, Trumbauer, and
Zantzinger
Philadelphia Museum of Art
Perspective from east without
dome
December 26, 1911
Horace Trumbauer office,
delineators
Blue-line print
11½ x 26½" (29.2 x 67.3 cm)
Inscribed: *DEC. 26. 1911 C. L.
BORIE HORACE TRUMBAUER
C. C. ZANTZINGER ASSOCIATE
ARCHITECTS.*
Philadelphia Museum of Art,
Archives, 20.4
Fig. 32

44. Borie, Trumbauer, and
Zantzinger
Philadelphia Museum of Art
First-floor plan, showing
possible expansion
1912
Horace Trumbauer office,
delineators
Blue-line print
28 x 28¼" (71.1 x 71.7 cm)
Philadelphia Museum of Art,
Archives, 20.6

45. Borie, Trumbauer, and
Zantzinger
Philadelphia Museum of Art
Southeast elevation
Spring 1912
Horace Trumbauer office,
delineators
Hand-colored photograph of
lost watercolor
City Archives of Philadelphia,
140.3, 81, PW 1210
Fig. 33

46. Borie, Trumbauer, and
Zantzinger
Philadelphia Museum of Art
Southeast perspective
September 1912
Horace Trumbauer office,
delineators
Watercolor and graphite on
paper
23¼ x 51½" (59 x 130.8 cm)
Philadelphia Museum of Art,
Archives, 20.7
Fig. 34

47. Borie, Trumbauer, and
Zantzinger
Philadelphia Museum of Art
First-floor plan, first phase only
September 1912
Horace Trumbauer office,
delineators
Photograph of lost drawing
Philadelphia Museum of Art,
Archives, SF/PHO, Box 1

48. Borie, Trumbauer, and
Zantzinger
Philadelphia Museum of Art
Porticoed model from east
1914
Photograph of lost model
Philadelphia Museum of Art,
Archives, SF/PHO, PMA
Proposed Models
Fig. 35

49. Borie, Trumbauer, and
Zantzinger
Philadelphia Museum of Art
Colonnaded model from south,
with triumphal arch in fore-
court and future galleries
indicated
1914
Photograph of lost model
Philadelphia Museum of Art,
Archives, SF/PHO, PMA
Proposed Models

50. Borie, Trumbauer, and
Zantzinger
Philadelphia Museum of Art
Colonnaded model from south,
with monument in forecourt
and future galleries indicated
1914
Photograph of lost model
Philadelphia Museum of Art,
Archives, SF/PHO, PMA
Proposed Models

51. Borie, Trumbauer, and
Zantzinger
Philadelphia Museum of Art
Astylar model from south,
with screened forecourt and
no future galleries indicated
1914
Photograph of lost model
Philadelphia Museum of Art,
Archives, SF/PHO, PMA
Proposed Models
Fig. 36

52. Borie, Trumbauer, and
Zantzinger
Philadelphia Museum of Art
Southeast elevation of colonnaded variant with arch in
forecourt
1914
Zantzinger, Borie, and Medary
office, delineators
Graphite, ink, colored crayon,
and watercolor on illustration
board

9¾ x 27¾″ (24.8 x 70.5 cm)
Philadelphia Museum of Art,
Archives, 30.5

53. Borie, Trumbauer, and
Zantzinger
Philadelphia Museum of Art
Entrance and typical gallery
floor plans of astylar variant
September 24, 1914
Zantzinger, Borie, and Medary
office, delineators
Graphite, wash, watercolor,
and colored pencil on illustra-
tion board
20 x 24¼″ (50.8 x 61.6 cm)
Inscribed: SEPTEMBER 24 1914
Philadelphia Museum of Art,
Archives, 30.6
Fig. 39

54. Borie, Trumbauer, and
Zantzinger
Philadelphia Museum of Art
Southeast elevation of arcuated
variant
1914
Zantzinger, Borie, and Medary
office, delineators
Graphite, ink, watercolor, and
wash on illustration board
10¼ x 23¾″ (26 x 60.3 cm)
Philadelphia Museum of Art,
Archives, 30.7
Fig. 40

55. Borie, Trumbauer, and
Zantzinger
Philadelphia Museum of Art
Northwest elevation of arcuated
variant
1914
Zantzinger, Borie, and Medary
office, delineators
Graphite, ink, and wash on
illustration board
10¼ x 23¼″ (26 x 59.1 cm)
Philadelphia Museum of Art,
Archives, 30.8

56. Borie, Trumbauer, and
Zantzinger
Philadelphia Museum of Art
Northeast elevation of arcuated
variant
1914
Zantzinger, Borie, and Medary
office, delineators
Graphite, ink, and wash on
illustration board
10⅛ x 15¼″ (25.7 x 38.7 cm)
Philadelphia Museum of Art,
Archives, 30.9

57. Borie, Trumbauer, and
Zantzinger
Philadelphia Museum of Art
Entrance-floor plan of arcuated
variant
1914
Zantzinger, Borie, and Medary
office, delineators
Graphite, ink, and wash on
illustration board
15 x 25″ (38.1 x 63.5 cm)
Philadelphia Museum of Art,
Archives, 30.10

58. Borie, Trumbauer, and
Zantzinger
Philadelphia Museum of Art
First gallery-floor plan of
arcuated variant
1914
Zantzinger, Borie, and Medary
office, delineators
Graphite, ink, and wash on
illustration board
15 x 25″ (38.1 x 63.5 cm)
Inscribed: C. L. BORIE JR.
HORACE TRUMBAUER C. C.
ZANTZINGER ASSOCIATE
ARCHITECTS.
Philadelphia Museum of Art,
Archives, 30.11

59. Borie, Trumbauer, and
Zantzinger
Philadelphia Museum of Art
Transverse section of arcuated
variant

1914
Zantzinger, Borie, and Medary
office, delineators
Graphite and ink on illustration
board
14½ x 23½″ (36.8 x 59.7 cm)
Philadelphia Museum of Art,
Archives, 30.12

60. Borie, Trumbauer, and
Zantzinger
Philadelphia Museum of Art
Close perspective of arcuated
variant from east
1914
Zantzinger, Borie, and Medary
office, delineators
Graphite on illustration board
21⅞ x 29⅞″ (55.6 x 75.9 cm)
Philadelphia Museum of Art,
Archives, 30.13
Fig. 41

61. Borie, Trumbauer, and
Zantzinger
Philadelphia Museum of Art
Sketch perspective from east,
bird's-eye perspective from
east, transverse section, and
northeast elevation of colonnaded variant
1914
Zantzinger, Borie, and Medary
office, delineators
Graphite and colored crayon on
tracing paper
14⅜ x 15¾″ (36.4 x 40 cm)
Philadelphia Museum of Art,
Archives, 30.4
Fig. 37

62. Borie, Trumbauer, and
Zantzinger
Philadelphia Museum of Art
Sketch entrance-floor plan
1914
Zantzinger, Borie, and Medary
office, delineators
Graphite on tracing paper

14¼ x 14⅛″ (36.1 x 36 cm)
Philadelphia Museum of Art,
Archives, 30.14

63. Borie, Trumbauer, and
Zantzinger
Philadelphia Museum of Art
Sketch southeast elevation of
colonnaded variant with obelisk
in forecourt
1914
Zantzinger, Borie, and Medary
office, delineators
Graphite and colored crayon on
tracing paper
9½ x 18¼″ (24.1 x 46.3 cm)
Philadelphia Museum of Art,
Archives, 30.15
Fig. 38

64. Borie, Trumbauer, and
Zantzinger
Philadelphia Museum of Art
Sketch southeast elevation of
colonnaded variant with monu-
ment in forecourt
1914
Zantzinger, Borie, and Medary
office, delineators
Graphite and colored crayon on
tracing paper
9 x 19″ (22.9 x 48.3 cm)
Philadelphia Museum of Art,
Archives, 30.16

65. Borie, Trumbauer, and
Zantzinger
Philadelphia Museum of Art
Sketch southeast elevation of
colonnaded variant
1914
Zantzinger, Borie, and Medary
office, delineators
Graphite on tracing paper
7⅜ x 19″ (18.7 x 48.2 cm)
Philadelphia Museum of Art,
Archives, 30.17

66. Borie, Trumbauer, and
Zantzinger
Philadelphia Museum of Art

Three sketch elevations of the
forecourt, shown with monument, obelisk, and fountain
1914
Zantzinger, Borie, and Medary
office, delineators
Graphite and colored crayon on
tracing paper
12 x 18″ (30.5 x 45.7 cm)
Inscribed: *Borie*
Philadelphia Museum of Art,
Archives, 30.18

67. Borie, Trumbauer, and
Zantzinger
Philadelphia Museum of Art
Ground-floor plan
April 20, 1915
William Pope Barney (1890–
1970), delineator
Graphite, ink, and crayon on
tracing paper, mounted on card
24½ x 27⅛″ (62.2 x 68.9 cm)
Inscribed: APRIL 20 1915 WPB
Philadelphia Museum of Art,
Archives, 40.2

68. Borie, Trumbauer, and
Zantzinger
Philadelphia Museum of Art
Southeast elevation
May 1, 1915
William Pope Barney,
delineator
Graphite, ink, crayon, and
watercolor on paper
15 x 43¼″ (38.1 x 109.9 cm)
Inscribed: *May 1 1915* WPB
Philadelphia Museum of Art,
Archives, 40.3
Fig. 42

69. Borie, Trumbauer, and
Zantzinger
Philadelphia Museum of Art
Bird's-eye perspective from east
May 1915
William Pope Barney,
delineator
Graphite on tracing paper
11¾ x 17¾″ (29.8 x 45.1 cm)

Philadelphia Museum of Art,
Archives, 40.7
Fig. 43

70. Borie, Trumbauer, and
Zantzinger
Philadelphia Museum of Art
Perspective from southeast
June 1915
Howell Lewis Shay (1884–
1975), delineator
Photograph of lost drawing
Inscribed: *Rec'd by Art Jury June
21, 1915. Approved . . . Andrew
Wright Crawford 6-29-15 Secre-
tary Date of Action by Art Jury
June 25, 1915.*
Philadelphia Museum of Art,
Archives, SF/PHO, Box 1
Fig. 44

71. Borie, Trumbauer, and
Zantzinger
Philadelphia Museum of Art
Perspective from east and
second-floor plan
June 1915
Howell Lewis Shay, delineator
Two photographs of lost draw-
ings, mounted together
Inscribed: *Rec'd by Art Jury June
21, 1915. Approved . . . Andrew
Wright Crawford 6-29-15 Secre-
tary Date of Action by Art Jury
June 25, 1915.*
Philadelphia Museum of Art,
Archives, SF/PHO, Box 1

72. Borie, Trumbauer, and
Zantzinger
Philadelphia Museum of Art
First-floor plan
June 1915
Howell Lewis Shay, delineator
Photograph of lost drawing
Inscribed: *Rec'd by Art Jury June
21, 19[15.] Approved . . . Andrew
Wright Crawford 6-29-15 Secre-
tary Date of Action by Art Jury
June 25, 1915.*

Philadelphia Museum of Art,
Archives, SF/PHO, Box 1
Fig. 45

73. Borie, Trumbauer, and
Zantzinger
Philadelphia Museum of Art
Northeast elevation and
longitudinal section
June 1915
Howell Lewis Shay, delineator
Two photographs of lost draw-
ings, mounted together
Inscribed: *Rec'd by Art Jury June
21, 1915. Approved . . . Andrew
Wright Crawford 6-29-15 Secre-
tary Date of Action by Art Jury
June 25, 1915.*
Philadelphia Museum of Art,
Archives, SF/PHO, Box 1

74. Borie, Trumbauer, and
Zantzinger
Philadelphia Museum of Art
Model seen from southeast,
before and after installation of
trees and bushes
Fall 1915
Two photographs of lost model,
mounted together
Philadelphia Museum of Art,
Archives, SF/PHO, PMA
Proposed Models

75. Borie, Trumbauer, and
Zantzinger
Philadelphia Museum of Art
Model seen from southwest
Fall 1915
Photograph of lost model
City Archives of Philadelphia,
140.3, 81, PW 1209
Fig. 46

76. Borie, Trumbauer, and
Zantzinger
Philadelphia Museum of Art
Perspective from east
Fall 1915
Photograph of lost drawing

Philadelphia Museum of Art,
Archives, SF/PHO, Box 1
Fig. 47

77. Borie, Trumbauer, and
Zantzinger
Philadelphia Museum of Art
Ground-floor plan
Fall 1915
Photograph of lost drawing
Philadelphia Museum of Art,
Archives, SF/PHO, Box 1

78. Borie, Trumbauer, and
Zantzinger
Philadelphia Museum of Art
First-floor plan
Fall 1915
Photograph of lost drawing
Philadelphia Museum of Art,
Archives, SF/PHO, Box 1

79. Borie, Trumbauer, and
Zantzinger
Philadelphia Museum of Art
Perspective of stair hall
Fall 1915
From *Yearbook of the Twenty-
Second Annual Architectural Exhi-
bition Held by the Philadelphia
Chapter of the American Institute
of Architects and the T-Square Club*
(Philadelphia, 1916)
The Athenaeum of Philadelphia
Fig. 48

80. Borie, Trumbauer, and
Zantzinger
Philadelphia Museum of Art
Ground-floor plan
Late 1916–early 1917
Detail photograph of damaged
blueprint
39¼ x 43½" (99.7 x 110.5 cm)
(original blueprint)
City Archives of Philadelphia,
140.3, 81, V
Fig. 49

81. Borie, Trumbauer, and
Zantzinger
Philadelphia Museum of Art
Northwest elevation (revised)
Late 1916–early 1917
Blueprint
26½ x 34½" (67.3 x 87.6 cm)
Inscribed: *CHARLES L. BORIE JR.
HORACE TRUMBAUER CLARENCE
C. ZANTZINGER ASSOCIATE
ARCHITECTS*
City Archives of Philadelphia,
140.3, 81, N

82. Borie, Trumbauer, and
Zantzinger
Philadelphia Museum of Art
Perspective of stair hall
Late 1916–early 1917
Blueprint
16⅜ x 15¼" (41.6 x 38.8 cm)
City Archives of Philadelphia,
140.3, 81, Q
Fig. 50

83. Borie, Trumbauer, and
Zantzinger
Philadelphia Museum of Art
Perspective from east
1917–18
Jacques Gréber, delineator
Ink and crayon on tracing
paper, mounted on card
26 x 34" (66 x 86.4 cm)
Inscribed: *J. GREBER*
Philadelphia Museum of Art,
Archives, 50.1

84. Borie, Trumbauer, and
Zantzinger
Philadelphia Museum of Art
Perspective of south corner
1917–18
Jacques Gréber, delineator
Ink and crayon on tracing
paper, mounted on illustration
board
26 x 34" (66 x 86.4 cm)
Inscribed: *J. Gréber*
Philadelphia Museum of Art,
Archives, 50.2

85. Borie, Trumbauer, and
Zantzinger
Philadelphia Museum of Art
Longitudinal section
October 20, 1917
Jacques Gréber office,
delineators
Watercolor and ink on paper
32⁵⁄₁₆ x 82¼" (82.1 x 208.9 cm)
(plexiglass package)
Inscribed: *J. GRÉBER. S.A.D.G.,
PARIS, X-20th 1917*
Philadelphia Museum of Art,
Archives, 50.3
Fig. 53

86. Borie, Trumbauer, and
Zantzinger
Philadelphia Museum of Art
Northwest elevation
1917–18
Jacques Gréber office,
delineators
Watercolor and ink on paper
26⅛ x 63⅝" (66.4 x 161.6 cm)
Philadelphia Museum of Art,
Archives, 50.5

87. Borie, Trumbauer, and
Zantzinger
Philadelphia Museum of Art
Perspective from north
1917–18
Gouache, crayon, and graphite
on tracing paper, mounted on
card
25 x 51¾" (63.5 x 131.4 cm)
Philadelphia Museum of Art,
Archives, 50.7
Fig. 54

88. Borie, Trumbauer, and
Zantzinger
Philadelphia Museum of Art
Perspective from southeast
1917–18
Ink and crayon on paper
32 x 75" (81.3 x 190.5 cm)
Philadelphia Museum of Art,
Archives, 50.6

89. Borie, Trumbauer, and Zantzinger
Philadelphia Museum of Art
First-floor plan
Summer 1917
Photographic print, mounted on linen
31¾ x 37¼″ (80.6 x 94.6 cm)
Inscribed: *C. L. BORIE, JR. HORACE TRUMBAUER C. C. ZANTZINGER ASSOCIATE ARCHITECTS.*
Philadelphia Museum of Art, Archives, 50.24
Fig. 51

90. Borie, Trumbauer, and Zantzinger
Philadelphia Museum of Art
Northeast elevation of south pavilion
c. 1920
Crayon and graphite on tracing paper
36 x 48″ (91.4 x 121.9 cm)
Philadelphia Museum of Art, Archives, 50.26

91. Borie, Trumbauer, and Zantzinger
Philadelphia Museum of Art
Perspective from southeast
1925
Hugh Ferriss (1889–1962), delineator
Crayon on paper
19½ x 34¾″ (49.5 x 88.3 cm)
Inscribed: *Hugh Ferriss del*
Philadelphia Museum of Art, Archives, 50.30
Fig. 56

92. Borie, Trumbauer, and Zantzinger
Philadelphia Museum of Art
Perspective of stair hall
c. 1927
Crayon on tracing paper, mounted on card
16 x 18⅞″ (40.6 x 47.9 cm)

Philadelphia Museum of Art, Archives, 60.1
Fig. 58

93. Borie, Trumbauer, and Zantzinger
Philadelphia Museum of Art
Perspective of room from the Treaty House, Upminster, England
c. 1927
Crayon on tracing paper, mounted on illustration board
22¼ x 23¾″ (56.5 x 60.3 cm)
Philadelphia Museum of Art, Archives, 60.2
Fig. 57

94. Borie, Trumbauer, and Zantzinger
Philadelphia Museum of Art
Foundations under construction, with the parkway in the background
January 26, 1923
Photograph
City Archives of Philadelphia, 117.01, 9992
Fig. 55

95. Borie, Trumbauer, and Zantzinger
Philadelphia Museum of Art
Installation of the wall covering in an axial gallery on the second floor of the north wing, two days after the first press tour of the new building
January 5, 1928
Photograph
Philadelphia Museum of Art, Archives, Book 4, No. 80

96. Borie, Trumbauer, and Zantzinger
Philadelphia Museum of Art
The large exhibition hall at the head of the stairs, its unfinished ceiling hidden by painted canvas, five days before the official opening by the mayor

March 21, 1928
Photograph
Philadelphia Museum of Art, Archives, Book 4, No. 128

97. Horace Trumbauer
Free Library
Perspective from southeast
1912
Photograph of lost watercolor
Free Library of Philadelphia, Print and Picture Department
Fig. 59

98. Horace Trumbauer
Free Library
Perspective from southwest
c. 1916
Watercolor and ink on paper
25 x 53″ (63.5 x 134.6 cm)
Free Library of Philadelphia
Fig. 60

99. Horace Trumbauer
Free Library
"Report on Central Library Building" by Paul P. Cret
May 4, 1922
Typescript
City Archives of Philadelphia, 140.3, 1434

100. Horace Trumbauer
Free Library
Groundbreaking ceremony
May 12, 1917
Photograph
Free Library of Philadelphia, Print and Picture Department

101. Horace Trumbauer
Free Library
Erection of steelwork
February 2, 1923
Photograph
Free Library of Philadelphia, Print and Picture Department

102. Horace Trumbauer
Free Library
Entrance hall

c. 1930
Photograph
Free Library of Philadelphia, Print and Picture Department

103. Horace Trumbauer
Free Library
Entrance hall at night
c. 1930
Photograph
Free Library of Philadelphia, Print and Picture Department

104. Horace Trumbauer
Free Library
Main reading room
c. 1930
Photograph
Free Library of Philadelphia, Print and Picture Department
Fig. 61

105. Horace Trumbauer
Free Library
Periodicals room
c. 1930
Photograph
Free Library of Philadelphia, Print and Picture Department

106. Horace Trumbauer
Johnson Collection Gallery
Perspective
1919
Jacques Gréber, delineator
Photograph of lost crayon drawing
Inscribed: *J. Greber del. Paris 1919*
The Commissioners of Fairmount Park, Philadelphia
Fig. 63

107. Paul P. Cret and Jacques Gréber
Rodin Museum
Sketch southwest elevation
September 1926
Paul P. Cret, delineator
Graphite on tracing paper
5⅝ x 12¼″ (14.3 x 31.1 cm)

University of Pennsylvania, Architectural Archives, Philadelphia. Gift of John F. Harbeson, 176.2
Fig. 64

108. Paul P. Cret and Jacques Gréber
Rodin Museum
Southeast elevation
November 19, 1926
Graphite and colored pencil on tracing paper
12¼ x 21¾″ (31.1 x 55.2 cm)
Inscribed: *Nov. 19. 26.*
The partners of H2L2 Architects/Planners, Philadelphia

109. Paul P. Cret and Jacques Gréber
Rodin Museum
Southwest elevation
November 29, 1926
Blue-line print, revised in colored crayon
10⅞ x 20¾″ (27.7 x 52.7 cm)
Inscribed: *November 29, 1926*
Philadelphia Museum of Art, Archives, 100.1

110. Paul P. Cret and Jacques Gréber
Rodin Museum
Northwest elevation
December 1926
Graphite on tracing paper
10¾ x 18¾″ (27.3 x 47.6 cm)
The partners of H2L2 Architects/Planners, Philadelphia

111. Paul P. Cret and Jacques Gréber
Rodin Museum
Southwest elevation
July 22, 1927
Graphite and colored pencil on tracing paper
17⅞ x 32¼″ (45.3 x 82 cm)
Inscribed: *P. P. CRET AND J.*

GREBER ASSOCIATED ARCHITECTS
JULY 22 1927
The partners of H2L2
Architects/Planners,
Philadelphia
Fig. 65

112. Paul P. Cret and Jacques
Gréber
Rodin Museum
Transverse section
July 25, 1927
Graphite and colored pencil on
tracing paper
17¼ x 36″ (43.8 x 91.4 cm)
Inscribed: *P. P. CRET AND
J. GREBER ASSOCIATE ARCHI-
TECTS JULY 25, 1927*
Philadelphia Museum of Art,
Archives, 100.3
Fig. 66

113. Paul P. Cret and Jacques
Gréber
Rodin Museum
Southwest elevation
August 1927
Graphite and colored pencil on
tracing paper
18½ x 41¾″ (47 x 106 cm)
The partners of H2L2
Architects/Planners,
Philadelphia
Fig. 67

114. Paul P. Cret and Jacques
Gréber
Rodin Museum
Northwest elevation
August 1927
Graphite and colored pencil on
tracing paper
17¾ x 42″ (45.1 x 106.7 cm)
The partners of H2L2
Architects/Planners,
Philadelphia

115. Paul P. Cret and Jacques
Gréber
Rodin Museum
Ceiling plasterwork detail

August 16, 1928
Charles F. Ward, Jr., delineator
Crayon and colored crayon on
tracing paper
31½ x 50⅝″ (80 x 128.6 cm)
Inscribed: *8-16-28 WARD PAUL
PHILIPPE CRET AND JACQUES
GREBER ASSOCIATED ARCHITECTS*
The partners of H2L2
Architects/Planners,
Philadelphia

116. Paul P. Cret and Jacques
Gréber
Rodin Museum
Longitudinal section, showing
Mastbaum memorial
October 29, 1928
William J. H. Hough (1888–
1969), delineator
Graphite and colored pencil on
tracing paper
20 x 33″ (50.8 x 83.8 cm)
Inscribed: *10-29-28 W.J.H.H.
PAUL PHILIPPE CRET AND JACQUES
GREBER ASSOCIATED ARCHITECTS*
The partners of H2L2
Architects/Planners,
Philadelphia

117. Paul P. Cret and Jacques
Gréber
Rodin Museum
Model
c. 1929
44 x 32″ (111.8 x 81.3 cm) (base)
Rodin Museum, Philadelphia

118. Paul P. Cret
American Philosophical Society
Perspective of neo-Georgian
design from southwest
c. 1925–26
Watercolor, ink, graphite,
gouache, and crayon on paper
11½ x 28¾″ (29.2 x 73 cm)
Inscribed: *Paul P. Cret*
American Philosophical
Society, Philadelphia
Fig. 69

119. Paul P. Cret
American Philosophical Society
Transverse section of
neo-Georgian design
c. 1925–26
Graphite and colored pencil on
illustration board
10½ x 20⅛″ (26.7 x 51.1 cm)
Inscribed: *PAUL PHILIPPE CRET.
ARCHITECT.*
American Philosophical
Society, Philadelphia

120. Paul P. Cret
American Philosophical Society
First-floor plan of neo-Georgian
design
c. 1925–26
Graphite and colored pencil on
illustration board
17 x 32¾″ (43.2 x 83.2 cm)
Inscribed: *PAUL PHILIPPE CRET.
ARCHITECT.*
American Philosophical
Society, Philadelphia

121. Paul P. Cret
American Philosophical Society
Southwest elevation of seven-
bay neoclassical design
December 28, 1927
Photographic print of lost
drawing
10¼ x 19¼″ (26 x 48.9 cm)
Inscribed: *DEC. 28, 1927 Paul P.
Cret, Architect*
American Philosophical
Society, Philadelphia
Fig. 70

122. Paul P. Cret
American Philosophical Society
Southwest perspective of five-
bay neoclassical design
May 1929
Photograph of lost drawing
American Philosophical
Society, Philadelphia
Fig. 71

123. Paul P. Cret
American Philosophical Society
Southwest study elevation with
square piers
January 29, 1932
Graphite on tracing paper
19¼ x 34½″ (48.9 x 87.6 cm)
Inscribed: *JAN 29. '32.*
American Philosophical
Society, Philadelphia
Fig. 72

124. Paul P. Cret
American Philosophical Society
Southwest study elevation with
Aeolic columns
January 1932
Graphite on tracing paper
19¼ x 34½″ (48.9 x 87.6 cm)
American Philosophical
Society, Philadelphia

125. Paul P. Cret
American Philosophical Society
Southwest study elevation with
Doric columns
January 1932
Graphite on tracing paper
19¼ x 34½″ (48.9 x 87.6 cm)
American Philosophical
Society, Philadelphia
Fig. 73

126. Paul P. Cret
American Philosophical Society
Southwest study elevation with
square piers and attic windows
January 1932
Graphite on tracing paper
19¼ x 34½″ (48.9 x 87.6 cm)
American Philosophical
Society, Philadelphia

127. Paul P. Cret
American Philosophical Society
First-floor plan
February 15, 1932
Graphite and colored pencil on
tracing paper
16 x 28½″ (40.6 x 72.4 cm)
Inscribed: *PAUL P. CRET,*

ARCHITECT FEB 15, 1932.
American Philosophical
Society, Philadelphia

128. Paul P. Cret
American Philosophical Society
Sections through exhibition
lobby, main stair hall, and
auditorium
February 15, 1932
Graphite and colored pencil on
tracing paper
18¾ x 31⅜″ (47.6 x 79.7 cm)
Inscribed: *PAUL P. CRET,
ARCHITECT FEB. 15, 1932*
American Philosophical
Society, Philadelphia

129. Paul P. Cret
American Philosophical Society
Southwest elevation
May–June 1932
Graphite on tracing paper
21 x 41½″ (53.3 x 105.4 cm)
Inscribed: *REVISED JUNE 21. 1932
PAUL P. CRET ARCHITECT 5.31.32.*
American Philosophical
Society, Philadelphia
Fig. 74

130. Paul P. Cret
American Philosophical Society
Interior elevation of auditorium
1932
Graphite and colored pencil on
tracing paper
17½ x 59″ (44.5 x 149.9 cm)
Inscribed: *Paul P. Cret Architect*
American Philosophical
Society, Philadelphia

131. Paul P. Cret
American Philosophical Society
Entrance elevation
1932
Graphite and colored pencil on
tracing paper
59 x 41¾″ (149.9 x 106 cm)
American Philosophical
Society, Philadelphia

132. Paul P. Cret
American Philosophical Society
Sections through lobby and
meeting rooms
1932
Graphite and colored pencil on
tracing paper
21 x 38½" (53.3 x 97.8 cm)
Inscribed: PAUL P. CRET,
ARCHITECT
American Philosophical
Society, Philadelphia
Fig. 75

133. Paul P. Cret and Harry
Sternfeld (1888–1976)
City Hall Tower
South elevation showing
resheathing
May 24, 1927
Harry Sternfeld, delineator (?)
Graphite on paper
approx. 48 x 30½" (121.9 x
77.5 cm)
Inscribed: *May 24, 1927 Paul P.
Cret Harry Sternfeld*
University of Pennsylvania,
Architectural Archives,
Philadelphia. On permanent
loan from the City Planning
Commission, Philadelphia
Fig. 76

134. Paul P. Cret
Victory Hall
Perspective from southwest
1925
Photographic print of lost
drawing
8 x 20" (20.3 x 50.8 cm)
Inscribed: PAUL P. CRET,
ARCHITECT
University of Pennsylvania,
Architectural Archives,
Philadelphia. Gift of John F.
Harbeson, 185.3
Fig. 93

135. Paul P. Cret
Franklin Memorial
First-floor plan ("Scheme A")

1927
Graphite and colored pencil on
tracing paper
14 x 19¾" (35.6 x 50 cm)
The partners of H2L2
Architects/Planners,
Philadelphia
Fig. 94

136. Paul P. Cret
Franklin Memorial
Sketch first-floor plan ("Scheme
No. 2")
1927
Graphite on tracing paper
9¼ x 14½" (23.5 x 36.8 cm)
The partners of H2L2
Architects/Planners,
Philadelphia

137. Paul P. Cret
Franklin Memorial
First-floor plan ("Scheme
No. 2")
1927
Graphite and colored pencil on
tracing paper
14½ x 22¼" (36.8 x 56.4 cm)
The partners of H2L2
Architects/Planners,
Philadelphia

138. Paul P. Cret
2601 Parkway
Perspective of classical design
from south
c. 1931
Crayon and colored crayon on
tracing paper
9½ x 13¾" (24.1 x 34.9 cm)
The partners of H2L2
Architects/Planners,
Philadelphia
Fig. 77

139. Paul P. Cret
2601 Parkway
Perspective of Romanesque
design from southwest
c. 1931
Crayon and colored crayon on

tracing paper
8¾ x 13¾" (22.2 x 34.9 cm)
The partners of H2L2
Architects/Planners,
Philadelphia

140. Paul P. Cret
2601 Parkway
Perspective of Gothic design
from southwest
c. 1931
Crayon and colored crayon on
tracing paper
11¾ x 15½" (29.8 x 39.4 cm)
Inscribed: PAUL P. CRET
ARCHITECT
The partners of H2L2
Architects/Planners,
Philadelphia

141. Paul P. Cret
2601 Parkway
Perspective massing study from
southwest
May 5, 1932
Crayon on tracing paper
11½ x 17" (29.2 x 43.2 cm)
Inscribed: MAY 5, 1932.
The partners of H2L2
Architects/Planners,
Philadelphia

142. Paul P. Cret
2601 Parkway
Perspective of "moderne"
design from south
c. 1932
Crayon and colored crayon on
tracing paper
7 x 15¼" (17.8 x 38.7 cm)
The partners of H2L2
Architects/Planners,
Philadelphia
Fig. 78

143. Paul P. Cret
2601 Parkway
Perspective of modern design
from southwest
Late 1930s
Graphite on tracing paper

4½ x 7¼" (11.4 x 18.4 cm)
The partners of H2L2
Architects/Planners,
Philadelphia
Fig. 79

144. Cope and Stewardson
The Franklin Institute
East elevation
April 1907
Blueprint
8½ x 15¼" (21.6 x 38.7 cm)
The Franklin Institute Science
Museum, Philadelphia
Fig. 83

145. Cope and Stewardson
The Franklin Institute
First-floor plan
April 19, 1907
Graphite and colored pencil on
tracing paper
12¾ x 12¼" (32.4 x 31.1 cm)
Inscribed: *April 19, 1907. Cope
& Stewardson Archts.*
The Franklin Institute Science
Museum, Philadelphia

146. John T. Windrim
The Franklin Institute
Perspective from east
Early 1908
Halftone reproduction
5⅜ x 6¼" (13.7 x 15.9 cm)
The Franklin Institute Science
Museum, Philadelphia
Fig. 84

147. John T. Windrim
The Franklin Institute
East elevation
October–December 1909
Photograph of lost drawing
Inscribed: *John T. Windrim
Architect*
The Franklin Institute Science
Museum, Philadelphia
Fig. 85

148. John T. Windrim
The Franklin Institute
First-floor plan
October 15, 1909
Photograph of lost drawing
Inscribed: *15-X-09 John-
T.-Windrim-Architect*
The Franklin Institute Science
Museum, Philadelphia

149. John T. Windrim
The Franklin Institute
Perspective from east
c. June 1930
From The Franklin Institute, *A
Living Memorial* (Philadelphia,
[1930])
The Franklin Institute Science
Museum, Philadelphia
Fig. 86

150. John T. Windrim
The Franklin Institute
Model seen from southeast
October 1930
Photograph of lost model
The Franklin Institute Science
Museum, Philadelphia
Fig. 87

151. John T. Windrim
The Franklin Institute
Perspective from northeast
March 23, 1931
Photographic print of lost
drawing
Inscribed: JOHN T. WINDRIM
ARCHITECT 3.23.31.
City Archives of Philadelphia,
140.3, 2285, 0
Fig. 88

152. John T. Windrim
The Franklin Institute
East elevation
November 1931–February 1932
Ink on linen
25¾ x 44" (65.4 x 111.8 cm)
Inscribed: *Nov 2 1931 Jan 11 1932
Feb. 2, 1932*

The Franklin Institute Science Museum, Philadelphia

153. John T. Windrim
Bell Telephone Building
Parkway and Arch Street elevations
Early 1914
Photograph of lost drawing
City Archives of Philadelphia, 140.3, 106
Fig. 81

154. John T. Windrim
Convention Hall
Perspective from south
September 1916
Photograph of lost drawing
Inscribed: JOHN T. WINDRIM, ARCHITECT.
City Archives of Philadelphia, 117.01, 15593
Fig. 91

155. John T. Windrim
Convention Hall
First-floor plan
September 1916
Photograph of lost drawing
Inscribed: JOHN T. WINDRIM, ARCHITECT
City Archives of Philadelphia, 117.01, 12512

156. John T. Windrim
Municipal Court
First-floor plan for site on west side of Logan Square
May 1920
Blueprint
43½ x 34¾" (110.5 x 88.3 cm)
Inscribed: *May 1920* JOHN T. WINDRIM ARCHITECT
City Archives of Philadelphia, 140.3, 1216, B
Fig. 92

157. John T. Windrim succeeded by W. R. Morton Keast
(1888–1973)
Municipal Court

Perspective of southwest corner
1932
Photograph of lost drawing
Inscribed: *John T. Windrim, Architect 1932*
The Athenaeum of Philadelphia. Gift of Mrs. Grace G. Keast
Fig. 95

158. John T. Windrim succeeded by W. R. Morton Keast
Municipal Court
Cartoon for stained-glass window *Justice Is the Queen of the Virtues* by D'Ascenzo Studios
c. 1939
Graphite and watercolor on paper
24½ x 11½" (62.2 x 29.2 cm) (sight)
The Athenaeum of Philadelphia. Gift of Mrs. Betty Bramnick
Fig. 97

159. W. R. Morton Keast
Pennsylvania Academy of the Fine Arts
Southwest elevation
February 14, 1935
Photograph of lost drawing
Inscribed: *February 14, 1935. Morton Keast, Architect.*
Pennsylvania Academy of the Fine Arts, Archives, Philadelphia
Fig. 99

160. W. R. Morton Keast
Pennsylvania Academy of the Fine Arts
Longitudinal section
February 14, 1935
Photograph of lost drawing
Inscribed: *February 14, 1935. Morton Keast, Architect.*
Pennsylvania Academy of the Fine Arts, Archives, Philadelphia

161. W. R. Morton Keast
Pennsylvania Academy of the Fine Arts
First-floor plan
February 14, 1935
Photograph of lost drawing
Inscribed: *Morton Keast, Architect. February 14, 1935.*
Pennsylvania Academy of the Fine Arts, Archives, Philadelphia

162. W. R. Morton Keast
Pennsylvania Academy of the Fine Arts
Second-floor plan
February 14, 1935
Photograph of lost drawing
Inscribed: *Morton Keast, Architect. February 14, 1935.*
Pennsylvania Academy of the Fine Arts, Archives, Philadelphia
Fig. 98

163. W. R. Morton Keast
Fairmount Community Center
Southwest elevation
May 7, 1935
Hand-colored photograph of lost drawing
Inscribed: *May 7, 1935 Morton Keast, Architect.*
Pennsylvania Academy of the Fine Arts, Archives, Philadelphia
Fig. 100

164. W. R. Morton Keast
Fairmount Community Center
Typical floor plan
May 6, 1935
Hand-colored photograph of lost drawing
Inscribed: *May 6, 1935 Morton Keast, Architect.*
Pennsylvania Academy of the Fine Arts, Archives, Philadelphia

165. Charles Z. Klauder
(1872–1938)
Philadelphia Council, Boy Scouts of America
Perspective from northeast
January 1929
Photographic print of lost drawing, with graphite additions
8¼ x 13⅞" (21 x 35.2 cm)
Inscribed: *C Z Klauder*
City Archives of Philadelphia, 140.3, 2137, B
Fig. 101

166. Charles Z. Klauder
Philadelphia Council, Boy Scouts of America
First-floor plan
January 9, 1929
Photographic print of lost drawing, with graphite additions
14½ x 16¼" (36.8 x 41.3 cm)
Inscribed: *JAN. 9, 1929. CHARLES Z KLAUDER ARCHITECT*
City Archives of Philadelphia, 140.3, 2137, F

167. Stewardson and Page
Insurance Company of North America
Perspective from northeast
Early 1923
From *Building for the Insurance Company of North America, Philadelphia. Stewardson and Page Architects* (Philadelphia, [c. 1923])
CIGNA Archives, Philadelphia, 13/8
Fig. 102

168. Stewardson and Page
Insurance Company of North America
Perspective of central hall
November 1923
William E. White (dates unknown), delineator
Graphite on paper

14⅞ x 22¹/₁₆" (37.8 x 56 cm)
Inscribed: *W.E.W. del Nov 1923*
CIGNA Archives, Philadelphia, 20/1.24
Fig. 104

169. Stewardson and Page
Insurance Company of North America
Perspective of central hall
1923
Graphite on paper
25⅜ x 20¾" (64.4 x 52.7 cm)
CIGNA Archives, Philadelphia, 20/1.39
Fig. 105

170. Stewardson and Page
Insurance Company of North America
Perspective of board room
1923
Graphite and crayon on poster board
22¾ x 22½" (57.8 x 57.2 cm)
CIGNA Archives, Philadelphia, 20/1.12

171. Zantzinger, Borie, and Medary
Fidelity Mutual Life Insurance Company
Southwest elevation
March 31, 1925
Watercolor and graphite on paper, mounted on card
12¾ x 20½" (32.4 x 52.1 cm)
Inscribed: *ZANTZINGER BORIE & MEDARY ARCHITECTS MARCH 31 1925*
The Athenaeum of Philadelphia. Gift of Dr. Vaughan P. Simmons
Fig. 106

172. Zantzinger, Borie, and Medary
Fidelity Mutual Life Insurance Company
Perspective from southwest
1926

Birch Burdette Long (1878–
1927), delineator
Lithograph on paper, mounted
on card
23½ x 40″ (59.7 x 101.6 cm)
Inscribed: BBL (monogram)
The Athenaeum of Philadel-
phia. Gift of Dr. Vaughan P.
Simmons
Fig. 107

173. Irwin T. Catharine
(1884–1944)
School Administration Building
Sketch perspective from north-
east
June 1928
Photographic print of lost
crayon drawing
24½ x 18″ (62.2 x 45.7 cm)
City Archives of Philadelphia,
140.3, 2111, B
Fig. 109

174. Irwin T. Catharine
School Administration Building
North elevation
June 12, 1928
Blueprint, with building short-
ened in colored crayon
30½ x 21″ (77.5 x 53.3 cm)
Inscribed: *Irwin T. Catharine*
R.A. ARCHITECT JUNE 12, 1928
City Archives of Philadelphia,
140.3, 2111, D

175. Irwin T. Catharine
School Administration Building
Perspective from northeast
1928, with later changes of
detail
Chester B. Price (1884/85–
1962), delineator
Crayon on paper
32 x 43″ (81.3 x 109.2 cm)
Inscribed: *Chester B. Price 1928*
The School District of
Philadelphia
Fig. 110

176. Irwin T. Catharine
School Administration Building
Study of lower corner
February 1930
Graphite on tracing paper
12 x 13″ (30.5 x 33 cm)
City Archives of Philadelphia,
140.3, 2111
Fig. 111

177. Irwin T. Catharine
School Administration Building
Study of top
February 1930
Graphite on tracing paper
11½ x 12¾″ (29.2 x 32.4 cm)
City Archives of Philadelphia,
140.3, 2111

178. Irwin T. Catharine
School Administration Building
Full-scale details of auditorium
ceiling plasterwork
May 13, 1931
T. L. Sime (dates unknown),
delineator
Crayon and colored crayon on
tracing paper
77½ x 42″ (196.8 x 106.7 cm)
Inscribed: *T. Sime Irwin T.*
Catharine 5/13/31
The School District of
Philadelphia
Fig. 113

179. Irwin T. Catharine
School Administration Building
Full-scale details of auditorium
wall plasterwork
May 20, 1931
T. L. Sime, delineator
Graphite on tracing paper
42 x 53½″ (106.7 x 135.9 cm)
Inscribed: *T. Sime Irwin T.*
Catharine R.A. 5/20/31 Revised
June 3-31
The School District of
Philadelphia

180. Irwin T. Catharine
School Administration Building
Perspective and elevation of
auditorium chair
May 19, 1931
Emil Schmidt (dates unknown),
delineator
Ink on linen
14⅜ x 17¼″ (36.5 x 43.8 cm)
Inscribed: *E.S. 5/19/'31 Irwin T.*
Catharine RA Architect
The School District of
Philadelphia

181. Irwin T. Catharine
School Administration Building
Four stained-glass panels of
Fairmount and the Acropolis
(never installed as intended in
the second-floor exhibition
room) by Columbia Art Glass
Company, after a design by
Herman Schuh (in Catharine's
office)
c. 1931
90 x 46¾″ (228.6 x 118.7 cm)
(each)
The School District of
Philadelphia
Fig. 114

182. Voorhees, Gmelin, and
Walker
Concert Hall for the Philadelphia
Arts Association
Perspective at night from
northeast
1932
Chester B. Price, delineator
Photograph of lost drawing
Inscribed: *Voorhees Gmelin &*
Walker 1932 Chester B. Price 1932
The Athenaeum of Philadel-
phia. Gift of the Bok Tower
Gardens
Fig. 115

183. Voorhees, Gmelin, and
Walker
Concert Hall for the Philadelphia
Arts Association

Perspective of small concert hall
1932
Reproduction of lost drawing
Inscribed: *Voorhees Gmelin &*
Walker 1932
The Athenaeum of
Philadelphia. Gift of the Bok
Tower Gardens